WRITING
the
BLOCK BUSTER NOVEL

WRITING

the

BLOCK BUSTER NOVEL

ALBERT ZUCKERMAN

WRITER'S DIGEST BOOKS
Cincinnati, Ohio

Four unpublished outlines and two unpublished first-draft scenes from *The Man From St. Petersburg* used with permission of Ken Follett.

Writing the Blockbuster Novel. Copyright © 1994 by Albert Zuckerman. Printed and bound in the United States of America. All rights reserved. No part of this book may be reproduced in any form or by any electronic or mechanical means including information storage and retrieval systems without permission in writing from the publisher, except by a reviewer, who may quote brief passages in a review. Published by Writer's Digest Books, an imprint of F&W Publications, Inc., 1507 Dana Avenue, Cincinnati, Ohio, 45207. (800) 289-0963. First paperback edition 2002.

Other fine Writer's Digest Books are available from your local bookstore or direct from the publisher.

Visit our Website at www.writersdigest.com for information on more resources for writers.

To receive a free weekly E-mail newsletter delivering tips and updates about writing and about Writer's Digest products, send an E-mail with the message "Subscribe Newsletter" to newsletter-request@writersdigest.com, or register directly at our Web site atwww.writersdigest.com.

06   05   04   03   02   5   4   3   2   1

Library of Congress has catalogued hardcover edition as follows:

Zuckerman, Albert.
    Writing the blockbuster novel / by Albert Zuckerman : with an introduction by Ken Follett.
        p.   cm.
    Includes index.
    ISBN 0-89879-598-2 (hardcover)
    1. Fiction—Technique. I. Title.
PN3365.Z83   1993
808.3—dc20   93-28427
ISBN 1-58297-127-7 (pbk. : alk. paper)   CIP

Edited by Jack Heffron
Cover designed by Brian Roeth
Interior designed by Ten Speed Press

ABOUT THE AUTHOR

Albert Zuckerman has been literary agent and book doctor to some two dozen blockbuster novels. At Writers House, he presides over a firm which represents hundreds of leading writers in all categories. Author of two published novels, winner of the 1964 Stanley Drama Award, former writer for three television series, he also taught playwriting at the Yale School of Drama. He lives in New York with his wife.

ACKNOWLEDGMENTS

Writers as a rule are chary of exposing their mistakes, false starts, anything less than their polished final work. That Ken Follett is allowing me to publish a goodly amount of his first-draft material is a little amazing and most generous. What this book hopes to accomplish and what gives it great potential value to you the reader would not exist without his extraordinary courage and kindness in allowing me to use this material.

My former wife, Eileen Goudge, read the entire manuscript in first draft and made shrewd and perceptive editorial suggestions for which I thank her, as well as for her limitless moral support.

As an author, Eileen Goudge also deserves my gratitude. Without her fine work on *Garden of Lies*, this would be a much poorer book. And I acknowledge, too, my great debt to Mario Puzo for providing me with so many wonderful examples from *The Godfather*, to Colleen McCullough for doing the same with *The Thorn Birds*, and last but certainly not least, to the memory of Margaret Mitchell for providing us with so brilliant a demonstration of the novelist's craft in *Gone With The Wind*.

Also, six editors at Dan Weiss Associates made comments on the first draft, some of them scathing, which actually were useful, and I am grateful to them and to Dan for having organized this critical effort.

Simon Lipskar, my brilliant son-in-law and a colleague at Writers House, deserves a special word of appreciation for setting up the first few chapters and especially for the laborious task of going through all four drafts of the outline of *The Man From St. Petersburg* and eliminating the repetitive material from draft to draft as well as summarizing sections of it to create continuity. He also read the completed first draft and made some sharply insightful suggestions for revision, and I thank him for those, too.

My former assistant, Todd Wiggins, did yeoman's work in deciphering my handwritten scrawl and typing the bulk of the manuscript. And he, too, made some excellent comments and suggestions.

Finally, I want to thank Jack Heffron, my editor at Writer's Digest Books, for his careful reading of the text and for his thoughtful editorial input.

I dedicate this book to all the authors who have written blockbuster novels that, for one reason or another, never achieved the huge recognition that they deserved.

Among my own such friends and clients are

Michael Peterson for *A Time of War*,

Robert Shea for *Shike*,

William Cobb for *A Walk Through Fire*,

Ridley Pearson for *The Angel Maker*,

and F. Paul Wilson for *The Keep*.

TABLE OF CONTENTS

☙

INTRODUCTION

by

Ken Follett

THERE ARE THREE QUALITIES A STORYTELLER NEEDS ABOVE ALL OTHERS. He or she must be (a) imaginative, (b) literate and (c) stubborn. But you can have all three and still write a bad book. I know. I wrote several.

Ever since I can remember, I've had elaborate daydreams, about what I would do if I were shipwrecked on a desert island, or became a millionaire, or had to fight in a war.

When I was a baby my mother told me stories all the time. I don't know whether this nurtured my imagination or I simply inherited her ability. Either way, by the time I got to school I could make up stories as easily as kick a football.

When my own children were young I would tell them fantastic tales extempore. Standing at a bus stop, my son would ask me why some buses were red and others green. (In those days London buses were all bright red and country buses were green.) I would say, "The one to get on is the blue bus. It takes you anywhere you want to go in the twinkling of an eye, but it only comes along once in a lifetime. If we catch it I want to go to the Wild West and meet Billy the Kid. Where do you want to go?"

If you are the kind of person who can do that, you're imaginative. But don't be swollen-headed. Thank your mother.

Writers also need to be more literate than the average. Most people find it fairly difficult to put their thoughts down in writing. They can write a letter to a friend or send a memo to a colleague, but ask them to write a four-page report or an article for the local newspaper and they get nervous.

I feel the same way if someone asks me to help fix a car that won't start: I sort of know what is required but it will take me all day to do what another person would achieve in five minutes. I wasn't brought up in a car-fixing family, I was brought up in a reading family. The only way you get to be highly literate is through years of reading and writing.

Most writers I know are interested in obscure questions of spelling and grammar. For example, is there a difference in meaning between "each other" and "one another"? Some people say that "each other" should be used where just two people are involved and "one another" for three or more. Copyeditors may correct a writer who fails to follow this rule. But some authorities maintain there is no difference, and certainly ordinary speech does not distinguish the two.

Are you thinking this is a perfectly trivial question? If so, you probably aren't going to be a professional writer. Words are our tools, and subtle distinctions are important even if readers are not consciously aware of them. When I first came across this business about "each other" and "one another," I was mildly panicked at the thought that I might have been misusing these phrases all my life.

Writers are generally fascinated by puns, word games, variant spellings, regional dialects, forms of Pidgin English, new coinages, and everything to do with the language they use. In the same way, painters are usually fascinated by the way light falls on surfaces and changes the way things look. You'll never be a writer if you don't love the language you use.

Finally, you need to be stubborn. Most people who set out to write a novel never finish it.

At first you're kept going by the novelty (pardon the pun) of the process: inventing characters and drama right out of your head. But when you have fifty or a hundred pages written, you realize that you're going to have to do this for another six months or a year to finish it. You think of all the movies you'll miss, all the evenings in the pub with your friends, all the TV shows you won't see, all the jobs around the house that won't get done—and for what? For a novel that in all probability no one will ever want to read. At this point most people give up. A few, however, say, "The heck with it, maybe nobody will ever want to read it, but I've started it and I'm going to finish it."

Anyone with these three qualities can write a novel. If you want to write a *successful* novel, you need more. You need this book.

My first novel was not a big best-seller. It was published as a paperback original in Britain, the United States and Germany. You can still get it in the States. It's called *The Big Needle*, and the only reason it's still selling is that people mix it up with *Eye of the Needle*.

If you read it you'll see what kind of book a person writes who has the three qualities I've mentioned but totally lacks craft.

My journey from *The Big Needle* to *Eye of the Needle* was taken in the company of Al Zuckerman, the author of the book you hold in your hand.

At first I thought Al was a knowall. He always had something negative to say about my ideas for books, my outlines and my drafts. I was being published in Britain, but after *The Big Needle* he could never sell my stuff to American publishers, and he always had some damn excuse.

I would send him an outline or a draft, and back would come a little homily. It invariably began: "I cannot sell this book in the U.S. because——." What followed purported to be a comment on the American publishing business, but in reality it was a little lesson in what it takes to write a best-seller: I needed a character with whom readers would readily identify; or the book should be set in a milieu people would like to visit rather than a poor working-class district of England; or the story lacked a big dramatic question that would engage the reader's attention from beginning to end.

But what did he know? He was just a small-time agent who had written a couple of novels that were no more successful than my own. The trouble with Al was that, no matter how small-time he was, I could generally see, on reflection, that he was right. Gradually I began to learn from his advice. "The people in your story have no past," he said once, and that was when I started to give each of my major characters two parents, a childhood, painful memories of adolescence and so on. When I first tried to write an outline for the story that became *The Pillars of the Earth*, Al commented, "You have created a tapestry of medieval life, but what I need is a series of linked melodramas." Linked melodramas is what I gave him, years later, and people loved it.

Very few people can give this kind of advice, and no one does it as well as Al Zuckerman. I've never had him all to myself, but now that he's written this book I have to share him with thousands of other writers. To tell you the truth, I'm feeling a little jealous. But what the heck, I shouldn't be selfish.

So here he is. Enjoy him. Learn from him. He's the best. And good luck with your writing.

Chapter One

GETTING STARTED

THIS BOOK IS FOR WRITERS—for storytellers who have had a novel published, maybe several; for authors who believe they have wrestled with and mastered the essentials of the craft of fiction but who can't break into hardcover; for authors whose books have been praised, awarded prizes, yet who can't earn a living from their work; and for authors who receive advances and royalties that are a fraction of what they feel they deserve.

It will also benefit beginners and veteran writers who have yet to publish a novel. But if you belong in these groups, remember that Rome wasn't built in a day. For a beginner, trying to write a blockbuster novel might be likened to a high school athlete trying to play with the Dallas Cowboys or a first-year piano student trying to perform Beethoven's Emperor Concerto with the New York Philharmonic. These things sometimes happen, but chances are you'll stand a better chance getting your first novel published if it's a work less ambitious in scope and scale, say, a category romance or mystery.

This book is by no means intended for all published novelists. It will offer no help to authors who mean to forge new paths in literature, to dazzle serious readers with a contemporary equivalent of Proust, Joyce, Kafka or even Faulkner, or who aim to replicate the success of such recent "literary" best-sellers as *The White Hotel, The Name of the Rose* or *Possession*. Rather, it will dissect and hopefully illuminate what in today's book publishing industry is generally called "the commercial best-seller."

The creation of any novel that succeeds in stirring the hearts of millions of readers around the world must involve an element of indescribable magic, akin in a way to the human soul. The miracle of divine or evolutionary engineering has resulted in a human body with myriad organs, glands, bones, veins and tissues that can be x-rayed, sono-grammed, microscopically examined. Science can determine the quali-ties that set apart the ill from the healthy, the weak from the strong. With popular fiction, too, it is possible to peel away the surfaces of individual words and show how a blockbuster novel—like a watch—is built with a multitude of interlocking parts, all of which are needed precisely to move each other. In the best-loved novels, these parts are designed in ways that are on one hand unique but on the other appear to follow certain rules.

If you aspire to seeing your name on best-seller lists, you probably are familiar with the names of the authors who often appear there. Albert Zuckerman is not one of these. You may ask, Who is this guy? What are his qualifications? What gives him the authority to assert knowledge that many top publishing professionals—writers, editors, agents—freely admit eludes them?

The answer is that I have been midwife to more than a dozen mega-books—*New York Times* best-sellers, Literary Guild and Book-of-the-Month Club Main Selections, choices of Readers Digest Condensed Books, novels made into motion pictures and TV mini-series. I've worked with their authors from their stories' initial conception through constructing and reconstructing plot outlines, developing characters and intensifying their relationships, to rebuilding scenes and chapters in first-draft manuscripts, and finally enriching, rewriting and polishing second and final drafts before delivery to their publishers.

Ken Follett has been generous enough to call me "the best editor in the world." A great compliment, but I may not be. What is clear, though, is that my working with him has in some measure helped bring about the sale of more than thirty-five million copies of his books. Particularly exciting to me has been working with an unpublished author, and then rocketing him into the publishing industry's strato-sphere. My first such thrill came with Anne Tolstoi Wallach, whose *Women's Work* in 1982 garnered a then-record advance for a first novel: $850,000. My talented wife, Eileen Goudge, after producing a bunch of young adult romances, set out in 1986 to write a mainstream wom-en's novel on which I worked at her side. *Garden of Lies*, as part of a two-book contract, brought an advance of almost a million dollars, enjoyed nineteen weeks on the *New York Times* hardcover and paperback best-seller lists, and has been published in seventeen languages.

These large sums help spread the word about a new author and incite a commitment to strong promotion from a publishing house, but you must not conclude that a small advance will necessarily doom your book to a tiny print run and obscurity. *Jaws*, including the movie income, is reputed to have earned Peter Benchley around ten million dollars. His guarantee from Doubleday was $7,500. For *The Godfather*, Mario Puzo's contract with Putnam provided $5,000. Paramount, however, paid him $25,000 (based on an outline and four chapters) for an option on the movie rights. Without that, Puzo could not have afforded to write his book.

Eye of the Needle found no takers among U.S. publishers when I first submitted it in outline form. In the mid-1970s, Follett was supporting a family with two small children and living hand-to-mouth, grinding out genre books and chasing after freelance writing jobs. He managed to get the book commissioned in England as a paperback original for a pittance. In this country, Follett's outline got no more than a yawn from publishers. But when the first-draft manuscript arrived in the spring of 1977, I got all excited. Here was a crackling thriller that had a shot at becoming a best-seller. To get a new author widely recognized, however, is murder, one of the hardest things in the world. Everything would depend on how well it was published.

I had been an agent for only three years and had placed a fair number of books but nothing with such great potential. How should I handle this, I nervously asked myself, not wanting to screw up my big chance. Traditional wisdom would have had me send out copies to the dozen or so major publishers and sell to the highest bidder. But I saw a danger in that. The big houses, the ones most likely to offer hefty advances, all had (and generally always do have) name authors under contract whose work would inevitably take precedence on their lists over that of an unknown. I wanted a publisher who would push like crazy for Follett and on whose list *Eye of the Needle* would be the top book.

Arbor House was a dynamic small publisher who, through clever advertising and production, had made a minor best-seller out of a less-than-wonderful biography of Montgomery Clift, which they had acquired from me for an advance of $5,000 after it had been rejected by thirty-nine other houses. What, I asked myself, might this little house be able to do with a strong book? The most Arbor would or could afford was $20,000. I explained to Follett that better up-front deals probably could be had, but I advised him to take this one, and he went along. *Eye of the Needle* was given an inspired title (in England it was published under its original title, *Storm Island*). The book was well edited, released in an appropriate and superb jacket, and promoted brilliantly and with fantastic energy. It garnered $700,000 in paperback sales, lasted more than thirty weeks on the hardcover best-seller list, was made into a feature film, and transformed this author overnight from a poor young man into a rich one.

But be prepared for rejection. Steel yourself to persevere and keep laboring until you overcome it. Prior to *Eye of the Needle*, Follett wrote six novels that were published in a minor way in England, but that I failed utterly to place here. *Garden of Lies* was by no means Goudge's first book. After dozens of nonfiction magazine pieces, she wrote several novels, finally getting one published, a paperback original for $1,500. Then she found work writing teenage romances and developed her craft, producing twenty or so of those, some under harrowing deadlines of two and three weeks.

Having thus achieved a bit of financial stability, she was able to devote herself to a long dreamt-of adult story. I advised her to forge ahead and write the entire book as opposed to my offering it to publishers on the basis of an outline and sample chapters. She demurred, feeling that if she had a contract before she undertook the bulk of the work, she would feel more secure—financially and psychologically—even if it meant receiving a much smaller advance than she might obtain with a finished manuscript.

With a detailed outline and three sample chapters, a presentation of about 150 pages, I was able to get her a guarantee of $75,000 from Atheneum, the only house to whom I had submitted the material. We chose Atheneum because Eileen liked and trusted Susan Ginsburg, who in 1987 was editor in chief there, and wanted Susan to work with her. But jobs in publishing houses are volatile. Editors get fired, take higher-paying positions at other houses, go to law school, try some other career, or stay home and raise the kids. I represent authors who have had as many as five editors from the time their books were contracted until they were published. To have two or three is quite common. So I demanded and was able to get an "editor clause," a provision that if Susan Ginsburg was for any reason not employed at Atheneum when the final manuscript was delivered, Goudge, by repaying the money she'd received (which was $25,000), could regain all rights to her work.

As it happened, during the year between the contract-signing and the manuscript's completion, Ginsburg left the firm. We judged that, without her, Atheneum at that time would not be the ideal home for *Garden of Lies*, which I believed could become a blockbuster.

Excitedly, I called the head of a major house, one of the most powerful women in the business, and told her I had a terrific completed novel available. She encouraged me to messenger it to her apartment, which I did. A week later, she told me no thanks, she wasn't interested. A little disheartened but still enthused about the book, I contacted the editor in chief of a second house, a man I like and respect and with whom I'd had many mutually profitable dealings. He promptly agreed to read it and just as promptly declined it.

What now? I can't deny that I was discouraged, but I'd learned through hard experience that a good agent has to stand by his own judgment, cleave to his belief in a project. If publishers don't reject a book, they will, even when enthused, almost inevitably try to offer as little as they can. Authors often think their works are worth far more than their market value, that is, the number of copies likely to be sold. An agent must navigate a steady course between the two, not letting himself be buffeted by one side or the other, or his strength as the author's true advocate goes out the window.

I submitted *Garden of Lies* to the dozen or so remaining houses active as publishers of mainstream women's fiction. More than half rejected it outright. Two others, thank heaven, were thrilled with it. They bid against each other for the rights, which led to the large advance. The point here is that because this highly successful novel's author was unknown, it was turned down cold by almost all the publishers to whom it was submitted. It's a common story. New York City is full of rueful and even embarrassed editors who declined *The Firm*, a true mega-hit by John Grisham. On the other hand, all an author needs is one good publisher, and these manuscripts both found one.

The expertise that I used to counsel Follett and Goudge and other widely read writers, such as F. Paul Wilson, Olivia Goldsmith, Michael Peterson, Ridley Pearson and Robert Shea, came from my background of sixteen years as a playwright, television writer, novelist and teacher. In 1964, I won the nationwide Stanley Drama Award for the best full-length play by a new dramatist; dozens of my television scripts for *The Edge of Night*, *Love of Life* and *Somerset* have been aired; Doubleday and Dell published two of my novels; and for five years, I taught playwriting to graduate students at the Yale School of Drama.

To get the most from this book, read it in conjunction with others. First, the more current best-sellers you acquaint yourself with, the better. More specifically, you will find the following chapters peppered with references and examples from five novels: *The Godfather* by Mario Puzo, *Gone With the Wind* by Margaret Mitchell, *The Thorn Birds* by Colleen McCullough, *The Man From St. Petersburg* by Ken Follett, and *Garden of Lies* by Eileen Goudge. The first three, in my view, are classics of modern popular literature as well as mega-best-sellers. The latter two, also highly successful, are works whose origins and step-by-step development I can illuminate with a minimum of guesswork, having been a part of their creation. Again, to assist you in translating to your own writing the techniques and processes I'll be describing, you should read these books and also keep them at your side as you wend your way through this book.

In fact, if you haven't read one or more of these novels, I suggest that you put this book down after you finish chapter two and pick up *The Man From St. Petersburg*. If you have already read it, consider refreshing yourself with a rereading. After you complete chapter three, you should acquaint or reacquaint yourself with the other four novels. I will, in the course of these pages, dig deeply into the underpinnings and mechanics of all five novels. For you to derive the fullest benefit from this book, you will need to be familiar with them all.

Now for some caveats. There is, I feel I should point out, an articulate school of thought that maintains that writing fiction cannot be taught. Yet most colleges and universities offer whole menus of fiction-writing courses. In some institutions it can be a field of major concentration; indeed, graduate writing programs such as the one at the University of Iowa have produced dozens of estimable writers, including some Pulitzer Prize winners. Plainly, certain essential aspects of writing fiction can be taught. I know this because I've been the teacher, and I've enjoyed sharing in the profits, both financial and emotional. But just as a deaf person would have a rough time trying to become a musician, there are brilliant and gifted people who, no matter how hard they work at it, will not become novelists. And there are some vital aspects in the art and craft of fiction that are extremely difficult to teach or to learn.

Keep in mind that learning how to write novels is a process. It takes a lot of time and infinite labor. After only a few months of lessons you would be foolish to conclude that you were unfit to become a concert violinist. With writing novels too, if you have a passion for it, you must give yourself years to practice, to learn to overcome your mistakes, and to prove to yourself that you possess the necessary skills.

One precious quality in the best authors, which I believe is largely innate but is sometimes slowly acquired over time, is what editors and critics call "a voice." The line-by-line writing of J.D. Salinger (*The Catcher in the Rye*) doesn't sound like anyone else's. Stephen King's reputation among those unfamiliar with his work seems to rest largely on his bizarre and otherworldly plots, yet he has a sublime gift for the cadences and nuances of small-town American idiomatic speech, rendering its gross and subtle tones and rhythms with a uniqueness and an artistry that, to me, rivals Mozart's or Van Gogh's.

The writing of Susan Isaacs (*Compromising Positions*) is permeated with an acerbic wit, a hip New York jokiness that is emblematic only to her. To point to but a few other popular novelists whose individual prose styles can be picked out within several lines or a page, I would name Tom Wolfe, Anne Tyler, Pat Conroy and Norman Mailer. The list could go on and on.

This book, if studied carefully, will teach you a great deal about how blockbuster novels are constructed. But a distinctive voice, if you don't already have one, must grow out of your own special affinity for the English language, out of the rhythms, tones and nuances you hear and weave into your own mind of people's speech, out of your own highly personal and somewhat skewed vision of the world. But take heart. This is an issue that should not worry you unduly. While a unique or distinctive voice is an important asset, and often a decisive one in literary fiction, it is a less vital component in blockbuster novels. In fact, quite a few best-sellers are written in voices you would be hard put to categorize or to describe as in any way unique.

Another skill of the very best writers and one which, again, is more instinctive than acquired is an eye for detail. But not for all details, only the most telling ones. The great storyteller has an acuity of perception as sharp as that of a visual artist and can make music in words. Not only in dialogue, but in characters' thoughts and emotions, in visual perceptions, sounds, smells, palpable sensations, visceral reactions. Some of us are born with the literary equivalents of 20/20 eyesight and perfect pitch; a few can learn to develop these; some cannot.

A cold person, a dyed-in-the-wool cynic, a misanthrope, misogynist, homophobe, any man or woman who is not brimming with love and admiration for at least some of the people in his or her own life will find it difficult, if not impossible, to create fictional characters deeply involved with each other; and it's only about such characters that readers care. And for a novel to become popular, and to live on, we the readers *must* care.

Long after the twists and turns of a wonderful story such as *Gone With the Wind* fade from our memories, we remember Scarlett O'Hara and her unquenchable passion. Anton Chekhov wrote short stories, novels and four great plays, *The Seagull, The Three Sisters, Uncle Vanya* and *The Cherry Orchard*, all of which are populated by large extended families with mothers, sisters, aunts, cousins, and in-laws, but in not one of them is there a father. Chekhov hated his own father, recognized that he could not render such a character sympathetically, and so chose never to include one.

Energy, willpower and grit are also qualities of the novelist that cannot be taught. Anyone who thinks writing novels may be an easy way to make a buck is kidding himself. Perseverance and determination to climb not one lofty mountain, but peak after exhausting peak, a whole range of mountains—that's the doggedness it takes to complete a blockbuster novel. The author who cannot set aside a completed five- or eight-hundred-page draft and start all over from page one, throwing out scenes and entire chapters, altering and enriching relationships, characters and locales, intensifying conflicts and climaxes, is also un- likely to attain the high level of sustained drama contained in most best-selling novels.

Nor is there much place in the ranks of top popular novelists for writers who are defensive or protective about their plot notions, oddball characters, first drafts, favorite scenes, bons mots, and so on. The most widely read authors are almost invariably those most open to sugges- tions and constructive criticism from trusted editors, agents and fellow professional writers. But the author in the end must also possess her own keen critical sense, so she can accurately judge which suggestions to take up and which to reject. She must also be her own harshest critic, ruthless in anatomizing her text and seeking out ways, again and again, to strengthen it.

A final crucial and unteachable (at least in a book such as this) element in a leading novelist's toolbox is culture, widespread general knowledge, rich and varied life experience. The writer who has a close

acquaintance with the works of Plato, Shakespeare, Tolstoy, Dostoyev-
ski, Proust and Hemingway, to name a few, has an invaluable resource
of plots, dramatic situations, formulations of character, insights into
human nature, exquisite metaphors, and other brilliant uses of language. A familiarity with history, politics, the mores of the rich and
famous, or of gangsters, athletes and cowboys, the hotels, restaurants,
shops and clubs of the great cities of the world, the inner workings of
corporations, hospitals, law firms, bureaucracies, military units, and
high-tech weapons systems will enable the writer to weave a seamless
background of hard fact that helps compel the reader to suspend disbelief and to accept the authenticity of the novelist's imaginatively created
world.

In its essence, however, a novel is emotion. A novelist's true lode,
his font of inspiration, if you will, is in the feelings, passions, sufferings
and ecstasies that he himself has experienced and that, in the process
of writing, he transmutes through his characters. Francoise Sagan with
Bonjour Tristesse wrote perhaps the best-known coming-of-age novel of
the twentieth century. She herself was at the time a teenage girl and
rendered sublimely the angst, pain and tenderness of that difficult period of life. But she would have fared less well, I believe, if she, as a
postadolescent, had tried to bring alive a mother's passion for her child
or, say, a husband's feeling for his dying wife. In Ken Follett's *The
Pillars of the Earth*, a wonderful strand is made up of the domestic
jealousies and conflicts within the family of a newly married couple,
each of whom has children by previous liaisons. There is no such element in Follett's six previous best-sellers. But when writing *Pillars*,
he, a father of two, was well into his second marriage to a lady with
three children. I'm certain it never occurred to him deliberately to use
this aspect of his life in his novel. But through personally experiencing
these familial bickerings and tensions on a daily basis, they literally
had become a part of him, and it is this soaking up of everyday emotion
that becomes the unconscious wellspring from which every novelist
must draw.

To look at this more simplistically, female authors generally do a
better job with the pangs of childbirth and male authors with the
tensions and horrors of battle; and it is novelists who are forty or older
who usually succeed best with both mature and young characters.

All right, I've laid out some limiting factors that may or may not
apply to you, certain aspects of the novelist's art and craft that I doubt

can readily be taught or learned overnight. But don't be discouraged. If you're reading this book, many of you already possess, I would hope, some or all of these attributes. And if you do not, there is nothing to prevent you from setting about, little by little, to acquire them. Regardless of your current stage of development as a writer, you should find the approaches and techniques contained in the following chapters to be of solid value.

Chapter Two

THE BIG BOOK:
WHAT IS IT?

―――――――――――――――― ⌘ ――――――――――――――――

WHAT'S WRONG WITH MY BOOK?''a distraught author will growl at me. "If only the damn publisher would tour me in a few cities to do publicity, run some decent consumer advertising, it would be sure to catch on. Look at these reviews—'as good a mystery as I've read this year,' 'reminds me a lot of John D. MacDonald at his best,' 'a compelling, even hair-raising finale.' "

My answer might be, "Hey, there's absolutely nothing wrong with your book. In fact, it's a wonderful and highly accomplished piece of work, but from a publisher's point of view, it's a small book."

"Small, schmall, what are you talking about? A good book is a good book. Shouldn't that be enough?"

Unfortunately, as writers discover every day, simply because a book is praised by reviewers and even by many discriminating readers, because it really is good, doesn't necessarily mean it will be discovered by much of the reading public. Even a novel deemed worthy of the National Book Award or the Pulitzer Prize may sell only a few thousand copies. And New York publishers, with their large staffs of managers, editors, salespeople, publicists, warehouse clerks, and bookkeepers have massive overheads. They cannot afford to stay in business, cannot continue issuing new works of fiction, unless a minimum of two or three of their titles in any given year sell in the hundreds of thousands.

It's not uncommon for authors with important reputations acquired over years and years of distinguished publication to become disgusted or even furious when they learn that some first novelist is receiving a half-million-dollar advance or that some "name brand" (but in their view inferior) writer is getting millions. Indeed, to most writers, publishers appear to be grudging skinflints. Actually, publishers often are happier and more comfortable agreeing to a million-dollar guarantee for a novel than to a ten-thousand-dollar one. For the seven-figure payment, they presumably are acquiring a book whose author talk-show hosts will interview, that bookstores will display in their windows, that drugstores, supermarkets and airport newsstands will stock, that film and television producers will compete for, that, despite the intense competition from movies, TV, sports and other activities for people's leisure, will somehow break through and penetrate the vast public's consciousness.

The book that accomplishes this is (for want of a better term) the Big Book. Editors and publishers pursue manuscripts and proposals that possess such potential (and of course, popular authors, too) with demonic intensity and will compete for them almost ferociously. So, what exactly is this thing? In the rest of this chapter I'll point out the main characteristics of the Big Book, and in later chapters I'll delve into these in detail.

HIGH STAKES

The first thing to note about a big novel is that what's at stake is high—for a character, a family, sometimes a whole nation. The life of at least one major character is usually in peril. But more than that, in this type of book the individual at risk often represents not just himself, but a community, a city, an entire country. Feliks in *The Man From St. Petersburg* is both hunter and hunted. As hunter, if he succeeds as an assassin, he not only kills a man, but by doing so he deters Russia from allying with England against Germany; he will thus save millions of his young compatriots from being slaughtered in an insane war. To Lord Walden and the British agents pursuing Feliks, the stakes are equally high. If they prevail in safeguarding the threatened Russian prince, not only do they save a human life, but indirectly, by preserving an alliance with the Czar, they also save their beloved England from being overwhelmed by the Kaiser.

In many major women's novels, however, the principal stake is not life or death but personal fulfillment, as with Scarlett in *Gone With the Wind* or Meggie in *The Thorn Birds*. Although this stake—the consummating or the not consummating of a love relationship—may in itself seem mundane, no more than the stuff of everyday life, these heroines' lusts, longings and passions are imbued by their creators with such fierce and unrelenting intensity that what is at issue for them strikes the reader as powerfully as mayhem, murder or national catastrophe.

LARGER-THAN-LIFE CHARACTERS

A second key characteristic of the mega-best-seller is larger-than-life characters. Characters in fiction, as in life, are defined by what they do, and in big novels the main characters do extraordinary things. Don Corleone in *The Godfather* lets it be known that he wants an acting role in a big Hollywood movie for his godson. The studio head, outraged at being subtly threatened, refuses his request. The Don, to demonstrate his power and seriousness of purpose, arranges for the executive's prize possession, a costly thoroughbred racehorse, to be slaughtered and its severed head placed in the man's bed. Puzo establishes Corleone as existing outside the law of the land, the self-made ruler of an independent nation, with virtually absolute power over his relatives, retainers, employees, and vast areas of illicit enterprise.

In the opening chapters of *Gone With the Wind*, Scarlett is portrayed as a willful, mercurial, outrageously flirtatious and selfishly bratty teenager. But later in the novel, when the tide of war turns against the Confederacy, and Atlanta, an inferno of noise and flame, is being invaded by hostile Union troops, she, with no knowledge or experience, delivers Melanie's baby. Then she dares to flee into the night (despite exploding bombs and cannon-fire) with only comatose Melanie, her newborn, terrorized Prissy and no protection.

At Tara, Scarlett finds her mother dead, her father growing senile, her sisters bedridden, the plantation devastated, and no money or food. She, who never did a lick of work in her life, summons the energy and guts to till the fields and compel her rebellious house servants and sisters to help. When a menacing Yankee scavenger slips into the house, the terror-stricken young woman who could never bear the squealing of a pig at slaughter has the presence of mind to sneak off for a pistol and then finds the courage to shoot the thief. The only way she can think of to keep from losing her beloved plantation at a tax sale is to con Rhett Butler into marrying her. But she won't go to him like a beggar. No, overriding Mammy's fierce protests, she cuts up her mother's velvet curtains to be sewn into a new dress, so that when she *does* go to him, she can appear like a queen granting favors.

THE DRAMATIC QUESTION

The plots of big novels may at first glance seem highly complicated. And a thorough synopsis of the action in, say, *Gone With the Wind* would be long and involved. A closer and more careful look, though, would reveal that the book's *spine*—the ongoing central conflict around which its major characters interact, the main issue that drives and unites its myriad scenes—couldn't be more basic and clear-cut. This novelistic foundation is its suspense factor, which I call the dramatic question. In *Gone With the Wind* there are three dramatic questions: Will Scarlett succeed in getting Ashley to return her love? And later in the novel, once it's clear that Ashley is not the right man for her: Will she recognize that it's really Rhett she loves, and will Rhett ever manage to win her love?

In thrillers, the dramatic question as an underlying organizing principle is even more evident than in sprawling works such as *Gone With the Wind* or *The Godfather*. In *Eye of the Needle*, it's this: Will the Needle be able to escape to Germany with the Allies' D-Day invasion plans, or will British intelligence catch him first? Frederick Forsyth's most popular book, *The Day of the Jackal*, pivots on an attempt to assassinate Charles de Gaulle. Here the dramatic question quite simply is this: Will the Jackal manage to knock off the French president, or will the police inspector, hot on the killer's heels, somehow get to the Jackal first and prevent this from happening?

Not only big books, but genre novels such as mysteries and romances are also structured on a straightforward dramatic question: Will the sleuth track down the killer? Will the heroine get together with the man of her dreams? Such books lack other characteristics of the big novel. Yet genre authors such as Danielle Steele, Dick Francis and Tony Hillerman, who initially won a following in paperback and whose popularity has grown from book to book, demonstrate that there are routes other than through "the big book" to publishing stardom.

HIGH CONCEPT

Combine "high concept" with a strong dramatic question and you may have an even better chance of coming up with a big book. High concept, if you are not familiar with the term, is in essence a radical or even somewhat outlandish premise. Can a young lawyer escape a seemingly respectable law firm that secretly launders money for the Mafia, whose hoods kill any attorney who even talks about trying to leave? There in a sentence is the dramatic question and high concept of *The Firm* by John Grisham. In *The First Wives Club* by Olivia Goldsmith, three middle-aged women are tossed aside by their callous multi-millionaire husbands, who then all take up with younger women. The badly treated ex-wives are provoked into seeking revenge. Will they be able to carry it off? The unifying suspense factor is clearly present, but, even more important is the freshness of the plot situation and its trendy topicality. With business tycoons these days almost routinely acquiring trophy wives, it's not surprising that Sherry Lansing, a female producer with Paramount in 1991, was attracted to this high-concept story and paid a hefty sum for the film rights even before I placed this book with Poseidon/Simon & Schuster.

Garden of Lies is built on a high-concept premise that some publishers to whom the manuscript was submitted found too far-fetched. A poor girl, Sylvie, married to a rich man (who's away on business) gives birth to a dark-complected child obviously fathered by Sylvie's Greek handyman lover and not by her fair-skinned husband, who had been openly suspicious of her relations with the Greek. That very night there's a fire in the hospital. In the confusion Sylvie rescues a baby, a fair-haired girl belonging to a woman who perishes in the fire. The nuns don't realize that this infant isn't Sylvie's, and she, to save her marriage, decides to keep it and to abandon her own baby.

Equally farfetched and fraught with coincidences is the subsequent story of the two switched children. Sylvie's real daughter, Rose, who would have been reared a rich Jewess, grows up in poverty, parentless, with two sisters and a cruel and fanatically Catholic grandmother. Sylvie's stolen child, Rachel, is raised in a luxurious upper-class Jewish home and becomes a doctor. During the Vietnam War, Rachel saves the life of and then marries the man to whom Rose was betrothed and whom Rose loves more than anything or anyone. Later, even more improbably, Rose becomes a lawyer, and later in the novel is the one who defends Rachel in a fierce malpractice suit.

The point here is that big books need to be built on highly dramatic situations, plots that include bizarre and surprising actions and that lead to one powerful confrontation after the next. In real life, events do not occur with such gross yet highly ordered unlikeliness. Has anyone ever heard of a young man coming home from college to find that his uncle has killed his father and married his mother? Shakespeare's insights into character, family relations, young love, political in-fighting, theatrical lore, his magic with language—in short, his literary art-istry—make us believe in Hamlet and in his peculiar dilemma. So too, in her way, does Goudge with her switched babies who so coincidentally keep meeting up. No author sells more books than Stephen King and no author contrives more outlandish plots. But King's skill, genius even—and that of most superior popular authors—is, on the one hand, in recreating the dialogue and details of everyday life as he experiences them and, on the other, in orchestrating his story with such a high level of excitement that despite the contrived fantasy elements we quite happily suspend our disbelief.

MULTIPLE POINTS OF VIEW

Another important facet of the big novel is that it involves the reader emotionally with more than one character. It contains multiple points of view. The story is not primarily narrated by an omniscient author or by a single character in the novel in the first person, but rather expressed through the feelings, thoughts and sensibilities of a small number of major characters. It is not the voice of the novelist that impersonally describes the settings and other physical details. Instead we are led to perceive and experience the uniquely created world through the character's own senses. Her feelings and emotions alone provide the sometimes skewed but usually highly colored light by which we see her and the other characters she deals with.

A novel such as *The Man From St. Petersburg* provides a good exam-ple. Each chapter, either in its entirety or in a substantial subsection, is written exclusively from the point of view of one of the book's four principal characters. Follett's action stays highly charged because in each scene we experience the action through the point-of-view charac-ter, the one who has the greatest emotional involvement, the largest stake in what's happening. When Feliks is pursued through London and he's desperately afraid of being caught, we experience the frenzied flight through his sensibility and not through the point of view of his pursuer.

Unfolding a story through the interior feelings, hopes and longings of two men and two women of highly different ages, backgrounds and nationalities endows this text with a psychological complexity and richness, a minispectrum of colors, which, in a private-eye novel or romance told from only one point of view, is largely absent.

It's almost as if Follett has written four separate novels that keep colliding at key dramatic intersections.

SETTING

The last of the big novel's components I'll point to for now is setting. Readers of popular books enjoy escaping into the minds, hearts and vicissitudes of fictional characters, but they also like to be drawn into new, unfamiliar and even exotic environments. Novels such as *Hotel* and *Airport* by Arthur Hailey are permeated with thousands of details on every facet of what's involved in running a huge metropolitan hotel or busy airport. Most of us pass through such places on a regular basis, but we know little or nothing of the goings-on behind the scenes, the day-to-day problems, the technical intricacies. Coupled with a good story, such a body of information becomes a learning experience; and readers, by and large, are people who do like to learn.

A more contemporary example, *The Hunt for Red October* by Tom Clancy probably contains as much technical information about submarines and undersea warfare as one might find in a Naval Academy textbook. James Michener's vast popularity stems from the combination of his novelistic skills with his judicious culling of history for dramatic episodes, physical descriptions, ways of behaving and thinking, all of which he weaves into fiction to build such works as *Hawaii*, *Chesapeake* and *Poland*.

For a writer attempting a blockbuster novel now, however, I would not recommend a historical setting. An established author like Ken Follett can attract readers with a medieval saga such as *The Pillars of the Earth*, but it's relatively rare these days for a book club to choose a historical novel as a main selection, and the clubs do reflect the taste of the hardcover fiction-buying public. That public, which is affluent (with novels these days costing between twenty and thirty dollars) and which comprises no more than 3 percent of our population, also tends to favor stories set in the worlds of characters who are powerful, rich and famous, as opposed to environments inhabited by convicts, small farmers, blue-collar workers, welfare recipients or even "average" middle-class families.

A FINAL CAVEAT

Before we move into the nitty-gritty of techniques and working methods, however, another caveat. Fiction is an art, and art is not mathematics. I can and will lay out and analyze in considerable detail elements, techniques and structures with which most major best-sellers have been built. But in the end, in fiction as in art, there are no precise rules. If an author is brilliant enough to make his book work and at the same time disregard what is generally accepted as a key element of craft, then it works. One or another of the building blocks that I deem essential to constructing a blockbuster novel you will inevitably discern to be absent from this or that huge best-seller. For every precept I propound, you may be able to pick out a book you love that ignores it.

For example, I suggest several major point-of-view characters for a big novel (a methodology to which chapter six will be devoted), usually at least three. Yet two of the most wonderful and successful novels in recent years, *Presumed Innocent* and *The Burden of Proof*, both by Scott Turow, are written entirely from within the point of view of only one character.

Coming-of-age stories, I believe, are a big no-no for the author who aspires to write a big book. But of all the novels by Philip Roth, *Portnoy's Complaint* has been far and away his most successful. And J.D. Salinger, more than forty years after he wrote it, most vigorously lives on with *The Catcher in the Rye*.

For a novel to be big, the reader, I maintain, must empathize (or better, care passionately) about one or even two or three of the major characters. So what about *The Bonfire of the Vanities* by Tom Wolfe? you may ask. Line by line his writing crackles with wit, innuendo, fresh and brilliant language, and his plot is intricately and cannily woven together; his story's background, replete with telling details, topically epitomized the excesses of the 1980s. So his satire worked, and the rule of art in his case just did not apply.

But the chances of your snagging a spot on the best-seller list—and no matter how talented and assiduous you are, these chances are slim—will improve if you ask yourself, Is what's at stake in my story monumental, at least for my main characters? Am I creating a character (or maybe two) who is extraordinary in some way, even larger than life? Can the thrust of my novel be summarized in a simple but strong dramatic question? Is my plot built around a high-concept conflict such as one finds in almost any book by Sidney Sheldon or Michael Crichton? Am I developing at least one character (and preferably more than one) with whom the reader will become emotionally involved? Am I placing my characters in an environment that is in some way unusual or exciting, one that will cause the reader to feel she's entering a largely new world?

The following chapters will point the way on how to go about doing these things. But don't expect me to take you by the hand and explain (much less guarantee) how, by proceeding from A to Z, you'll be sure to come up with a blockbuster. What I will do, assuming you already have some solid material of your own to work with, is teach you by example. I'll illuminate how five very different authors have gone about organizing and employing the specific techniques that make their books work so wonderfully well. If you can then transpose this to your own writing and at the same time bring to it qualities that are unique to you, some measure of your own individual artistry, you could be on your way to becoming the author of a blockbuster novel.

Chapter Three

SETTING YOUR NOVEL

❧

WE READ NOVELS TO BE ENTERTAINED; but most readers are looking for more than the momentary excitement of, say, a sporting event or even a motion picture when they delve into a novel. They take pleasure in being transported not only into the dilemmas and sensibilities of characters different from themselves. Readers also enjoy being introduced to exotic environments where, almost as tourists or students, they can observe and learn about customs, mores, rituals, modes of dress and etiquette, social and business practices largely or wholly alien to those with which they are familiar.

THE IMPORTANCE OF SETTING

The setting of a novel can be the key determinant in the foundation of a plot and in the establishment of characters. In *The Man From St. Petersburg*, Lord Walden, seen in his splendiferous country and city homes, his London clubs, his assigned place at the Royal Court, surrounded by so many servants that he doesn't even know their names, becomes a quintessential symbol of pre-1914 imperial Britain. At the same time, as a literary character, he acquires added reality, credibility and depth, participating as he must in the everyday demands of eating, dressing, attending official functions, trying to be the devoted husband and father, all presented by Follett from within the perspective of a man of Walden's time and elevated social class.

In terms of plot, in Walden's case, it's the historical and offstage threat of an imminent war with Germany that provides the impetus for the story. In *Gone With the Wind*, the cataclysmic background of the Civil War as it affects Clayton County and the state of Georgia not only sets off the action, but Mitchell then makes use of actual recorded battles and of the subsequent Reconstruction period for major events in her plot. The invasion of Atlanta by Yankee forces, to mention but one example, provides the harrowing setting that makes the flight of Scarlett, Melanie and Melanie's newborn from the beleaguered city so powerfully dramatic.

Some blockbuster novels seem simpler, more basic, than an epic such as *Gone With the Wind*. These may be built around struggles for bare necessities, food, warm clothing, shelter, sheer physical survival, along with love and human closeness. But when artfully colored with the special hues and intimate details of a little-known environment, such books, when skillfully written, can become hugely popular. Witness the prehistoric hunters and gatherers in Jean Auel's *The Clan of the Cave Bear*, the nearly starving Chinese peasants in Pearl Buck's masterpiece, *The Good Earth*, or John Steinbeck's wandering and homeless 1930s Oakies in *The Grapes of Wrath*.

The novels of Arthur Hailey (*Airport, Hotel, Overload, Wheels, The Moneychangers*), James Michener (*Alaska, Chesapeake, Poland, Hawaii, Texas*) and James Clavell (*Tai-Pan, Noble House, Shogun*) provide some of the best-known examples of environmentally dominated best-sellers. Hailey chooses niches in contemporary America, ones that we the readers know about somewhat in passing, but only from the outside. Immersing us in the day-to-day workings of a major bank, a great hotel, a vast electrical utility, a frantically busy airport, Hailey at the same time builds a compelling story around a cast of characters whose interaction provides narrative excitement while bringing to life the doings of people in one of these unfamiliar workplaces. To us, the uninitiated, these settings are so out of the ordinary that they seem fascinating. Hailey is known to take three years on a novel, one of which he is said to devote entirely to researching its technical background.

Michener's forte is history. His settings can be the worlds of astronauts or World War II U.S. sailors in the South Pacific or a dozen equally far-flung others. It's the wars, revolutions, grabs for power and/ or economic dominance, or the scramble for sheer physical survival, usually over a period of generations, that give direction to the actions of Michener's characters and in the end control their destinies. The reader, through this history lesson, gains knowledge of courtship ways, religious practices, building techniques, burial ceremonies, methods of crop cultivation—in short, most of the key activities in these disparate characters' lives. Michener is said to employ a team of researchers to help come up with all the facts in his books, but he is also a constant globe-girdling traveler acquiring atmosphere, impressions and information firsthand.

Louis L'Amour, whose western novels dominated the field for more than thirty years (and still do), would interview every old-time lawman, cowpoke and ex-con he could find, recording their recollections on tape. He was an inveterate collector of original source materials about the old West—diaries, old books, journals, letters—and he would also visit the places where he set his novels.

A recent trend in popular fiction and an interesting variation on the above is what's known in publishing circles as the techno-thriller. A book such as *The Hunt for Red October* by Tom Clancy is built with the overall architecture of such now-classic thrillers as *Eye of the Needle* and *The Day of the Jackal*. But, as mentioned in the previous chapter, Clancy combines this structure with a Hailey-like background of high-tech, high-powered military, naval and aeronautical technical equipment. In this type of novel, the intricate and complex workings of machines with extraordinary capabilities, such as a new type of nuclear-powered Soviet submarine undetectable by sonar, a DSRV (Deep Submergence Submarine Rescue Vehicle), a Super Stallion long-range heavy lift helicopter, or an F-14 Tomcat jet-fighter plane, become as important to the story as most of its characters. Less high-tech is Follett's *Night Over Water*, but its 1939 Pan-Am Clipper is again a physical element that largely shapes the story. The plane's rate of fuel consumption, passenger cabin layout, baggage storage areas, take-off and landing capabilities, crewing arrangements, scheduled stops en route, all become controlling factors in the plot.

RESEARCH

For an author to create any of these types of richly textured out-of-the-way settings, it certainly gives her a tremendous edge to have actually lived or worked within one of these environments. Robin Cook, a doctor, writes medical thrillers. *Presumed Innocent* and *The Burden of Proof* are built around lawyers, and Scott Turow is a lawyer. Alex Delaware, the hero of Jonathan Kellerman's superb mysteries, is a child psychologist, as is the author. Hemingway's *A Farewell to Arms* and Jones's *From Here to Eternity* would not be the books they are had Hemingway not served as an ambulance driver in World War I and Jones in the U.S. Army in Hawaii prior to World War II.

But Arthur Hailey never worked as an air traffic controller, nor Mario Puzo as a Mafia leader, nor Ken Follett as a spy; and Margaret Mitchell was born several decades after the Civil War had ended. These authors' environments had to be created from research. For some projects, written materials—books, periodicals, newspapers, unpublished letters and diaries—can provide the requisite essentials. For novels set in the distant past such as *The Pillars of the Earth*, these texts often are the only available resources except, of course, for monuments such as the medieval cathedrals themselves. For books set in the present or recent past, visits to the particular environment, prolonged stays even, and interviews with people who have personal experience within the subject background can immeasurably enrich a novel.

Though *The Key to Rebecca* is set in World War II, Ken Follett traveled to Egypt in 1979 to acquire a feel for the country and its people, to soak up its atmosphere and see with his own eyes locations that would figure in his story. For *Night Over Water*, to find out at firsthand what flying the Pan-Am Clipper was like, he journeyed from London to Florida to interview the few surviving former crew members, who in 1990 were in their late seventies and eighties. Eileen Goudge was never in Vietnam, but some of the most powerful chapters in *Garden of Lies* are set there. The bulk of her information came from such war novels as *The Thirteenth Valley* by John Del Vecchio, but she also interviewed combat veterans for additional facts and anecdotes. And one veteran read and vetted the chapters for accuracy, as did a lawyer for the legal chapters and a doctor for the medical ones.

If you are unable to visit the site of your story, try to interview people who have been there, or who have flown the planes, sailed the ships, conducted the experiments you're writing about. Track them down, telephone, go to them. Lots of wonderful novels have been written based largely on library research, but the more firsthand information you can gather, the better your chances to imbue your work with a freshness that will make your story feel authentic.

WEAVING INFORMATION INTO ACTION

Background information derived from personal knowledge or from research is clearly valuable and in some books vital; but if it is not carefully woven into the fabric of the story, it can also deaden a book. Readers these days, accustomed to films and television, have little patience with long descriptive passages, especially at the start of a work before character interest has been established and the beginnings of the plot set in motion. It's all too easy for a writer to become enamored of delicious tidbits of information discovered while doing research and then to force-feed these into his novel. The result can be a bored agent or editor who rejects the manuscript or, if the book is published, a frustrated reader who's been diverted from the story of the characters with whom he's become involved, and who then skips over this informational section to get back to the action. So, unless this great research item can be worked into your novel in a way that helps illuminate your characters and/or serves to advance your plot, your book could be better off without it.

Now for you to see specifics, let's take a close look at just how a few bits of research are used and woven into two of our core titles, *The Man From St. Petersburg* and *The Godfather*.

Weaving in The Man From St. Petersburg

By a few pages into chapter two of the Follett novel, the four major characters have been introduced and the assassination plot has been set in motion. Now abruptly the problem becomes this: Can Charlotte learn to deftly gather and walk with her ball gown's four-yard train of cloth-of-silver lined with pale pink chiffon and caught at the end by a huge white and silken bow? The real essence of this little scene between Charlotte and her mother is, of course, to show how unconventional and outspoken Charlotte can be. It also prepares us for the debutante presentation at court, after which Feliks will try to kill Orlov. The little details of Charlotte standing in her dress of white tulle embroidered with crystals before a large pier-glass being fussed over by a dressmaker and coached in deportment by her mother bring us intimately into the texture of these characters' daily lives. And these descriptive details don't seem extraneous or boring, because Follett neatly integrates them into the action between Charlotte and Lydia.

In chapter nine, Walden goes to his comfortable old club in Pall Mall (as opposed to his spic-and-span and female-dominated home) to meet Basil Thomson of the Special Branch, hoping to find that the police have caught the assassin. Over an elaborate lunch, Walden unhappily learns from Thomson most of what the reader already knows about Feliks's vicious past, and then is badly shaken when told that he, Walden, may be the Russian's next target. But Follett humorously intersperses and counterpoints Thomson's shocking (to Walden) revelations with details of a gargantuan clubman's meal representative of the period. The two start with sherry, Brown Windsor soup, poached salmon and a bottle of hock to wash it down. Their main course, sliced from a joint before them, is mutton with red currant jelly, roast potatoes and asparagus, which is then followed by a savory of foie gras. Both men refuse Black Forest gateau, choosing ices instead, and Walden orders half a bottle of champagne. After this they have Stilton cheese and sweet biscuits with some of the club's vintage port. To finish, Walden takes a peach, Thomson a Melba pear, and they adjourn to the smoking room for coffee and biscuits. The research here is tasty in itself. It portrays how rich Edwardians comported themselves, illumines amusingly the gastronomic excesses of the period, and is woven seamlessly into the action.

Weaving in The Godfather

Toward the end of the sixty-four-page opening chapter of *The Godfather*, after the Corleone family has been introduced and several secondary plot strands set in motion, Puzo sets out the organizational structure of a Mafia family. We learn that between the head of the family, the Don, and the operating level of men who carry out his orders there are three layers, or buffers, so that nothing that these men do can be traced back to the top. We also learn about the role of the Consiglieri, the right hand to the Don, his auxiliary brain, the one person who would know everything the Don knows or nearly everything.

The point is that this information in the novel is not flatly presented as above but is imparted within a dramatic context, within the novel's ongoing action. The hidden chain of command gets brought into play because a beating is to be administered to the two punks who tried to rape Amerigo Bonasera's daughter. The order from the Don needs to work its way down to the men who will do the actual work.

As to the Consiglieri, Tom Hagen, he is given a more delicate and difficult task: to fly to California and persuade a Hollywood studio head, who has already said a definitive no, to change his mind and cast Johnny Fontaine as the lead in a big war movie. Hagen and his role of Consiglieri get defined then, not in the abstract, but through the specific mission that he's given and then undertakes.

The dramatic event in chapter six is the rubbing out of Paulie Gatto, who is suspected of being a traitor. Clemenza, his caporegime, or boss, has two problems: First, to whom does he now give Gatto's job, and second, how does he smoothly knock off Paulie? Puzo takes the opportunity of Clemenza's dealing with these two issues to discourse on promotion procedures within the Mafia; executive personnel selection; public body disposal versus discreet disappearance of a corpse; and on how, in a war between the families, secret apartments must be located where the "soldiers" hide out and sleep on mattresses scattered through the rooms. Finally, there is even an informational element in the killing of Gatto, after which the body is abandoned in one car and the killers move off to a second vehicle left parked nearby purposely for their escape. Mafia mores and techniques may seem a little commonplace now, what with the proliferation of gangster novels and films since *The Godfather*, but at the time, Puzo's information was fresh and exotic, especially since it was integrated so masterfully into his story.

Using Emotion

A precept for you to keep in mind when you set the scene in your own book is to color your descriptions with emotion. If we as readers find out about a sunset, a house, a submarine, through how a character feels about its qualities, we'll feel it's an ongoing part of the story; we'll relate to it more easily than if it sticks out because it's described impersonally as you the author narrate these details. This is also true with characters; the reader needs to be able to see them. If your character looks in the mirror and comments on his own appearance, or we find out how a character looks through the eyes and critical sensibility of a second character, the description will flow into the action much more smoothly than will a straightforward descriptive statement about clothes and physiognomy.

In your book, as in the examples I've cited, try to avoid flatly presenting information. Search for ways to weave it into the action. If, for example, you're writing about drug dealers, and you feel it's important to convey exactly how the heroin or cocaine is processed, what are your options? You could create a scene in which one character wants to hasten the processing in some way, while a second is opposed and fearful of the results. As they thrash things out between them, the details of the processing can easily emerge. Or their processing site could be raided; and in the still-tense aftermath, their methods could be excitingly reconstructed by a cop. Or you could have a scene of buying, selling or bargaining that would make it necessary to flaunt the process. The possibilities are endless.

CHOOSING YOUR SETTING

Okay, we've looked a bit at how Follett and Puzo have handled their settings. Now how do you go about deciding on an environment for your novel? For commercial purposes, the ideal choice would be a background that is topical, trendy, "sexy," and one with which you are already personally familiar. That would spare you from having to spend a lot of time on research, but keep in mind that any novel is going to involve at least some digging around for vital factual information.

What is topical, of course, changes with the times. While the Cold War was going on, novels such as *The Spy Who Came in From the Cold* by John Le Carré could become blockbusters. In 1993 publishers won't even consider a Cold War story. For a dozen or so years after the Vietnam War, the public seemed to want to forget it completely. Then in the 1980s, a spate of novels set in that bloody conflict was published, and some, such as *The Thirteenth Valley* by John Del Vecchio, became best-sellers. But in 1993, that war too is no longer a fertile ground for popular fiction.

Sexy Settings

So what's topical and trendy—not to mention "sexy"—right now, you ask? I'll make some suggestions, but keep in mind that these are being made in 1993, and how valid they'll be if you're reading this book five years from now is an open question. More importantly, though, I shall try to show how you can ascertain for yourself whether an environment you are considering possesses some "heat."

The United States has been economically at odds with Japan for more than twenty years, and a competitive and somewhat hostile relationship between our two countries seems bound to endure. For as long as it does, here is a terrific potential subject, as Michael Crichton has already shown with his hugely popular *Rising Sun*. The accomplishments of biological and genetic engineers in recent years have been and continue to be astounding. For his blockbuster *Jurassic Park*, Crichton chose that "sexy" background. This, however, is a field of constant surprises and discoveries, and it could accommodate dozens more good novels.

Other trendy backgrounds you might consider: computer technology, software, AIDS research, organ transplants, pollution control, currency speculation, money-laundering, licit and illicit arms dealing, nuclear power, electronic toys, credit card wars, organic food production, in short, most any subject area that gets dealt with regularly in the news media. Although not particularly topical, some of the standbys that seem to work again and again are law, medicine, dealing in precious metals and gems, high finance and professional spooks.

New environments, ones that appear never to have been previously opened up to the novel-reading public, when written about in a distinctive voice, can generate enormous excitement. *The Joy Luck Club* by Amy Tan introduced fascinated readers to the closed-off and exotic world of Chinese immigrants. Terry McMillan's *Waiting to Exhale* was a mega-success, revealing for the first time in popular fiction what life is like for single, middle-class black women in the 1990s. And Puzo, of course, did much the same kind of thing years ago with his Mafiosi.

Settings to Avoid

There are settings, too, that you should avoid. Some are out-of-vogue because their time has passed, some because they've been written about so much that the public seems to have grown tired of them, and some because they are too remote from the interests and concerns of people who can afford to spend twenty dollars or more for a novel. In addition to the Cold War and the Vietnam War, the Broadway theater is an example of a subject whose time has passed. The entertainment industry generally—movies, rock music, ballet, opera, television—has been dealt with in so many novels that agents and publishers look askance at stories with these settings. Politics and political campaigns also are often considered to have had overexposure.

Despite the fact that *A Thousand Acres* by Jane Smiley won the Pulitzer Prize for 1992 and was a best-seller, I would not recommend that you set your novel on a farm. Less than 1 percent of the population can afford to buy hardcover fiction with any regularity, and that affluent group tends to be more interested in rich people than in poor ones, in city dwellers rather than in rural folk, in movers and shakers rather than in the downtrodden. And all cities are not equal. New York and San Francisco, for example, are invested with an appeal and glamour hard to duplicate in, say, Hartford or Kansas City. I'm not suggesting that your novel be set exclusively in penthouses and corporate boardrooms. However, it's sad but true that you may find it impossible to get a publisher if your principal location is a prison or a shelter for the homeless.

Historical Settings

Three of the five novels you are reading in conjunction with this book are set more than fifty years ago. And some of your other great favorites might be *Shogun* by James Clavell, *Aztec* by Gary Jennings, or *The Pillars of the Earth* by Ken Follett. This quite naturally could lead you to assume that I recommend such a course for you. As I've earlier mentioned, I do not. Simply put, a better and more ready market exists for contemporary stories than for historical ones. And this is even more strongly the case if you're hoping to sell your book to the movies. *Dances With Wolves* and *The Last of the Mohicans* notwithstanding, Hollywood producers are terribly fearful of the huge costs involved in constructing period settings and costumes. I would estimate that, in recent years, more than 90 percent of the novels made into films have had contemporary settings. Ken Follett, when I first began working with him, was eager to write a novel set around the building of a medieval cathedral. I advised him to wait, and he did. After producing six thrillers, he had built up a worldwide following. Then he risked writing *The Pillars of the Earth*. Happily, readers in every country loved it. But had he not first developed that audience, the book almost surely would have fared less well. Nicholas Guild, another client of mine, wrote two excellent novels set in ancient Assyria that passed almost unnoticed in this country, whereas in Germany and Italy they achieved considerable success. But authors want to be recognized where they live, and Guild is now writing contemporary fiction.

Chapter Four

THE OUTLINE PROCESS

NO SANE PERSON WOULD THINK OF SETTING OUT TO CON-
STRUCT a skyscraper or even a one-family home without a detailed
set of plans. A big novel must have the literary equivalents of beams
and joists strong enough to sustain it excitingly from beginning to end,
and it also must contain myriad interlocking parts fully as complex as
those in any building type. Yet there are authors who commence a
novel without first working up an outline. Outlines, they say, cramp
their creativity, inhibit their characters from roaming free and becoming interesting, and take the joy out of writing because this planning
process denies them the possibility of making wonderful discoveries
that come to them only while they're setting down the novel itself.

My surmise is that few writers who talk this way ever see their
books on the best-seller list. Every mega-book with which I've been
involved was planned and replanned and planned again, much the way
architectural drawings are continually revised. Some major authors
must first write the full text for a number of scenes as a way of getting
to know their characters before they put together their outlines, while
others can start cold with a first-draft synopsis. Margaret Mitchell, an
exception, appears not to have used a written outline for *Gone With the
Wind*. What she did do, though, to ensure a plot that would build
inexorably to the climax she envisaged was to write her last chapter
first and then work her way from back to front, chapter by chapter.

OUTLINING *THE MAN FROM ST. PETERSBURG*

The outlining process, like the writing of the book itself, is almost
always a matter of layering. No writer, I believe, comes up with a
wholly satisfying outline on his first attempt. To demonstrate this, I'm

now going to take you through four drafts of outlines for *The Man From St. Petersburg* written over an eight-month period from January through August 1980. What you will see is how Follett, step by step, consciously sets out to build a story that contains high stakes; larger-than-life characters; a strong dramatic question; a high concept; farfetched plot premise; intense emotional involvement between several point-of-view characters; and an exotic and interesting setting.

But first a word about the impetus for this particular novel, for the thinking process that preceded the outline. This was to be Follett's fourth major book. *Eye of the Needle* and *The Key to Rebecca* were both set in World War II, and *Triple* in the Arab-Israeli flare-ups of the 1960s. His publishing contract called for a thriller set "preferably in World War II," but he and I felt that the market at the time was glutted with World War II and Cold War stories, and that his existing readers and potentially new ones might prefer a fresh environment. I pointed out that for some years there had not been a best-selling work of fiction set in World War I. He decided that the London of 1914 could provide a marvelously colorful background for a novel of intrigue. He also liked a setting of wartime or a country on the verge of war because he sought a situation that involved not just individuals but also the fate of nations. So, even before he set a word to paper, he decided on a setting in which the stakes could be extraordinarily high and in which he could place larger-than-life characters in highly charged dramatic situations.

Follett's novels (and those of most best-selling authors) begin with plot. At the outset, it's often no more than a strong situation that can be summarized in a sentence or two. You'll see how Follett uses the outline form gradually to enrich and complicate his plot while at the same time to narrow and sharpen its focus. But character is equally crucial. And Follett, from outline to outline, adds and eliminates dramatis personae, as well as their past histories and unique idiosyncrasies—all with a view toward building up the stature of his people, making them interesting, exciting and enhancing our feelings for them.

The four outlines and the analyses that follow essentially contain the entire message of this book in microcosm. By carefully studying what Follett has done, you will be able to witness the actual gestation of a blockbuster novel's structure, coupled with the principles that guided its formation. Later chapters will then amplify, expand on and reemphasize the ideas first presented here. After you complete the book,

I would recommend reading this chapter a second time. What Follett has done and my analysis may then be doubly meaningful to you.

But a warning. Unless you are dead serious about racking your brain to try and absorb the outlining process, you may find the rest of the chapter dense, tedious and maybe even boring. So if your aim in reading this book is to quickly glean a few nuggets that may help your own writing, I suggest that you either skip ahead to chapter five or read only the first outline and the last one. Constructing a novel such as *The Man From St. Petersburg* is a brain-twisting, time-consuming, complex process for the author. Anyone who wants to follow and understand this process must have patience and perseverence. You must be prepared to dig into the nitty-gritty of small details and to cope with the complexity of false starts and trial and error. And if you really want to challenge yourself, you might after reading each successive outline write what you feel is a better one of your own. Then delve into Follett's next draft, compare and contrast yours with his. After that, dig into my analysis of the novelistic principles governing the choices that Follett made.

THE OUTLINES
First Outline

BACKGROUND: ORIGINS OF THE FIRST WORLD WAR

Serbia was a small country in what is now Yugoslavia. It was dominated by its neighbour Austria, which was then large and powerful and known as the Austro-Hungarian Empire. Austria wanted to absorb Serbia, so Serbia sought the protection of Russia. Nevertheless, in 1908 Austria annexed a big piece of Serbia, a province called Bosnia. In 1914 a group of Serbian nationalist students assassinated a visiting Austrian Archduke in the town of Sarajevo, the capital of Bosnia. Then:

1. The Austrians, who already had designs on Serbia, used the assassination as a pretext and declared war on Serbia. (However, they did not actually attack.)

2. Russia, which was supposed to be Serbia's patron, reluctantly mobilized her army. (Mobilization meant calling-up the conscripts, arming them, and sending them to the border in railway trains.) At first Russia mobilized only partially, against Austria; but then the Russian generals realized that partial mobilization left them vulnerable to an

attack by Austria's ally, Germany; so the Russians ordered full mobilization.

3. Once Russia had mobilized against Austria and Germany, of course, Germany had to mobilize. However, Germany's problem was that Russia was allied with France, and the German generals were afraid that while they mobilized against Russia in the east France would attack them in the west. They decided to solve this problem by trying to put France out of the war with a lightning knockout blow. So Germany invaded France.

4. The German plan for invading France involved going through Belgium. Nobody cared much about Belgium, although there was an ancient treaty (1839) which permitted (but did not oblige) Britain to defend the neutrality of Belgium. However, Britain did care about Germany, which was growing fast and threatened British domination of the seas, world trade and the colonies. So when Germany invaded Belgium, Britain used the 1839 treaty as an excuse to declare war on Germany.

This is how a quarrel between Austria and Serbia led to war between England and Germany.

PART ONE

1. The slums of Edwardian London are no better than they were in Dickens's time. They are characterized by dirt, disease, awful poverty, drunkenness and fierce exploitation. One in three babies dies before its first birthday. When school medical examinations are introduced, one child in six is found to be too starved, verminous or sick to benefit from education. In some homes, people eat standing up because there are no chairs. In Whitechapel, where the official overcrowding level is 214 inhabitants per acre, there are in fact 6,000 people per acre.

In the East End, the poorest of Englishmen mingle with even poorer immigrants from Eastern Europe. Refugee Russians, Poles, Germans, Latvians, and Letts import far-left political ideas, which take root in the richly rotting soil of London poverty. The most powerful political organization is the Federation of Jewish Anarchist Groups, which publishes its own newspaper, *Der Arbeter Fraint*—in Yiddish—and organizes a successful strike of sweatshop workers.

Early in 1914, a German spy appears in this milieu. He is calling himself Feliks Murontziv and posing as a Russian anarchist. His brief is to report on the many refugee revolutionists in London, paying particular attention to expatriate Germans who might be planning a comeback.

Feliks is a complex and driven man. At the age of eleven he discovered that the solid German bourgeois couple who brought him up were not his natural parents. In fact, he is the son of a now-dead peasant girl and an unidentified young aristocrat. Feliks is obsessed with deception in general and betrayal in particular. He both adores and hates the aristocracy, and posing as an anarchist while working for the ruling class symbolizes his inner conflict. On a more rational level he would like to become a big shot and sees secret intelligence work as his road to advancement. He yearns for war. He is twenty-five.

In playing his anarchist role, he lets some of his passions show through, and he appears as a Rasputin-like character, intense, magnetic, fiery and domineering.

He has a wife and child in Germany, but the first thing he does in England is to marry a London girl and make her pregnant. For Feliks there will never be love without betrayal.

2. MI5 was started in 1906, when it was called MO5 and had a staff of one: its founder, Captain Vernon Kell. Kell's superiors were horrified the first time he asked for an assistant, but it is a basic law of nature that Intelligence departments always get bigger, and by now— 1914—Kell had four officers, a lawyer, two investigators and seven clerks. His office is in the basement of the Little Theatre in John Street, off the Strand.

Kell is a curious man. The son of an English officer and a Polish countess, as a boy he traveled all over Europe and learned French, German, Italian and Polish. He served in China during the Boxer Rebellion and passed Army interpreter's exams in Chinese and Russian. The East broke his health and—it seemed—ended a promising military career. He has asthma, recurrent dysentery, and back pains so bad he can hardly sit upright and uses his car for even the shortest journeys.

This is a man with an iron will, very tough and deeply pious. With tongue in cheek he tells the editors of *Who's Who* that his interests are fishing and croquet. One of his colleagues is fond of saying that Kell can smell a spy the way a terrier smells a rat. It may not be true, but it is a sign of the attitude he inspires in his subordinates. Superficially he is an officer of the old school from his moustache to his mirror-bright toecaps, but in fact he is devious, flexible, unorthodox, and at times most ungentlemanly in his methods. He claims to be a brilliant forger, but this is both a joke and a cover story, for in fact he uses the services of jailed counterfeiters. He is referred to as "K," beginning the tradition that Intelligence chiefs in England will be known by an initial. Kell has a good relationship with the aggressive, mercurial young Winston Churchill, who has been Home Secretary and is now First Lord of the Admiralty. Churchill is keen on cloak-and-dagger stuff and helps Kell cut through red tape.

Kell's big break comes when a Prussian naval officer goes from the German Embassy to a barbershop in the Caledonian Road, which is a bit like going from Central Park South to Brooklyn for a haircut. The barber's name is Karl Gustav Ernst. Kell has Ernst's mail intercepted. The barbershop turns out to be the post office for the German spy network in England.

Kell begins to track down the individual spies, but—setting another MI5 tradition—when he identifies them he does not arrest them, unless they discover something really important or try to leave the country.

3. The British Establishment is at its peak. They rule half the world. They don't know it, but they will never have it this good again. The old playboy King Edward VII died in 1910, but this is still the Edwardian era: the wealth, power and prestige amassed during the sixty-three solemn years of Victoria's reign are being spent with gusto. People eat and drink hugely. Houses are enormous, clothes are gorgeous, entertainment is lavish. The rules of etiquette have attained unparalleled complexity—for example, brown boots may not be worn closer to London than Ascot. Small fortunes are made by the Bond Street and Savile Row outfitters who supply the many clothes essential for different times of day and different social occasions. More than a million people, out of a working population of eighteen million, are employed as domestic servants. It is a time of hypocrisy: Everyone pays lip service to Victorian morality, and the homosexual intelligentsia have been driven abroad by the Oscar Wilde trial; but royalty patronise the Paris brothels and syphilis is rampant.

The Earl of Walden is a rich man. Most of his wealth is in London property, so he has survived the collapse of agricultural prices which has reduced the fortunes of some of his friends. To look after himself, his wife and his two teenage daughters, he employs more than one hundred servants at his homes in London, Surrey, Monte Carlo and Scotland. This year his elder daughter, Charlotte, is eighteen and is "coming out"—that is, she will put her hair up, be presented at court, and go to the endless parties and balls of the London "season" in order to meet a suitable husband.

Charlotte is pretty, protected, innocent, cultured, willful and idealistic. Her education has been narrow and impractical. A year ago she was wearing pigtails and knee socks. She asked her governess: "What will I do when I come out?"

"Oh, go to parties and balls and picnics and just have a wonderful time until you get married."

"And what will I do after I get married?"

"Why, my child, you will do *nothing*." This conversation continues to be on Charlotte's mind.

The London season is a marriage market for the ruling class, and this year's top prize is Prince Aleksei Andreivitch Oblomov, a handsome, enormously wealthy Russian of thirty. He is related to half the crowned heads of Europe, including George V of England; he is a favourite of the Czar, his uncle; and he is the man every debutante's mother wants for her son-in-law.

Charlotte meets him at her own coming-out ball and quickly discovers why he has escaped marriage so long: He is chronically shy with women. She succeeds in bringing him out of his shell a little, and he talks earnestly about the need for reform in Russia: for mechanised agriculture, free speech, land reform, industry and democracy.

Of course he is only a young hothead, and his elders are confident that, once he finds a wife and settles down, he will realize that in Russia all is for the best in the best of all possible worlds.

4. While Charlotte has been growing up cocooned in Walden Hall, European statesmen have been forging the alliances which will ensure that when one of them goes to war the rest will follow. The Central Powers—Germany and Austria-Hungary—are encircled by hostile nations: France, Belgium, England, Russia and the Balkans. As always, the problem facing German military planners is the danger of war on two fronts, against Russia in the east and France in the west. The aim of German diplomacy, therefore, is to neutralise Russia. One attempt to do this has already failed: In 1905 the Kaiser and the Czar signed the Treaty of Bjorko, but their officials tore it up immediately afterward.

The head of German espionage at this time is Gustav Steinhauer, an overblown, ambitious, scheming former Pinkerton detective (really). He was the "Prussian naval officer" who had his hair cut in the

Caledonian Road. He has twenty-two spies in England. As war looms in 1914, Steinhauer reads in an English newspaper that Prince Oblomov is in London, and he has a bright idea.

If England and Russia could be made to quarrel, and if the timing of the quarrel were just right, then Russia might be kept out of the coming war. Now, there is already a cause of friction between Russia and England, in that England shelters refugee Russian revolutionists. (England does this because public opinion and the Liberal government disapprove of the brutal Czarist regime.) Steinhauer thinks that if the Czar's favourite nephew were to be assassinated in England by refugee Russian revolutionists, the consequent cooling of relations between the two countries might be crucial.

Steinhauer goes to England to brief Feliks.

5. Coming home from a party at dawn, Charlotte is thunderstruck to see a woman asleep on the pavement. Her chaperone explains that thousands of men, women and children have nowhere to sleep but the streets of London. Charlotte just did not know that there were really poor people in the world. She goes home and screams at her mother: "Why didn't anyone *tell* me?" Her hysteria has another, secret source: She has just found out how babies are made. It seems that her education so far has been little better than a conspiracy to deceive her. Charlotte has her father's strong will as well as her mother's soft heart, and she won't stand still for this kind of treatment.

Now that she has begun to find out how things are in the real world, what can she do about it? She learns that as a woman she cannot even vote! She forgets Prince Oblomov and seeks out a different, more arty kind of society. She cultivates avant-garde acquaintances and meets some of the intellectual subversives of the day: Thomas Hardy, Emmeline Pankhurst, Bertrand Russell, Bernard Shaw, D.H. Lawrence. She scandalizes her society friends by declaring an (entirely theoretical) belief in free love and terrifies her parents by planning to go on a suffragette demonstration.

6. Kell, the head of MI5, is still reading the mail of Ernst, the barber; so he learns in advance of Steinhauer's visit and has Steinhauer shadowed.

Steinhauer meets with Feliks and explains the idea. Feliks is very keen: For him to kill an aristocrat with his superior's approval is a way of getting as it were double stamps. Feliks wonders how to get next to Oblomov. Steinhauer shows him the English newspaper, in which

Oblomov is reported to have attended the coming-out ball of Charlotte, Viscountess Walden, at 19 Belgrave Square. Find Charlotte, says Steinhauer, and perhaps she will lead you to Oblomov.

7. Kell knows of this meeting but does not know what was said. He decides to take a closer look at Feliks. He manages to stand next to him in a pub one evening and even pass a few words of conversation. Kell feels instinctively that Feliks is interesting and dangerous. However Kell does not have the manpower to put a twenty-four-hour watch on every suspected spy. But he does have informants within the revolutionary underworld. One of these is Andre Barre, a Bolshevik. Kell asks Barre to learn what he can about Feliks.

This is Kell's big mistake.

8. Charlotte goes on her suffragette demonstration. The King has refused to give an audience to Mrs. Pankhurst, so the suffragettes march on Buckingham Palace. The police are ordered to repel them with a minimum of arrests (because the suffragettes are more trouble in jail than out), and the consequence of this policy is that the women get beaten up. Idle male bystanders join in the attacks. The most militant of the women wield Indian clubs and throw pepper.

Charlotte is rescued from a beating by a tall, bright-eyed, roughly dressed Russian who tells her his name is Feliks.

The Archduke Ferdinand is assassinated in Sarajevo.

PART TWO

9. Feliks had originally planned simply to follow Charlotte around until he found Oblomov, but seeing her at the demonstration gives him a better idea.

He cultivates her, takes over her political education and seduces her. They are not in love. Charlotte is continuing her teenage rebellion, and although Feliks has an almost hypnotic power to dominate her, she does not become very fond of him. Feliks is using her, and he gets a big kick out of screwing the aristocracy, but he is not under her spell, not yet.

He tells her about life in Russia and the unbelievable brutality of the Czarist regime. He makes her read Marx and Kropotkin. He explains about revolution and about propaganda by deed. He talks about maybe kidnapping Oblomov and holding him to ransom against the release of political prisoners. She thinks it's a grand idea.

10. Andre Barre, the Bolshevik, knows where to get bombs, and

now Feliks asks for his help. Barre takes Feliks to meet a mad little Latvian in Islington who agrees to make them a bomb.

Barre has a meeting with Kell. Barre tells Kell that Feliks is having an affair with Charlotte, but does not say anything about the Oblomov plot.

Why? Everyone in the revolutionary movement trusts Barre because he is known to have suffered unimaginable torture at the hands of the Czar's police, who pulled out his fingernails and cut off his penis. It is assumed that the Czar could not have a more implacable enemy. Wrong. Barre is in fact a shell of a man who completely lacks a will of his own. Not only is he reporting to Kell, he is basically working for the Ochrana, the Russian secret police, his torturers. He has reported the assassination plot to the Ochrana and they have instructed him to do all he can to *help*.

Why? (i) It is Ochrana policy to *encourage* anarchist outrages in order to justify their ever-harsher crackdowns. (ii) This is particularly so in London, where they use agents provocateurs in the hope of scaring the English into sending the revolutionists home to be jailed, tortured and executed. (iii) Although the Czar thinks Oblomov is a harmless young hothead who will soon settle down, the Ochrana are afraid that if he doesn't settle down he will be a dangerous social-democrat and a pernicious influence and may well reduce their powers, so they will be delighted to see him dead.

11. Charlotte begins to cultivate Oblomov again and persuades her mother to give a weekend party for him at Walden Hall in Surrey. Charlotte achieves this partly by hints that Oblomov may be in love with her. Oblomov, who is certainly in love with her, also draws the conclusion that any advances might be favorably received.

Charlotte arranges for Feliks to be hired as a gardener at Walden Hall.

Then she goes for the first time to Feliks's house, and meets his wife—who is now very pregnant. At this point Charlotte's trust in Feliks begins to fade.

12. Kell gets suspicious about the long silence from Barre and sends an investigator to see him. Feliks sees the investigator leaving Barre's house and follows the man to headquarters. Realizing that Barre is a police informer, Feliks kills him. Then he picks up the bomb and goes to Walden Hall for the weekend.

Austria declares war on Serbia.

PART THREE

13. On Saturday morning Oblomov asks Charlotte to marry him. The "kidnapping" is scheduled for that afternoon, and the plan is that Charlotte should lure Oblomov to a disused hut in the woods. Charlotte is afraid that if she refuses Oblomov he may leave Walden Hall immediately; so she says maybe, and promises to give him his answer that afternoon in the hut.

Among the guests is a distinguished surgeon. Hesitantly, embarrassed, Charlotte asks him, "When a woman stops . . . bleeding . . . is it serious?" The doctor says, "It usually means she's pregnant." Charlotte turns white.

14. Kell learns of Andre's death. He has lost contact with Feliks. He remembers another link to Feliks—Viscountess Walden. He goes to Belgrave Square and is told that the Waldens are in the country, giving a weekend party for Prince Oblomov. Kell suspects the truth and heads for Walden Hall. (Maybe he sends a cable which is intercepted by Feliks or Charlotte?)

15. Charlotte goes early to the hut to tell Feliks she is having his baby. She interrupts his setting the fuse to the bomb.

Kell arrives at Walden Hall and goes out searching for Oblomov.

Charlotte realizes this is not a kidnapping but a murder, and that she was to have died with Oblomov. She tells Feliks that he would have been killing his own child, too. Suddenly they both realize that, because Feliks was interrupted in the middle of setting the fuse, the bomb is about to go off. Feliks throws himself on the bomb. As he lies dying, with half his body blown away, he tells Charlotte not to have the baby adopted. She promises.

Oblomov arrrives. He assumes—as will everyone else—that quite by accident Charlotte has saved his life.

Charlotte agrees to marry Oblomov.

Russia mobilizes.

The end.

Analysis of First Outline

Having read this outline, you should feel encouraged. Here is the embryo of what grew into a book that enjoyed more than twenty weeks on the *New York Times* hardcover best-seller list, sold more than four million copies in two dozen languages—and you quite rightly may have concluded that it is not very good. Follett begins with at least some interesting material about the setting for his story and with a basic dramatic situation, the assassination attempt. But on this first go-round, he doesn't feel the need (nor should you) to develop the full histories of all his major characters or to work out all the seesawings of an intricate thriller plot.

So, the first thing to keep in mind about outlining is that you must not let yourself feel intimidated or discouraged by how hard it seems to sit down and in a day or a week write one that you can look at and say, Hey, this really works. You should expect your first outline to be perhaps a little vague or poorly focused, and that it most likely will end up with some loose ends, some unresolved plot strands. Then you'll have to go back and approach it afresh, adding twists to the plot, enriching the background of the characters and the complications between them, changing elements you previously have set down to make them conform to your new ideas. Chances are you'll find shortcomings in your second outline as well, and you'll have to repeat the process. Yet to come are three more versions of outlines for *The Man From St. Petersburg*. For *The Pillars of the Earth*, Follett wrote nine.

But take care. Planning a book is different from writing it. Your final outline will serve you better if you refrain from letting it become a mininovel. What will help you most is writing up a solid paragraph or so about each of your major characters as each one enters the story. As you go on, write a paragraph or so (but no more than a page) setting down the main action of each chapter or major scene. There is no specified length for an outline, but I would recommend between twenty and forty double-spaced pages. Try not to encumber yourself at this stage of your work with details of dialogue, description or interior monologue. When you come to the actual composing of your text, you want to feel as uninhibited as possible and let your inspiration take you where it will. And outlines, as you'll see in the next to last chapter of this book, do often need to be at least partially set aside and reconceived as you go about writing your text and your novel takes on a life of its own.

As in Follett's three previous major works, *Eye of the Needle*, *Triple*, and *The Key to Rebecca*, the main conflict in the outline you have just read is between two intelligence services, exemplified by Kell for the British and Steinhauer for the Germans. But these two never deal directly with each other. The closest they come is when Kell has one of his men shadow the German. And they are given no strong connections with any of the other characters, so that their roles seem to have not much more than a mechanical function. Feliks, the Prussian agent and would-be assassin, is painted all black, a remorseless killer, a deceiver of women who has two wives and who also seduces naive Charlotte and bends her to his will. Charlotte, in the end, saves the day by confronting Feliks, but neither she nor any other character is presented as a strong protagonist.

Note, too, that the characters' motivations are all primarily political. Having given these people no intense personal relationships, Follett has not yet set up high stakes on a personal level, except to a small degree between Charlotte and Feliks. Oblomov has no role in the action except to be a comical suitor to Charlotte and to provide a target— both the Germans and the Russian secret police want him terminated. Lord and Lady Walden, Charlotte's parents who own Walden Hall, the setting for the climactic action, are minor figures who do no more than provide some lavishly wealthy Edwardian local color. None of the characters are larger than life; and none, with the possible exception of Charlotte, who grows from a naive innocent into a courageous and outspoken young woman, promise emotional involvement from the reader.

The main problem with this outline, however, is its diffused focus. Who is this book about? Who, from beginning to end, is going to engage and lock in our interest? It's not enough, for example, that Steinhauer wants Oblomov assassinated; so do the Russian secret police, who in one scene pop in and then right out of the story and are never brought alive with a named character. Once he has briefed Feliks, Steinhauer, the main force behind the assassination, also disappears. Charlotte, though she knows Feliks has deceived her, continues to help him. And Kell, whose ostensible role it is to prevent the assassination, is given no part in the climactic ending, nor does he do anything else that is particularly exciting. The story's central conflict, such as it is, is between Kell and Feliks, but it never takes hold. Except for Kell's once standing next to Feliks in a pub, the two never confront each other.

Nonetheless, with this outline, the seeds for the book that eventually will evolve are already somewhat in place. The assassination plan does provide a clear and highly charged dramatic question. The stakes, at a global level, couldn't be higher. The setting, embryonic though it is here, is colorful and likely to become fascinating. And with such scenes as the seducing of a virginal aristocrat by a German spy, and his later falling on an exploding bomb to save her and his unborn child, we can at least hope for some good excitement.

Now see how Follett goes about building on this in the outline that follows.

The ellipses you'll see from time to time indicate omissions that replicate background material from the first outline. Italics denote summarized repetitions of major actions from the previous synopsis.

Second Outline

PROLOGUE

Two young tourists from the U.S., Peter and Lizzie, are visiting Walden Wildlife Park in Surrey, England. The park is in the grounds of Walden Hall, a stately home which is open to the public. What Peter and Lizzie like best is the fantastic landscaped garden with its vistas, waterfalls, lakes, artificial hills, secret pathways, and—best of all—the follies, which are whimsical little buildings in a variety of crazy styles dotted about the garden for decoration. One of these is a funny little gazebo about half a mile from the house and partly hidden by shrubbery. Peter and Lizzie find their way inside. The place is clean, with marble seats and a working fountain. They smoke a joint, enjoying the ambience and imagining the lives of the incredibly rich people who used to live here. They make love, pretending to be Lord and Lady Walden. A little later they hear a voice: "I heard heavy breathing so I waited outside." In comes a woman who must be eighty years old. Peter realises they are a little out of line and begins to apologise. The old lady has a twinkle in her eye. "Don't worry, there was a time when I used to get laid in here." Peter and Lizzie give each other a look which says: She's an original! It turns out she owns the place. "As well as getting laid in here, I almost got killed here," she says. Her name is Lady Walden, and this is the story she tells:

PART 1

1. In 1914 the gazebo is a den for two teenage sisters who live at Walden Hall. The girls are Charlotte and Belinda, ages eighteen and sixteen (although from their conversation they seem younger). Normally they are very closely supervised by their governess, but on her

day off an easygoing maid takes over. The maid, Sarah, meets her boy-friend while the girls go to the gazebo.

. . . Today Charlotte and Belinda are talking about sex, a subject on which they are by modern standards breathtakingly ignorant. They agree that babies grow inside women but cannot decide how they come out. Charlotte knows where eggs emerge from chickens, and once by accident Belinda saw a cow drop a calf, but they agree that their own bodies have no apertures big enough for a baby. They wonder whether they suffer from a congenital deformity. There is no one they can ask about this. They do not consider the question of how a baby gets started—they assume it happens spontaneously around the age of twenty-one, which for them explains why girls are pressured to marry at nineteen or twenty.

2. . . . Charlotte and Belinda are extreme victims of the notorious conspiracy of silence about sex. . . .

. . . The Earl of Walden, the father of Charlotte and Belinda, is a typical but likeable product of this elite. . . . He is fifty and one of those men who are in their prime at that age. His big, beefy body has yet to collapse into sagging fat. His hearty manner conceals a strong intelligence. But his full-blooded enjoyment of life is genuine. He likes hunting parties and society balls, the company of young men and ma-ture women, going to the opera and the music-hall (vaudeville), drink-ing ale and port, playing poker and chess. He has no real job, apart from a ceremonial post in the royal household, but he is a friend of several senior politicians, he is active in the House of Lords, and he often does confidential diplomatic work.

. . . *With the danger of war hanging over Europe, German diplomacy aims to neutralize Russia, and* the French and British are keen to extract from the Russians a firm commitment to attack Germany if Germany attacks France.

It is with this in mind that the Foreign Secretary, Sir Edward Grey—a weasel-faced birdwatcher—visits Walden. Grey explains that a young Russian general will be in London for the season (which is May, June, July). He is prince Alexei Andreivitch Oblomov, aged thirty, a nephew and favorite of the Czar and a distant relation of Walden's wife, Lydia. Ostensibly Oblomov will be here to find a bride, but he will also conduct secret talks about Anglo-Russian military cooperation. Walden, who speaks Russian, will negotiate on behalf of England. Frankly, says Grey, if you can make them commit themselves we will win the war. If you can't, Europe will be conquered by Germany.

3. . . . England is the only European country with *no* restrictions on immigration. Consequently, London is a haven for refugee revolutionists. The anarchists are particularly strong, with their own clubs and their own (Yiddish) newspaper. England's open-door policy infuriates the Russian secret police—the notorious Ochrana—but the Liberal government and British public opinion are out of sympathy with the cruel domestic policies of the Czar.

The Ochrana, using "attachés" at the Russian Embassy in London, tries to keep an eye on these expatriate troublemakers and does so more successfully than the cheerfully incompetent English secret police, Scotland Yard's "Special Branch," who do not know a Menshevik from a mensch. But the Ochrana does more than watch. . . .

The Ochrana's senior plotter in London is Serge Ferfichkin, a cool but not perfectly sane manipulator with an obsession for files. The Ochrana is in charge of encoding and decoding all cable traffic at the Russian Embassy, so Ferfichkin hears of Oblomov's forthcoming visit to London, and he begins to think.

. . . The revolutionists scorn him [Oblomov] publicly and secretly admit that the kind of democracy he wants is the greatest threat to the prospect of a real revolution. But the Ochrana, politically naive like all intelligence organizations, see him as a highly dangerous man. . . .

And suppose—Ferfichkin reasons—Oblomov were to be assassinated, while in England, by an expatriate Russian revolutionist? Would this not force the British to reverse their open-door policy? Indeed, given that the British are so desperate to squeeze a military commitment out of Russia, such an assassination might even prompt the Czar to demand extradition of the revolutionists as the price of the commitment.

The assassination of Oblomov would therefore serve the Ochrana doubly. (Is it not incredible that they should kill one of their own leaders? No. They have already killed the Grand Duke Sergius and the Minister of the Interior, both in the interests of provocation.)

Ferfichkin also knows from the cables that Oblomov will have talks with the Earl of Walden. The name Walden rings a bell, and Ferfichkin dives into his files. Walden is married to a Russian, Lydia. Lydia has a file: Before she married Walden she associated with a young St. Petersburg anarchist called Feliks Murontsiv. Feliks has a file . . . and, yes, he is in London.

Ferfichkin calls in one of his agents.

4. . . . When he [Feliks] was a student he had a brief but passionate affair with Lydia, the daughter of a count; but she broke it off (under parental pressure) and married an English earl. Later Feliks was tortured by the Ochrana, escaped from prison and fled to England. His opposition to the ruling class is therefore deeply personal as well as political.

Now forty . . . He is tall, thin, hairy and none too clean, but there is in him a kind of animal energy which some women find irresistible. Most evenings he may be found at the Jubilee Street Anarchist Club in Stepney, drinking and arguing politics.

Tonight the group around Feliks is joined by Andre Barre, a sly, nervous Bolshevik with contacts at the Russian Embassy. Barre announces that he has heard that Prince Oblomov will come to London for secret talks with the Earl of Walden.

Here is the opportunity for propaganda-by-deed, and around the table there is much talk of assassination. Feliks however is quiet. If he is going to do something he will not plan it in public.

Barre, who is an agent provocateur, reports back. Ferfichkin says: "Do you think he realizes who Lady Walden is?" Barre says he showed no sign. "Well," says Ferfichkin, "he'll soon find out."

PART 2

5. . . . He [Oblomov] makes his first appearance at Charlotte's coming-out ball at the Savoy Hotel. He turns out to be very handsome as well as high-born and incredibly rich. The ball is a glittering occasion, with the debs in fantastic gowns and the young men in white ties and tails. . . . Charlotte is fascinated *by his talk about the need for reform in Russia* and has to be dragged away to dance with other guests.

A little later, in the ladies' powder room, she has a girl-to-girl chat with a cousin who tells her the sexual facts of life.

6. Feliks is also at the ball. He has got a job as a temporary waiter with the object of taking a close look at Oblomov. He does not plan to kill the prince tonight, if only because right now he does not have the money to buy a weapon. In a corridor he sees Lydia and hears her addressed as Lady Walden. He is thunderstruck. He catches her eye. She turns white and walks away. He goes after her and asks her to meet him. She refuses. But he gets the impression that he still has some

power over her; and now he knows where to get the money to buy the weapon that will kill Oblomov.

7. . . . *On the way home, seeing a woman sleeping on the pavement, Charlotte* insists on stopping the carriage and speaking to the woman. It turns out to be Sarah, the maid who used to deputize for the governess at Walden Hall. Sarah says she was fired because she got pregnant. . . . *When she {Charlotte} gets home, she screams at her mother. . . . From now on, she decides, she will find out things for herself (rather than submit to an education which seems to be a conspiracy to deceive her).*

8. Lydia, thirty-nine and still beautiful, has problems of her own. Back in 1894 she married Walden after a whirlwind courtship in St. Petersburg. She has always liked her husband, but she has nourished the memory of her adolescent passion for Feliks, and she has never ceased to feel guilty because she was not a virgin when she married Walden. This guilt has clouded the marriage. Now Feliks has reappeared in her life, and she is distraught. Although she no longer feels any physical lust for him, the combination of guilt and remembered affection make her vulnerable to him. And in this turmoil she cannot look her husband in the eye, so she becomes cool to him and begins to shut him out of her life.

PART 3

9. Ferfichkin knows Oblomov's movements. Consequently he is able to give Barre information which makes Barre indispensable to Feliks; and in return Feliks is obliged to make Barre privy to his plans, so Ferfichkin knows what Feliks is doing.

Now, instructed by Ferfichkin, Barre takes Feliks to see a crazy old Polish chemist in Clerkenwell who makes bombs. Feliks says he will need a large bomb with a timing device. The chemist names a price. I'll get the money, says Feliks.

Feliks calls on Lydia while Walden is out. (He gains admittance by giving a false name.) He tells Lydia how much money he needs and asks her to meet him in a week's time. Lydia, desperate to get him out of the house and terrified Walden will learn of her premarital affair, agrees.

10. Walden and Oblomov exchange information on mobilization and military planning. They begin to draft an agreement whereby both will attack Germany if Germany attacks either France or Russia. Oblomov may be hopeless with women but he is a tough negotiator, and

the first meeting gets stuck on the definition of "attack."

Afterwards Walden walks around for a while. He has noticed Lydia's new mood and vaguely resents it. He finds himself walking past a small house in Chelsea. It is the home of Bonita Carlos, real name Myrtle Jenkins. Bonnie was the greatest courtesan in London in the 1890s. The young Walden was crazy for her and in fact gave her this little house. What is she like now? he wonders. My God, she must be fifty. He walks on.

11. *Charlotte meets people in the avant-garde, and horrifies her parents by announcing she's going on a suffragette demonstration.*

12. Lydia's problem now is that she has no money. The household shopping is done by servants, and they do not use cash—the shopkeepers send bills to Walden who pays by check. Lydia's dressmakers, hatters, etc. all send bills. If Lydia takes morning coffee at the Cafe Royal during a shopping expedition, she signs for it. Her personal fortune consists of property and shares which she cannot sell without the knowledge of the family solicitor, a personal friend of Walden. She has no bank account of her own. So, highly embarrassed, she takes some jewelry to Hatton Garden and sells it.

13-14. *At the suffragette demonstration, Charlotte is rescued from a beating by a tall, roughly dressed Russian who introduces himself as Feliks. . . . He takes Charlotte back to his lodgings and seduces her.*

15. Walden asks Lydia to wear one of the pieces of jewelry she has sold. She tells him she has sent it for repair. Next day he sees it for sale in a shop window. He storms in and accuses them of theft. The manager takes him into the office and explains that this happens not infrequently; a lady needs cash for a clandestine purpose and sells some jewelry unbeknown to her husband. . . . Humiliated, Walden buys the stuff back. Then he hires a private detective to follow Lydia.

16. Following Feliks's instructions, Lydia books a private room in a restaurant and meets him there for lunch. She gives him the money. Now he asks for something else: a job. She gives him a letter to the head groundsman at Walden Hall, telling him to take Feliks on as a gardener.

PART 4

17. Walden's detective reports that Lydia had lunch in a private room in a restaurant with a man of about her own age and that they

spoke Russian together. The detective followed the man home and so has his address.

Walden instructs the detective to find out all about Feliks.

Then Walden goes to see Bonnie. She is now a comfortable, plump, horny woman of fifty, no longer a courtesan, living on her investments and a little lonely. She is thrilled to see Walden. They spend a wonderful afternoon in bed. Walden begins to consider ways in which he could spend less time with Lydia and more with Bonnie.

18-19. *Feliks persuades Charlotte that Oblomov should be kidnapped, and she persuades her mother to give a weekend party for Oblomov at Walden Hall, hinting that he may propose.*

20. . . . Sir Edward Grey tells Walden that he must sign an agreement with Oblomov within the next few days. (Of course, the agreement will still have to be ratified by the governments.) Walden says he thinks Oblomov will sign next weekend at Walden Hall.

PART 5

21. On the Thursday before the weekend party Feliks goes to Clerkenwell to collect the bomb. The chemist explains the mechanism. Setting the timer is a delicate job: The bomb must first be armed, then the timer—an alarm clock—must be set. The alarm bell will ring two seconds before the explosion. The bomb will destroy everyone in the room, provided it is not muffled by something soft and heavy like a sandbag.

Feliks takes the bomb and leaves for Walden Hall.

22. On Friday morning the private detective reports to Walden. Feliks is an anarchist, he says, and yesterday visited a man known to the police as a bomb maker. He then caught a train to Surrey.

Of course, it occurs to Walden that Feliks may intend to assassinate Oblomov. He gets the Russian Embassy to provide bodyguards for the prince. He wonders what Lydia's role is in all this and is afraid to ask her.

It occurs to him that if Oblomov is assassinated, it could ruin the secret treaty and even keep Russia out of the war.

23. Feliks, now gardening at Walden Hall, hears about the bodyguard and contrives to stay well away from the house. (Nobody here knows he is Russian—he has given his name as Felix Morrow.)

On Friday evening he and Charlotte make love in the gazebo. Then he tells her to lure Oblomov to the gazebo at exactly four o'clock on Saturday afternoon.

24. On Saturday morning Lydia finds the jewelry she sold in Walden's wardrobe. She decides to confess. . . .

25. After lunch Ferfichkin, who knows Feliks's plans through Barre, calls off Oblomov's bodyguards, saying that Oblomov has refused to have them hanging around. (Ferfichkin figures that Oblomov will be dead before he can deny it.)

Lydia gets Walden alone and confesses all. Walden has no time to be glad that she still loves him, because of course her confession reveals that the assassin is right here at Walden Hall! Walden starts a search—but neither Feliks, Oblomov or Charlotte can be found.

26. Oblomov is walking in the woods alone, wondering whether Charlotte will say yes. . . .

Charlotte goes to the gazebo, finds Feliks arming a bomb, tells him he would have been killing his unborn child. He throws himself on the bomb . . .

27. . . . Walden and Lydia are reconciled and have a second honeymoon. . . . *Charlotte agrees to marry Oblomov.*

The world goes to war.

EPILOGUE

The eighty-five-year-old Charlotte has been talking to Peter and Lizzie all day. At lunchtime they shared sandwiches in the gazebo, and later they had dinner together in the Great Hall of the house after all the tourists had gone home. Now, at almost midnight, Charlotte winds up the loose ends. She did indeed marry Oblomov. He was made military liaison officer with the British and so stayed in London for the war. He lost all his fortune in the revolution, but Walden got him a directorship of a bank, and to everyone's surprise he became a very successful international banker. Walden lived to a ripe old age but lost his money in the Depression. Lydia's grandsons have revived the family fortunes by turning Walden Hall into a tourist attraction.

"It's a wonderful story," says Peter. "You should write a book."

Charlotte laughs. "Nobody would believe it."

"Maybe not." Peter thinks. "Well," he says after a while, "you could make it a novel."

Analysis of Second Outline

Follett, as you can see, has made dozens of changes between outlines one and two, all important and most solid improvements. A few, however, have the effect of altering the story in basic ways, and it's those that I'll point up.

No longer are the orchestrators of the main action two spy masters. Kell is gone, as is Steinhauer and indeed the entire German involvement. Narrowing the focus, the assassination attempt is now exclusively a Russian affair, with Feliks now a Russian who gets set in motion and aided somewhat by a new character, Ferfichkin. This Russian Secret Police agent, however, does not impact directly on any of the main characters. As you'll see in later drafts, Follett wisely removes both him and Barre, his pathetic agent provocateur, from the story.

But with Ferfichkin, Barre and Feliks all sharing the role of antagonist and with no protagonist figure moving strongly against them, the focus of the story remains diffused, but far less so than in Outline One. What was almost pure political melodrama is being transformed into one in which character and character relationships begin to drive the plot.

This second synopsis does somewhat point up four main characters—Feliks, Walden, Lydia and Charlotte—who each are more developed and have been given a new knot of personal involvement between them.

Feliks, no longer a mercenary German, becomes an idealistic Russian revolutionist, a man who during his youth in St. Petersburg as a poor student was madly in love with a rich and titled girl. Lady Walden, who in Outline One was purely English, is now of Russian origin. Indeed, she becomes none other than Feliks's girlfriend of yesteryear who still feels guilty about her youthful affair and at the same time retains powerful feelings for this man who once was her great love. Feliks is thunderstruck to discover her at Charlotte's coming-out ball and then, because of their past intimacy, is able to use her to get money to buy a bomb. The discovery of Lydia's missing jewelry in turn triggers Walden's suspicion of her, his hiring a detective to find out all about Feliks, and his resuming an affair with a former mistress. Notice this string of causal connections driving the plot, none of which existed in Outline One. Yet these are a paltry lot compared with the intricate series that will tie the story together in the final version.

Feliks, in this draft, takes on new interest. His tight link to the Walden family through Lydia begins to engage our sympathy; he is recast as a man with a quest and no mere hired gun. Now he gets offered no money and no preferment. He decides all on his own to go after Oblomov. He also is someone who has suffered imprisonment and torture, and who has had the love of his life cruelly stolen from him.

Thus we can feel pity for him and some understanding for his actions, but not much warmth with his cool slaying of Barre. He is still cold-blooded, a less-than-wonderful antagonist, a smaller, meaner figure than the powerful character who dominates the book in its final form.

Walden and Prince Oblomov, who were little more than scenery, now have expanded and important roles. The titled Russian bachelor, no longer merely the playboy prey of British debutantes seeking a rich and aristocratic husband, now comes to London on a top-secret mission as the Czar's nephew and personal envoy to negotiate a treaty with Britain. He is also made into Lydia's distant relation. But Follett gives him little to do, except for one negotiating session with Walden and his proposal to Charlotte.

His English counterpart becomes Lord Walden, who now speaks Russian, having met and married Lydia in St. Petersburg. Walden's charge is a heavy one. If he can get Oblomov to agree to His Majesty's government's terms, Britain can win the impending war with Germany. But what lead us now to relate to Walden and perhaps even begin to feel for him are his even heavier personal problems, betrayals by both his beloved wife and daughter. These are daggers, as it were, stuck into him, which at the same time become a deadly menace to Oblomov and to the desperately needed treaty. But Follett in this draft has yet to involve Walden dynamically in the assassination plot, so that his personality appears bland and not terribly interesting, especially with his resuming ties with a former mistress at the first sign of his wife's moodiness and his employing a detective as opposed to his personally taking action himself.

Lydia, who barely existed before, now becomes a mainspring in the plot because of her past. This leads to her conflicted feelings toward Feliks and toward her husband. Fearful of her youthful love affair becoming known, she feels she must get Feliks some money, so she pawns some jewelry, and she even gives him a recommendation for a job at Walden Hall. Walden catches her in her lie, and she is overwhelmed with guilt, in the end confessing everything to him. Given her terrible plight, she now begins to become a major player while acquiring humanity and the possibility of substantial sympathy as a character.

Charlotte, essentially the same in both outlines, is enhanced by scenes with Belinda in which her quite natural curiosity about sex smacks up against the prudishly Victorian conspiracy of silence on the subject. These actions become modified by the final draft, but in the fleshing out of Charlotte's character, these are good developmental steps.

Finally, a word about the new Prologue and Epilogue. I recall that Follett added these to bring a sixty-five-year-old story closer to the contemporary reader by introducing Walden Hall as a place that still exists and by setting up personal contact between Charlotte as an eccentric old lady and some present-day American characters who are casual visitors to the estate. In the book itself there is an epilogue, but you'll find it bears little resemblance to this one, and there is no prologue. Peter and Lizzie smoking a joint and making love in the gazebo set a lighthearted tone that bears no relation to the serious story that follows. The young tourists having fun could even seem to trivialize the impact of the novel. So see this as a mistake, a false start. And don't be discouraged when you, too, read over scenes and chapters you've written and you suddenly realize they don't belong in your novel.

Third Outline

Prologue is approximately the same as in previous draft.

ONE

1. It is 1894, and the seventh Earl Walden is dying. He is a typical Victorian aristocrat of the huntin', shootin' and fishin' variety, and what he is dying of is sixty years of good living. Today he insists on getting up. Wearing a heavy coat and well muffled up, he walks—attended by anxious servants—through the woods to Lady Walden's Folly. His late wife had this built, ostensibly for her daughters; but she had two sons and no daughters, and she was less than perfectly sane, and she used to play here herself. The old Earl walks around, remembering her, and finally rests on the battlements, exhausted and close to death, gazing at the view she loved so well. His younger son George arrives. The Earl asks for Stephen, his elder son. "He's in St. Petersburg," George says. The Earl grunts, "He won't get much shootin' there." Then he dies.

2. The belle of St. Petersburg in 1894 is Lydia, the daughter of a count. Aged nineteen, she is beautiful in a frail, colorless sort of way, and terribly respectable: modestly dressed, obedient to her parents, respectful to her elders, a devout churchgoer, hopelessly impractical, and liable to faint at the slightest suggestion of impropriety. However, all this is to some extent an act, for she is secretly conducting a mad, passionate affair with an anarchist student named Feliks Murontsiv.

. . . He [Feliks] grew up thinking of himself as something special, a V.I.P. temporarily lodging with the petite bourgeoisie. He developed a commanding manner and an intuitive grasp of the psychology of dominance. He first learned to despise the aristocracy (to which he fancies he belongs) when they failed to pay their bills in his foster-father's shop. He looks undernourished: tall, thin as a rail, with a gaunt white face and large, staring eyes. He is fiery, passionate, idealistic and mad as hell at the whole world. At the University he has become an anarchist. The intellectual rationale for his political views is reasonable enough, but his fervor comes from his personal confusions and hatreds.

This evening Lydia snatches an hour with Feliks on her way to a reception at the British Embassy. As always, when they make love she shouts "Help!" at the moment of climax.

She arrives at the embassy looking happy and delectable, and she captures the heart of a visiting Englishman, Stephen Walden.

Young Walden is like his father, the seventh Earl—so much so that they cannot live together. Stephen was born in 1864. He learned to ride before he could walk and to shoot before he could write. He went to Eton, where he misbehaved, and Oxford, where he surprised everyone by graduating (in history). In 1887 he made his first trip to Africa where he fell in love with big-game hunting.

On that first African trip he picked up a manservant who was to be with him for the rest of his life. Pritchard, then sixteen (Walden was twenty-three), was the intelligent, cynical son of a London shirt-maker. He had run away to sea and then jumped ship at Zanzibar. A close bond was forged between the two men on safari. Pritchard is intensely loyal to Walden while at the same time despising the British ruling class in general. In turn Walden, who is always aloof with ser-vants, talks to Pritchard—when they are alone—the way a company president might talk to his chief executive.

When in London, Walden pursues loose women. . . . But Bonnie, *a singer*, threw him over when the Prince of Wales took a fancy to her.

Even before that time Walden found England suffocating and spent little time there. He is a restless young man who lives for kicks. He goes on safari once a year and travels the world in between. Being the heir to an earldom, he is entertained by England's ambassadors in the world's capital cities. The diplomats, having heard of his reputation as a hell-raiser, are surprised to find that he is intelligent and knowledgeable about international politics and has a flair for languages. In fact he is laying the foundation for what will later be a considerable expertise in foreign affairs.

Tonight at dinner he is placed next to Lydia. She is much too demure to be his usual type, but nevertheless he finds her enchanting. He thinks, *If I wanted a wife . . . but I don't.* She, secure in her passion for Feliks, flirts with him just a little.

That night a cable comes from England informing him of the death of his father. The news has an odd effect on him. He does not shed tears, but he cancels a gambling date and sits up all night, thinking.

3. Next morning Lydia's father, the old count, tells her he has found out about Feliks. He is wild with rage. Lydia dashes out of the house and goes to Feliks's lodgings, determined to run away with him. But Feliks is gone—arrested, says his landlady, for being an anarchist.

Meanwhile Stephen, now the eighth Earl Walden and addressed by everyone as "my lord," calls on the count and formally asks permission to pay court to Lydia. The count says yes, come back tomorrow.

Lydia returns and accuses her father of having Feliks arrested. The count admits it. Furthermore, he says, Feliks is at this minute being tortured by the Ochrana, the Czarist secret police, in an attempt to make him reveal the names of other anarchists. Lydia is frantic. She first screams, then pleads with her father for Feliks's release. "I'll do anything," she says, "anything you want!" Her father says, "Will you marry Stephen Walden?" . . .

TWO

It is 1914 . . . the last long summer of the British empire . . .

1. After the death of his father, Stephen Walden married Lydia, brought her back to England, moved into Walden Hall, took his seat in the House of Lords and settled down.

He found the family fortunes somewhat diminished because of the late-Victorian collapse of agricultural prices. While other country land-owners clamored for tariff protection, Walden switched money into London property and railways, and he is now richer than his father ever was. . . . His big, beefy body has yet to collapse into fat, although he has a gouty leg and walks with a cane. . . . He hunts fox in Surrey and shoots grouse in Scotland, but it is not the same as big game, and late at night he and Pritchard often sit in the gun-room over a glass of port, surrounded by the stuffed and mounted heads of lion, elephant and rhinoceros, and reminisce about the Africa days. . . .

Viewed from England, Europe appears menaced by an increasingly wealthy and aggressive Germany. Germany's annual steel production, for example, has overtaken that of Britain and is still accelerating. England's navy, the guardian of the island's trading arteries, is supposed to be larger than the combined navies of the two next strongest powers, but Germany is catching up and refuses to negotiate an arms limitation treaty. In the past year, her war preparations have become increasingly obvious. The government has imposed a one-off special tax to raise one billion marks—the largest levy in European history—and the money is being used to step up conscription (so that it now includes all fit men without exemption) with corresponding increases in military hardware. On the London money market, German firms have been factoring credits, i.e., discounting bills for early payment, with the result that while the rest of the world is owed money by Germany, Germany has collected all her debts. In short, Germany is ready to fight.

. . . *Fearing a war on two fronts, the aim of German diplomacy is to neutralize Russia.* One attempt to do this was almost successful, and Walden was personally involved in frustrating it. In 1906 the Kaiser persuaded the weak-willed Czar to sign the Treaty of Bjorko. It would have radically changed the Balance of Power if it had ever been respected by its signatories; but in fact it was forgotten as rapidly as it had been signed, and some of the credit for this is due to Walden, who was dispatched to St. Petersburg to persuade the Czar to renege. Walden looks back on this as the triumph of his life. . . . *Now Walden is asked to represent Britain in secret talks with Oblomov who also will be staying at Walden's London house.*

Walden is no stranger to the world of international diplomacy, but even he is somewhat awestruck by the importance of his task, which is no less than to get the Russians on our team. Of course he has strong personal reasons for wanting this: he loves Russia, his wife is Russian, and he has a lot of money invested in the Trans-Siberian Railway. But more importantly, he believes that if Russia remains neutral, Germany will conquer Europe.

2. . . . Charlotte is an only child who has grown up among adoring family and servants. She is too good-natured to be quite spoiled, but she is at least willful (like her father). Back in 1894, both her parents in their different ways suppressed the libertarian sides of their personalities in favor of respectability, and the submerged drives have surfaced in the offspring. Whether they knew it or not, Walden and Lydia always

smiled when baby Charlotte escaped from her crib.

Nevertheless her upbringing has been narrowly restricted. She has always been educated at home. Her only real friend is *her cousin* Belinda, who is in a similar position (although she is not an only child, Belinda's three brothers are very small). Charlotte has never seen poor people's homes—indeed she has never seen the servants' quarters of her own home—and she was never allowed to play with the children of servants or tenants. (Lydia remembers the terrible temptations to which she succumbed when *she* encountered the common people in the shape of Feliks; and she is terrified that her daughter will suffer in the same way . . . although Charlotte does speak Russian and French. . . .)

Willful, cultured, overprotected . . . she has one more crucial trait: idealism. She realizes that only white European aristocrats are entitled to be wealthy, powerful and idle, but she knows of no reason why the whole world should not be fed, clothed and happy. And all the people she comes across are relatively fortunate, for her father is the archetypal paternal country squire who provides for his tenants in bad times (while collecting fat rents from them) and takes care of his servants (while paying them next to nothing in wages). But Charlotte is ignorant of the downside. All she knows is that old servants get a cottage and a pension, newly delivered mothers are sent a basket of provisions, and in a hard winter everyone gets hot soup.

Finally, Charlotte is as beautiful as her mother. At present her beauty is entirely natural: an innocent smile, a clear complexion, a graceful walk. But soon she will learn how to dress like a woman, and then she will be ravishing.

. . . Observing her mother and other Edwardian ladies, Charlotte realizes that, while they are always busy with social affairs, nevertheless it is true that they do nothing. She feels, like any teenager, that she is faced with a decision about what kind of person she is going to be, and she is not at all happy with the prospect of a life spent doing nothing. This is Charlotte's personal version of the perennial adolescent identity crisis; and in confronting it she will, as her parents did in 1894, face a choice between freedom and responsibility. . . .

(The Victorian conspiracy of silence about sex cannot often have been as completely effective as it is in this case. The children of the poor sleep in houses too small for secrets; middle-class children learn about sex from school friends; aristocratic boys go to boarding schools; even aristocratic girls learn from older brothers. Real ignorance is only possible for protected, isolated girls like Charlotte and Belinda.) . . .

3. Dieter Hartmann, senior aide to the German ambassador in London, has a picture of the European situation rather different from Walden's. He is proud of his country's uphill struggle to greatness; and where, he asks, is it written that Britain shall rule the world and Germany shall always be a second-class power?

The problem is that Germany is in danger of being cut off from the rest of the world—notably the U.S., Africa and the Far East—because of the policy of encirclement masterminded by Britain. Germany is largely surrounded by hostile nations: France, Belgium, England and Russia. Italy is wavering and the Balkans are turbulent. Germany's only route to North America is via the North Sea, where Britain rules the waves (so a naval limitation treaty, which Britain keeps proposing as though it were the essence of sweet reason, would simply maintain the status quo and keep Germany trapped). Her route to Africa and the Middle East is via her ally Austrio-Hungary and the Balkans, which is why Germany encourages Austria's aggressive domination of the Balkans. Her only way to the east is via Persia, a territory that England and Russia have just carved up between them (Britain incidentally securing Persia's oil, the fuel for the new generation of fast warships). Germany wants colonies like everyone else, but each move she makes in Africa is denounced as troublemaking by the Powers, which are already sitting on rich possessions. Is there any way for Germany to avoid being suffocated? Hartmann, a pessimist, sees only one: war.

Hartmann learns of the forthcoming visit of Oblomov through a well-placed spy in the Russian Embassy. . . . Just as Walden sees the road for a firm alliance between Russia and England, so Hartmann is desperate to drive a wedge between the two—and now he sees, in the visit of Oblomov, what may be his last chance of doing this. . . .

Hartmann sees how this friction between the two countries might be inflamed into a full-scale quarrel on the eve of war *if a Russian anarchist were to assassinate the Czar's favorite nephew in London.* . . . At a minimum, the talks would be sabotaged. At best, it could keep Russia out of the war.

Hartmann calls in an informant, Andre Barre, who poses as a French Bolshevik to keep an eye on expatriate German troublemakers who might be planning to return home in force. Hartmann asks Barre, "Who is the leading Russian revolutionist in London?"

"Well," says Barre, "now that little Joey Stalin has left, I suppose it's Feliks Murontsiv."

4. Feliks was released from jail the day after Lydia's wedding. He left the University and, dressed as a monk, wandered the Russian countryside preaching the anarchist gospel. Eventually he was arrested again and sentenced to life imprisonment in Siberia. After some years he escaped and made his way to England. He knows Lydia got married and left Russia, but he does not know where she went nor what her name is now. But he has not forgotten her: whenever he dreams about sex it is always with a woman who shouts "Help!" in Russian at the climax. . . .

Every few months he and a small gang of nonpolitical villains burgle a house for funds. Most of Feliks's share goes to the anarchist cause, for his own lifestyle is frugal. . . . He dominates any group by his autocratic manner and the evangelical fervor blazing in his eyes. However, he is secretly discontented, for in his three years in London he has done nothing to further the anarchist cause. Meanwhile Russia is in a turmoil: more than a million workers are on strike; the Duma (parliament) is a helpless sham; and the oil workers are literally at war with the Cossacks. The country is a powder-barrel waiting for a spark. Feliks wants to be that spark, but he knows that as soon as he sets foot in Russia he will be packed off to Siberia (as Stalin was). What good could he do in Siberia? But what can he do in London?

Today Feliks's acquaintance Andre Barre comes to the Jubilee Street club, bringing with him a German anarchist called Dieter . . . *and inquires if Feliks would be interested in helping to assassinate Oblomov.*

THREE

1. On June 4 Charlotte is presented at court. This is the biggest and most gorgeous ceremony of British royalty, when the aristocratic girls of the kingdom parade before the monarch at Buckingham Palace. "Court dress" is obligatory. For women this means a white dress with a low-cut bodice and a train three to four yards long, a tiara with three white plumes, and just about all the family jewels. Men wear velvet knee-britches with silk stockings and all their medals. In the main part of the ceremony, the King and Queen sit on thrones while the debutantes pass before them one at a time.

Charlotte's debut is marred by a (historically true) incident. The girl ahead of her in the line suddenly drops to one knee and says, "Your

Majesty, for God's sake stop torturing women!" She is hustled away by two footmen. The royal couple pretend not to notice, but Charlotte is flustered. She assumes the girl is completely mad, and for now nobody will tell her otherwise.

2. From the spy in the Russian Embassy, Hartmann learns the date and time of Oblomov's arrival. He and Feliks go to Victoria Station to take a look. They hardly see Oblomov. He has traveled in a private coach (borrowed from the King, to whom he is related). He steps from that straight into Walden's Rolls-Royce. Feliks and Hartmann get a glimpse of a handsome, expensively dressed young man. Feliks's thoughts are dark. Oblomov represents the regime that is responsible for torture, slavery and starvation in Russia—but he also represents an opportunity to bring that regime down. Two servants who have traveled with Oblomov load a mountain of luggage into the car. Feliks and Hartmann follow the entourage to a large house on the edge of St. James's Park, the town home of Earl Walden.

Inside the house Oblomov is greeted by Lydia. She is thirty-nine and still beautiful. Her public image is not much changed since 1894: she is still respectable, though Anglicized, and she plays the part of an Edwardian lady with conviction. But what is happening underneath?

. . . Her nonconformist impulses are not dead, only dormant. Oblomov, who was a ten-year-old boy at her wedding, is an uncomfortable reminder of all this.

Oblomov speaks good English. He talks about Russia; and this pillar of the Czarist regime turns out to be something of a radical. . . .

. . . As soon as Charlotte walks in (looking ravishing) he turns into a nervous wreck, dropping his teacup, suddenly acquiring a thick Russian accent, blushing and stammering. But now Charlotte's hidden talents begin to emerge, and with her unique naive charm she begins to put him at his ease.

Outside, Feliks and Hartmann walk in the park and discuss what they have seen. It seems that Oblomov is reluctant to show himself in public. He will not be an easy target. (Perhaps the possibility of assassination has occurred to him, too.)

"Somehow we'll have to get in the house," says Hartmann, "but how?"

"I have an answer to that," says Feliks; and he shows Hartmann an item in the society pages of a magazine: Walden is giving a fancy-dress ball to introduce Oblomov. "That's when I'll kill him," says Feliks.

FOUR

1. . . . . The talks *between Walden and Oblomov* are given added urgency by the news that the Germans have completed the widening of the Kiel Canal (in mid-June), enabling their Dreadnoughts to pass between the North Sea and the Baltic. This a strategically vital project without which they could not win a naval war.

But now Oblomov drops a bombshell.

Russia's great long-term aim is to have a warm-water port. She has her Black Sea coast, but the Black Sea is connected with the Mediterranean by a narrow strait, the Bosporus, off Constantinople. Both the European and the Asia Minor banks of the Bosporus are held by Turkey. Russia has been supporting Slav nationalism in the Balkans in the hope that when the Slavs throw out the Turks Russia will have free passage through the Bosporus. But better than Slav control would be Russian control; and Oblomov now announces that if Russia is to fight on the Allied side in the coming war, the price of her cooperation will be Britain's recognition of the Balkans as a Russian sphere of influence.

Of course Walden is not mandated even to discuss this, and the talks adjourn while he puts the question to the foreign office.

2. For the first time in her life Charlotte is reading the newspapers, and she learns of the suffragette movement. She disapproves strongly of women who break windows and slash paintings. She talks to Pritchard about the deb who made the scene at the court. Pritchard explains the reference to torture: Suffragettes who are jailed go on hunger strike, and consequently are force-fed by a degrading and painful process. Charlotte refuses to believe this.

But she does not give it much thought, for today is the day of the fancy-dress ball, and the house is full of people all day long. The ballroom is being turned into a Sultan's palace. Charlotte is to go as Little Bo Peep, and out in the stable is a darling fluffy white lamb which will complete her costume.

Meanwhile, Hartmann buys and tests a pair of duelling pistols, and Feliks rents a Dick Turpin outfit complete with mask.

At the start of the ball Charlotte, Lydia, Walden and Oblomov stand in line, in a reception room off the ballroom, to welcome the guests.

Feliks arrives in his costume. He bluffs his way through the front door (for he has no invitation) and gets to the door of the reception room. There he gives his name as Dick Turpin, and so the usher announces him. Everyone laughs. Ignoring the line, he approaches Oblomov and draws his pistols. Everyone still thinks it's probably a joke. Feliks shouts: "Your death will free Russia!" Lydia screams "Help!" in Russian—just as she used to when Feliks made love to her. Feliks is frozen in shock. He stares at Lydia, recognizing her. In the instant for which Feliks hesitates, Walden lifts his cane and whacks Feliks across both wrists. Feliks drops the guns. He stares at them a moment longer, then turns and runs out.

For a second everyone is too stunned to move. Then Walden picks up the dropped pistols and unloads them. "Blanks," he lies. "A joke that didn't come off. Wonder who the blighter was?"

And the ball goes on.

FIVE

1. Feliks broods over Lydia. He is sure he could seduce her all over again. But what he feels for her is not love. He daydreams that she is naked and begging him to make love to her, and in his fantasy he refuses. He also thinks of Walden. So that gouty old squire is the one who stole Lydia! Feliks's pride is wounded by the way Walden literally rapped his knuckles with the cane.

Feliks wants to destroy this family.

He thinks he can do that in the course of killing Oblomov.

But Oblomov has vanished.

Hartmann talks to the embassy spy. Although Walden diplomatically smoothed over the Dick Turpin incident, both he and Oblomov know it was a serious assassination attempt. Consequently, Oblomov left the house on the park. His luggage came to the embassy—and went straight out again by the back door, no one knows where. But the talks are still going on.

Back at his own embassy Hartmann hears the news that is about to convulse Europe: the Archduke Franz-Ferdinand has been assassinated at Sarajevo in Bosnia.

Oblomov *must* be found.

2. Feliks now makes an uncharacteristically bold move: When Walden is out, he knocks on the door and asks to see Lydia. He gives his name as David Ponsonby-Gore and is shown into the morning-room.

When Lydia sees him she turns white. She will not look at him or speak to him. (NB She does not connect him with the Dick Turpin incident.) He has to prevent her ringing for the butler. He did not anticipate such a hysterical reaction, and he realizes that here and now he is not going to be able to coax her into revealing Oblomov's whereabouts. But if he leaves empty-handed he may not get a second chance. Clutching at straws, he asks her for money. She says she has none. "Then I'll have to ask your husband," he says. "No!" she cries. Her reaction confirms what Feliks had guessed: Walden has absolutely no knowledge of Lydia's premarital affair. This puts her somewhat in Feliks's power. He tells her to meet him in a restaurant in three days' time—with the money. Then he leaves.

3. Charlotte attends Belinda's coming-out ball. This is a glittering occasion, with all the girls in fabulous gowns and the young men in white tie and tails. Belinda has joined the "fast" set: She wears ankle-revealing dresses, does the Turkey Trot, smokes cigarettes in restaurants, and goes to boxing matches. Since that afternoon in Lady Walden's Folly she has learned the sexual facts of life, and tonight, during a girl-to-girl chat in the ladies' powder room, she relays them to Charlotte, who is stunned and cannot take it in.

. . . *On the way home, discovering her former maid sleeping on the pavement*, Charlotte says, "Come home with me." Annie knows better than to accept. Charlotte makes Marya give Annie all the cash in her purse. . . .

4. . . . *Lydia sells some jewelry*. When the transaction is done she examines her emotions and realizes with a rather Russian sense of fatalism that she just longs to see Feliks again.

SIX

1. . . . *Walden asks Lydia to wear this jewelry, and she feels guilty*. Walden is vaguely aware of her mood but pays little attention to it. He is authorised by the Foreign Secretary to make a counteroffer to the Russians: the Bosporus to be an international waterway with freedom of passage for all nations in peacetime guaranteed jointly by England and Russia. . . .

He [Walden] *sees the jewelry in a shop window and* takes it home, intending to confront her with it. But on his way he gets more and more mad at her; and when he arrives he says nothing to her but confides in Pritchard. He tells Pritchard to spy on Lydia and find out whether she has a lover.

Pritchard, now forty-three, is Walden's valet and personal servant, and he is also responsible for motorcars, which are his great enthusiasm. He quarrels continually with Marya, the governess, who unlike Pritchard is more conservative than her employers. But perhaps their constant sniping serves to conceal an underlying mutual attraction.

2. Now that Charlotte is beginning to understand the real world, what can she do about it? As a woman, she cannot even vote! The action of Letitia de Vries, the deb in the court incident, now appears in a different light. Charlotte calls on her. The de Vries have been ostracised as a matter of course, so they are pleased to see Viscountess Walden. Mrs. Pankhurst is there. Charlotte is ripe for conversion. She promises to go on a suffragette march.

She comes home and defiantly tells her parents where she has been. They are horrified and forbid her to leave the house unaccompanied.

3. . . . *At lunch in a restaurant*, in a roundabout way he [Feliks] asks her [Lydia] where Oblomov is. She will not say. He spins her a yarn about wanting to get a message into Russia. Eventually he threatens to reveal all to Walden. Lydia does not imagine that Feliks wants to kill Oblomov, but she knows somebody wants to kill him, and she cannot trust Feliks to keep the secret; so, courageously, she still refuses the information.

Pritchard observes this meeting. . . . Naturally Walden and Pritchard assume the man is a lover. Their hunting instincts are aroused. They decide to find out all about the man.

Walden is distressed by all this. . . . *Walking in St. John's Wood, Walden sees* a carriage draw up, and a plump, well-dressed middle-aged woman gets out. It is she [Bonnie Carlos]. Walden watches from a distance. She smiles at the coachman, a great big beaming smile that Walden remembers well. Suddenly he is filled with a longing like a pain. She looks in his direction. He turns quickly and walks away, not knowing whether she has seen him or not.

4. Hartmann learns that the Kaiser has (July 5) promised Austria unconditional support in any action against Serbia. War comes daily closer. Meanwhile the Russians have presented Walden with a modified demand: They want the territory that is at present European Turkey. Hartmann thinks the British may well concede this. He asks Feliks what is happening. Feliks says he has drawn a blank with Lydia and will now try Charlotte.

SEVEN

Charlotte sneaks out of the house, wearing a coat and hat of her mother's, to go on a suffragette march. Feliks, waiting near the house, follows her. Pritchard, who is still shadowing Feliks, follows too; but Pritchard thinks it is *Lydia* in the coat and hat. . . .

. . . Pritchard now realizes that this is Charlotte, not Lydia; but he assumes wrongly that Feliks has made the same mistake. He sees Charlotte knocked down. Forgetting Feliks, he plunges into the melee to rescue her. He is hit over the head and falls unconscious.

. . . *Charlotte, trampled, is rescued by Feliks who takes her back to his lodgings and seduces her.* Charlotte is mesmerized by Feliks: first by the power and confidence he displayed in the riot when she was helpless and terrified; second by the convincing simplicity of his political ideas; third by his fevered eyes, his hairy hands, his animal smell, and—not to put too fine a point on it—his cock. Feliks makes love the way he does everything else—boldly, imaginatively and passionately. And Charlotte learns the one thing Belinda was unable to tell her about sex, namely how nice it is. . . .

"But where is Oblomov?" asks Feliks.

Charlotte says, "At Walden Hall."

"Aah," says Feliks.

EIGHT

1. Walden offers the Russians Constantinople and the Bosporus. They say they will consider it. Returning to London, he finds Pritchard having his head bandaged by Marya. Pritchard reports that Charlotte was at the suffragette march. When she gets home there is a godalmighty row. Deciding that she cannot be trusted to stay in London, Walden sends her to Surrey to keep her out of trouble.

She manages to send a note to Feliks telling him what has happened and asking him to meet her in Lady Walden's Folly.

2. Walden's world is falling apart. The Balance of Power is toppling irrevocably, his daughter is a subversive, and his wife is an adulteress. He calls on Bonnie. Yes, she did see him that day, and she has been waiting for him ever since. . . .

3. Pritchard, still spying on Feliks, observes a meeting in a park between Feliks and Hartmann. When they part company Pritchard, on a hunch, follows Hartmann—all the way to the German Embassy. Pritchard gives the doorman a sovereign and learns Hartmann's name.

Walden now realizes that Feliks may be more than Lydia's lover. He makes an appointment to see the Commissioner of Police the following day.

4. Down in Surrey, Charlotte has nothing to do but spend time with Oblomov. They ride together, dine together, play cards and explore the countryside. He is rapidly falling in love with her. She likes him a lot and is embarrassed to find herself wondering what he looks like with his clothes off. She is beginning to have second thoughts about the kidnap plan when Feliks arrives.

. . . *They make love and* Feliks cases the joint.

He decides the best plan would be to have Charlotte bring Oblomov to the Folly, then kill both of them there. (Charlotte must be killed because she is, as far as Feliks knows, the only one who could finger him for the murder.) He will leave a bicycle concealed in the woods near the road, at a spot ten minutes' fast walk from the Folly. The bike will take him to the railway line where he will jump a freight train. He works all this out with care, timing each move, even checking the train schedule so he can catch the train within minutes of the murder.

With what shall he kill them? A knife is silent, but messy and tricky to use; and besides, he does not quite trust himself—when it comes to the crunch—to plunge a blade into Charlotte's beautiful body. A gun is more impersonal and requires less anatomical skill, but the noise might bring people running and interfere with his getaway. A bomb makes even more noise, but by using a timer he could get some distance away before the explosion.

He decides to postpone the decision by bringing all three.

5. Walden sees the police commissioner. The commissioner proposes that Hartmann (who has diplomatic immunity) should be expelled for consorting with known subversives, and Feliks should be arrested on suspicion of attempted murder (i.e., the Dick Turpin incident). Walden is much relieved and prepares to go home to Surrey for the weekend.

6. Germany's gold reserves are at a record high and the British fleet is on maneuvers at Portland. Hartmann learns that the Russians have accepted the British offer of Constantinople and the Bosporus, and the secret treaty will be signed this weekend. Now he is told the game is up, and he must pack his bags and leave for Germany tomorrow.

Which gives him time to meet Feliks at the station and warn him not to go home.

NINE

On Thursday, 23 July, Austria sends an ultimatum to Serbia with a forty-eight-hour deadline for reply.

Feliks sees his criminal friends and collects knife, gun, burglar's tools including a roll of wire and a bomb with a timer. The bomb has a buzzer that will go off five seconds before the explosion (NB I have not yet finished researching homemade bombs of the period.) Then he heads for Surrey.

Lydia is now back at Walden Hall, the London season being more or less over. Walking in the woods, she sees Feliks entering Lady Walden's Folly. She knows nothing of the recent feverish activity in London and thinks Feliks is still in love with her. In a turmoil, she hurries back to the house. In Walden's room she finds her jewels, and realizes she has been found out after all. . . .

Feliks instructs Charlotte to bring Oblomov to the Folly tomorrow. . . . Lydia cannot sleep. She will surely now be divorced by Walden. She should never have given Feliks up; he is the only man for whom she ever felt real passion. She decides to go to him. In her nightdress she leaves the house and goes to the Folly to give herself to him. She sees him making love to Charlotte. She leaves silently.

Oblomov asks Charlotte to marry him . . . She says, maybe.

TEN

. . . Walden and Pritchard arrive home at the same time as a cable from London saying that Feliks has not been arrested as planned. They immediately realize he is probably around here somewhere. Walden suggests to Oblomov that he move away. Charlotte tries desperately to think of a way to prevent this. She suggests Oblomov could camp out in Lady Walden's Folly. Walden is not keen but Oblomov is, for he wants Charlotte's answer. So it is done—but Oblomov takes two servants with him.

Feliks sees three of them arrive early at the Folly, realizes something is amiss, and hides nearby, watching.

Walden gets another cable, this one from the Foreign Secretary. Austria has declared war on Serbia. Now it is not just Oblomov's life but the future of Europe that is at stake. Walden organises search parties to hunt for Feliks in the surrounding countryside.

A chambermaid tells Marya that Charlotte threw up this morning. Marya sees Charlotte and notices she is not wearing a corset. Charlotte says her breasts hurt. Marya says, "Did you miss your headache this month?" Yes. "You are pregnant," Marya tells her. Charlotte goes rushing off to tell Feliks.

One of Oblomov's servants comes out of the Folly for a pee. Feliks hits him over the head, ties him up, and waits for the other one to come out and investigate.

Lydia has been confined to her room all morning, contemplating suicide, hearing nothing of the excitement and the search parties. Now Marya tells her that Charlotte is pregnant, whereupon Lydia goes berserk. She fetches a shotgun from the gun-room and a horse from the stable and heads for the Folly, overtaking Charlotte.

Oblomov's second servant comes out. Feliks disposes of him, goes inside and ties Oblomov up.

Lydia arrives with the shotgun but Feliks disarms her easily and ties her up, too. He arms the bomb and sets the timer. When you hear a buzz, he tells them, you will have five seconds to live.

By now the woods are full of searchers, so Feliks really needs the few minutes' head start the timer will give him. He decides he cannot wait for Charlotte, but as he is leaving she arrives. Hastily he ties her up. Then she tells him she is pregnant. Feliks stares at her, thunderstruck, thinking of himself, an illegitimate child, knowing that he will be killing the unborn child if he kills Charlotte. He bends to untie her— and the buzzer sounds.

Five seconds.

There is no time to untie her, so he picks her up.

Four.

She struggles and he drops her.

Three, two.

Now nobody can get out in time.

"You fool!" he screams at her.

One.

Feliks throws himself on the bomb, covering it with his body. It explodes, killing him. The others are unhurt.

Lydia starts to scream.

EPILOGUE
. . . Lydia confessed all to Walden, and they were reconciled . . . and when he [Walden] died he left half his estate to the illegitimate son of

a singer called Bonnie Carlos. . . . Oh, and the motor museum is run by the grandson of Pritchard, who married—wait for it—Marya.

Analysis of Third Outline

In Outline Three, Follett deepens and more richly colors his characters, adds several new scenes and striking plot twists, but on the whole stays within the framework he established in Outline Two. A most useful lesson for you now to pursue on your own would be to study how newly added twists in the plot here enhance character interest, and how new aspects in the characters' pasts and presents lead to fresh plot complications. The building of plot and character, as you should now be learning from Follett's work, is a continuously interactive process.

One interesting change from Outline Two is Follett's starting the novel earlier in time, not in 1914 but in 1894, with Walden's bloated and satirized father dying, with young Walden meeting Lydia in St. Petersburg while she is in the midst of a mad affair with anarchist Feliks, and with her agreeing to marry Walden to obtain Feliks's release from prison. The backstory involving these characters is much enriched; but note that in the final outline yet to come and in the book itself, the action commences in the present, a much better way to begin. You will find no dipping back into the past there until we learn what Feliks is up to, the book's main issue is joined, and solid suspense is established. Then starting in chapter two of the novel, you'll see Follett gradually weaving in only the most relevant and powerful elements from the backstory.

The most important new action in Outline Three is Feliks's attempt to kill Oblomov at the ball given by Lord Walden. No longer coming to reconnoiter as a waiter, he comes to fulfill his murderous mission. The main action of the story is no longer held back until the final chapter but is thus powerfully planted early on. The anarchist cries, "Your death will free Russia," and is stunned to hear a cry of "Help!" It is the cry of his long-ago mistress at the point of orgasm, an odd idiosyncrasy that Follett carefully prepares for earlier in the outline. What a dramatic reunion for these two! But Follett puts Feliks in disguise, so that later when he approaches Lydia, she won't recognize him as the would-be assassin. With Feliks discombobulated by his shock at rediscovering Lydia, Walden manages to whack him with a cane; and the Russian, furious from both his past and present griefs, flees with a burning desire to seduce Lydia and to destroy this family.

This foiled assassination prompts something new in the story, the need to hide Oblomov. This then triggers the main thrust of the novel's midsection, which now gets built around Feliks's efforts to locate Oblomov. His daring calling on Lydia is now not for money but to worm from her the prince's whereabouts. It's only when he fails at that, still trying to assert some power over her, that he asks for cash. Earlier in this version, Follett dramatizes this same theme when Feliks strains to identify Oblomov when he first arrives at Victoria Station, and when he tries to learn where the Russian is staying by following him to Walden's house.

Feliks's personality, though he is now clearly being developed as a main character of the story, is still in a formative state. His desire to destroy the Walden family and his cruel and manipulative use of both Lydia and Charlotte denies most of the sympathy we might feel for him. We are still faced with the essential unsavoriness of his actions, which, though daring, are cold-blooded. And thus his last-minute throwing himself on the exploding bomb seems only marginally credible.

Feliks's shocking people at the ball with his pistols also makes it possible for Follett to spark a new counterthrust against him. In the previous synopsis, the reader learns about the Feliks-Ferfichkin assassination plan early in the action, but none of the British characters or Oblomov do much of anything to try and stop him until almost the last scene. Now with Pritchard identifying Feliks and then linking him to the German Embassy, a new element of suspense is introduced somewhat earlier and then sustained throughout the last third of the story. In a novel of this kind, however, a high level of suspense is needed usually from the first chapter until the end; and in the final version you will see Feliks identified as the assassin both sooner in the story and with more exactitude.

With respect to Charlotte, a small but interesting addition is the scene at court where a debutante asks the King to stop torturing women, which is based on a true historical incident. In the book itself, this becomes a bit of gorgeous pageantry, but in terms of the plot, it serves as an excellent bit of preparation for the revolution in Charlotte's attitudes and character. Follett's changing Belinda from a younger sister to a "fast" cousin of Charlotte's age is also useful. Belinda can now teach Charlotte about sex. Another neat bit of history woven into the story is Charlotte's meeting Mrs. Pankhurst. This gives her a strong motive to march with the suffragettes and to defy the authority of her parents. Longing for answers to basic life questions, Charlotte now is an almost fully developed character, one with whom we can empathize. Even though she epitomizes a narrowly specific stage of life, Follett portrays her as outstandingly courageous for a girl of her class and upbringing, also brimming over with kindness and decency. She is both a larger-than-life character and one who is very human and down-to-earth.

The negotiations between Walden and Oblomov are much more extensive and take up a fair bit of space in this outline; but in the book itself, these diminish. Business discussions, which in essence these are, rarely work in fiction. What's at issue must be personal, something that intensely involves individuals with each other. A discussion about whether or not Russia should control the Bosporus is tough to make dramatic.

Although Andre Barre in his role as intermediary to Feliks is retained from the last outline, Ferfichkin of the Russian secret police is replaced by Dieter Hartmann, senior aide to the German ambassador, a man to whom Follett gives a clearer and less oblique motive than Ferfichkin had for arranging Oblomov's assassination. However, none of these professional spies or agents provocateurs—Kell, Steinhauer, Ferfichkin, Hartmann or Barre—are ever given personal connections to any of the main characters, so the reader fails to become interested in any of them as characters in themselves. Their only functions are to "set up" and to abet the assassination plot, functions that rarely, if ever, become the core of scenes of high drama. In Outline Four, you'll see how Follett wisely manages to do without any of them, and thus frees himself to focus on his totally involved principals.

Follett's heightening of Lydia's relationship with Feliks when she was young and her agreement to marry Walden only as a condition of securing Feliks's release from prison create new and interesting dramatic ramifications. We learn, for example, that she allows no contact between her children and those of her servants and tenants. God forbid her daughter should be exposed to the same terrible temptation to which she succumbed. The news of Oblomov's coming, which brings back into her life a strong reminder of St. Petersburg, throws her into turmoil. These new elements excitingly set the stage for her reunion with Feliks, which becomes fraught with all the more tension. After their first meeting, she now longs to see him again and grows cold to her husband. This coldness (coupled with her lie about the jewels) leads Walden to have Pritchard spy on her. Later, rather than confess to her husband about why she sold the jewels, she goes to Feliks wanting to make love with him. When Lydia discovers that Feliks is doing it with her daughter, she becomes incensed; she goes off and comes back with a shotgun, which leads to her then becoming a new factor in the climax.

Walden's character, too, is built up in a number of ways. The creation of Pritchard as a lifelong companion and devoted servant gives Walden the aura of a man worthy of devotion. And Pritchard can then serve the plot as Walden's personal, not hired, private eye who watches over Lydia and then Feliks. Walden, having in 1906 persuaded the Czar to renege on a treaty with Germany, is given credentials as a diplomat, which prepares for and makes credible his being chosen as the British negotiator. On the other hand, the love affair he resumes with the show-girl flame of his youth shows him to be a man turning his back on difficulty. This detracts from his stature as a character and from the main thrust of the action, and you will not find this episode in the book itself.

Walden's best facet now is his being enlarged as a semitragic figure. A King Lear would be out of place in a thriller, but Follett, even in outline, establishes a poignancy for this character, what with the crumbling of the world order on which his position in society rests and his discovery that his beloved daughter is a subversive and his wife an adulteress. Except for his caning Feliks at the Oblomov ball and organizing a fruitless search for the Russian toward the end, however, Walden does pitifully little to counteract Feliks or to play a strong role as the novel's protagonist. The dynamism Walden needs to fulfill this function, as you'll see, will be developed some in the final outline and more in the book itself.

Fourth Outline

BACKGROUND

Prologue from Outline Three now omitted. Economic and social conditions of the British rich and poor are established.

. . . Domestic politics were even hotter *than the weather in July 1914.* In 1905 a Liberal government had been elected. At first this made little difference to anything. Then in 1908 Prime Minister Campbell-Bannerman died, and a bunch of young firebrands came to power.

Asquith was the first Prime Minister in British history who did not have a country estate. His Home Secretary was the bellicose young Winston Churchill, and as Chancellor of the Exchequer he picked the Welsh nonconformist hothead Lloyd George. Thus began a period in politics more bitter and angry than any in this century. The Liberals introduced—or tried to introduce—a Land Tax, Home Rule for Ireland, a cheaper and more modern army and navy, old-age pensions, national health insurance, and—horror of horrors—a diminution in the powers of the House of Lords. Before it was over, the army would threaten mutiny, the Lords would defy the constitution, the monarchy would be dragged reluctantly into the political arena, and—a rare thing in Westminster—members of opposing parties would refuse to sit down at the same dinner table. Outside the framework of conventional politics, the status quo was under threat from the militant new trade unions, the nascent women's movement, the burgeoning Labour Party, and the anarchists. . . .

The German threat to Britain is restated.

CHARACTERS

Walden's relationship with his father and Walden's early years are sketched in again.

. . . The diplomats' wives never failed to be charmed by his gentility. Nevertheless, he would leave those elegant rooms in his immaculate evening clothes and spend the rest of the night drinking, gambling and whoring, and might even have to be got out of jail by the Ambassador in the morning. . . .

Returned to Walden Hall with his Russian wife, in the domestic political battle Walden is firmly on the side of the Conservatives and tradition, against the Liberals and change. Since he became the eighth earl he has found deep contentment in the life of an English aristocrat. . . . He adores his wife, although he feels vaguely that he has never really possessed her. Nevertheless, she is desirable, intelligent, and always good company, and he has no serious desire to wander. He is proud as Punch of his lovely daughter Charlotte and can hardly wait for the moment when she makes her debut in London society and all his friends say, "Damn fine filly, Walden!" He regrets not having more children, but it was not for the want of trying.

He represents the best of English aristocracy. His lands are scrupulously well maintained and scientifically farmed. His tenants' cottages are in good repair, his servants are well cared for, his home is beautiful, he is a patron of the arts. He is shrewd, knowledgeable and humane. He and his kind have ruled Britain during its period of greatest glory, and their worst fault is that they cannot see why things must change. His servants and his employees agree with him: They see no point in the government's taking money from him in the Land Tax in order to give them what they already get directly from him.

So Walden, a man who has found a happiness he thought would be permanent, feels that his whole way of life is under attack. But soon it will be threatened more seriously, this time from a foreign source.

Lydia is a woman haunted by a guilty secret. Her secret will be revealed, bit by bit, to her increasing dismay, during the summer of 1914. . . .

. . . *After nineteen years of marriage, the passionate side of her nature is well under control. She has grown enormously fond of Walden.* She loves Charlotte and feels protective toward her. Lydia's life task is to bring Charlotte up very properly and see her safely married. Lydia is superb at telling and showing her daughter how to walk, dress, talk and behave generally, but not much good at explaining more intimate or emotional matters.

. . . Charlotte loves her mother and regards her as the personification of feminine perfection . . . *but now, realizing that Edwardian ladies do nothing*, for the first time she is entertaining the unsettling idea that she may not want to be a replica of her mother. . . . It [Charlotte's identity crisis] will come to a head during the summer of 1914, and when it is over she will know who she is.

Feliks Murontsiv was born near Moscow in 1875. His father, a poor country priest, was a somewhat saintly man—dedicated, selfless and pious. Feliks inherited his selflessness but not his piety. He grew up with a deep and sincere compassion for the world's downtrodden and a bitter contempt for the church which supported and even profited from the status quo. Nevertheless the priesthood was the only way for a poor boy to get educated, and Feliks went to a theological college in St. Petersburg. There he discovered a system of belief more to his liking: anarchism.

Anarchists believe that all government is tyranny, all property is theft, and all organization is coercion. As soon as people realize this they will rise up and destroy the state. However, because anarchists are in principle opposed to organization, they cannot form a coherent political movement. The only way for them to encourage the revolution is by propaganda and by example, e.g., by assassinating politicians. So a caring political theory leads to murder. This is the central conflict of anarchism, and Feliks epitomises it with his contradictory qualities of compassion and ruthlessness.

. . . [he was] tender and vulnerable as a lover, and both passionate and lascivious in bed. . . . He escaped from there [Siberia], killing a guard (the only time he has killed despite his beliefs). He made his way to Switzerland—a journey which tapped his latent powers of ingenuity and hardihood . . .

In Switzerland he is deeply discontented *by the terrible situation of Russia and the Russians. But what can he do about it?. . .*

. . . In the servants' hall Pritchard will attack the Establishment, and Marya, who like many governesses is more royalist than the King, will defend it. Pritchard is always able to defeat her by descending to coarseness and embarrassing her into leaving the room. However, beneath this bickering is a weird mutual affection.

On Marya's day off, Charlotte is supervised by Annie, an easygoing young housemaid who has too much sensuality and too little sense and is disliked by Marya both for the excess and for the lack.

PLOT

One

"Churchill? Winston Churchill?" said Walden. "Here?"

"Yes, my lord," the butler said.

"Send the blighter away," Walden said. "I'm not at home." He turned and walked to the window, thinking: Young whippersnapper, I don't know where he gets the nerve, first calling on me in London then following me down here, he knows damn well I won't receive him.

The butler coughed.

Walden looked at him irritation. "Still here?"

"Mr. Churchill told me you'd be not at home, my lord, and said I must give you this."

Walden realized the butler was carrying a letter on a tray. "Give it back to him—no, wait." He had seen the seal on the envelope, and for once the Earl of Walden was intimidated. He opened the letter.

Buckingham Palace
24 May 1914

My dear Walden,
    You will see young Winston.
George R.

Walden recognized the handwriting. It was the King's.

He hesitated only a moment longer, then said, "Ask Mr. Churchill to come in."

Churchill is now First Lord of the Admiralty, which means not that he is a lord but that he is in charge of Britain's navy. He is of course a minister in the Liberal government, so from Walden's point of view he represents the people who are trying to destroy England. However, Churchill wants Walden to do a job which transcends domestic politics. He explains that he has arranged for a young Russian admiral to come to London for secret naval talks—at least, "naval" talks was the original proposal, but Churchill is parlaying the whole thing into a defense treaty. . . . It is the Czar who has insisted, in a personal telegram to his cousin King George V, that the English side be represented in the negotiations by Walden. *To obscure the real purpose of the visit, Oblomov will be introduced to society, while it is whispered about that he's looking for a wife.* . . .

Lydia leaves the men talking politics and strolls into the garden. She walks around the vast, lovely old house and wanders through the landscaped park . . . and she remembers *Oblomov as a ten-year-old at her wedding and that* [her wedding day] as the unhappiest day of her life. . . .

Lydia sees Charlotte deep in conversation with Belinda, and thinks, Please, God, let me keep my secrets. . . .

. . . Belinda is merely curious *about sex*, but Charlotte is made of sterner stuff. There are forbidden books in a locked cupboard in the library, and she knows where the key is. Belinda gets cold feet, but Charlotte overrules her. They get the books and sneak upstairs. (Annie, who is supposed to be supervising them, is meeting her boyfriend in the woods.) Charlotte leads the way through the disused nursery to an attic under the roof which used to be her hiding place when she was little. From here you can see across the several acres of roof which cover Walden Hall. There is a way to get up there from the stables, all across roofs, says Charlotte. They look at the forbidden books, but they get little help from the internal diagrams in the medical textbook and none at all from the bizarre, and to them incomprehensible, pornographic novel.

Meanwhile, Feliks's boat is docking at Dover.

The Swiss anarchists have learned, through a traitor in the Ochrana, of Oblomov's planned talks with Walden. Feliks is horrified by the prospect of a European war. The idea of young men being sent, by Kaisers and Czars and Kings, to be killed and maimed in a cause not their own is exactly the kind of thing that makes Feliks an anarchist. As far as he is concerned, Oblomov and Walden are conspiring to murder millions of Russians. So he plans to kill them both.

The effect of such a murder would be greater than might immediately be apparent. *It would halt the talks and cause antagonism between Britain and Russia.* . . . Thirdly, Feliks (or, if he is dead, his Swiss friends) will announce that Walden and Oblomov were killed because they were scheming to drag the Russian people into a war they do not want; and Russian popular reaction to that news might set off a chain reaction of revolt leading ultimately to revolution.

Feliks is tense, excited, apprehensive and happy. He may die soon, but for now life has suddenly started opening doors again.

As he sets foot on English soil for the first time in his life, there is something else on his mind. The woman he loved, nineteen years ago, married an Englishman. Feliks never knew the man's name, but he heard that they had gone to England. Now, after all this time, he will be in the same country as she. . . .

Two

. . . *At Victoria Station* two servants (who appear to be traveling with Oblomov) load a mountain of luggage on to the carriage and it drives away. Feliks, on a bicycle, follows it *to Walden's town home* . . .

. . . *Oblomov talks about the need for reform in Russia,* but Lydia is thinking: Could he possibly know about me? . . .

. . . *Charlotte with her unique, naive charm puts the stuttering Russian at ease.* Observing this [Charlotte's grace], Walden and Lydia exchange a secret smile of parental pride. . . .

. . . *Outside Feliks sees that Oblomov will not be an easy target.* Getting close to him [Oblomov] will tax Feliks's ingenuity . . .

. . . Walden has not anticipated this demand [for the Balkans as a

Russian sphere of influence]. He talks around it a bit, but before he can say anything of substance he must consult with Churchill.

Feliks learns from the society papers that the Waldens and Oblomov will be present at the King's Court on 4 June. He buys a gun. . . .

Three

. . . Meanwhile, outside in the Mall, the Waldens' footman William waits with their carriage (among a hundred others), watched by Feliks . . .

William goes into the park to take a leak. Feliks hits him over the head, takes his top hat and livery coat, and ties and gags him. Then he goes and sits in the Walden carriage.

At the supper after the ceremony Walden tells Churchill of Oblomov's proposal and suggests a counteroffer. . . . Churchill okays it.

Feliks hears the call: "The Earl of Walden's carriage." He drives up to the Palace gates. He keeps his back to the party as they get in. He drives away. He stops the carriage in the middle of the park. He pulls his scarf over his face (so that the women, whom he does not plan to kill, will not be able to describe him afterwards). He jumps down from his seat, takes his gun from his pocket, and flings open the carriage door.

Four

Lydia yells "Help!" in Russian—just as she used to when Feliks made love to her. Feliks freezes. Lydia! Here in *this carriage*! My own Lydia.

Walden, who is never frozen with shock, lashes out with his walking cane, hitting Feliks's wrist. Feliks drops the gun. He has forgotten the assassination and is staring at Lydia, who is hysterical. Walden hits him again. Feliks runs away.

Feliks remembers the last time he saw Lydia. . . . They [the Ochrana] beat the soles of his feet in an attempt to make him reveal the names of other anarchists. The torture stopped without explanation, and six weeks later—equally inexplicably—he was released. On the day he came out he learned that, the day before, Lydia had left for England with her new husband.

Walden, Oblomov and Churchill sit in the library. Churchill is mad at Walden for almost letting Oblomov get killed. Walden is angry, too, at himself and at the unknown assassin who hit William over the head and scared Lydia half to death. They agree to move Oblomov to a hotel and forget about introducing him to society. Churchill tells Walden, "I hold you personally responsible for the safety of the Prince." Oblomov says, "You too should be guarded, Walden. The gun was actually pointed at you."

Lydia has not recognized Feliks (except perhaps subconsciously). She fainted when he ran away. She believes that what happened was an attempted robbery. (So does Charlotte.) Lydia has been put to bed with a dose of laudanum. She dreams about Feliks. When Walden comes to bed she makes love to him without waking up.

Five

. . . That night her [Charlotte's] coming-out ball is held at a hotel . . . *a glittering occasion. On the way home Charlotte is horrified to see a woman sleeping on the pavement.*

. . . She [Annie] explains that she got pregnant and was fired without a "character." She subsequently had a miscarriage and is now destitute . . . but she asks for money. Charlotte tells her to come to the house tomorrow afternoon. . . .

. . . She [Charlotte] practically accuses her parents of murdering Annie's unborn child.

Walden and Lydia are somewhat thrown. Pregnant housemaids are always fired; it's the only way to run a respectable house. But in truth they cannot feel proud of this policy.

Walden in particular is really shaken. First an assassin attacks his family in the middle of London, then his daughter tells him his moral standards are evil. What is the world coming to?

Charlotte says she wants to take Annie as her personal maid. Lydia is aghast, Walden less so; reluctantly they consent.

Feliks is very down. He has lost the element of surprise. Oblomov's name no longer appears in the society papers, and the two Russian servants no longer go in and out of the house by the park; the prince has obviously gone into hiding somewhere. This is hardly surprising but it puts Feliks in a quandary. Oblomov could be anywhere. Feliks cannot check every hotel, every cabinet minister's residence, every London house owned by a Russian diplomat, etc. However there is one person who might simply *tell* him where Oblomov is: Lydia. . . .

Six

He gives his name as Constantine Dmitrich Levin and tells the butler that he must see Lady Walden immediately; it is a matter of urgency, and he is sure she will remember him from St. Petersburg. (The name he has chosen will be vaguely familiar to her as it is that of a character in *Anna Karenina*.)

The butler shows him into the morning-room where Lydia is writing letters. She looks up with an automatic smile, then frowns, then turns white as a sheet.

Eventually she tells Feliks how she came to marry Walden. . . .

As she tells this story, watching Feliks's face, she is consumed by a desperate need to touch him.

Feliks is much moved by the story. He goes to kiss her. No, she says; all that is half my life ago. Now that you know the truth, go away and never come back.

Feliks turns to go. Then: "I came to ask you something. . . ." He reminds himself of the importance of his mission and forces himself to repeat his prepared speech, a yarn about wanting to petition Oblomov personally for the release of a young anarchist sailor who has been jailed. Lydia tells him that Oblomov is at the Savoy Hotel.

As Feliks leaves, Lydia thinks: Thank God, he hasn't guessed the rest of the story.

Seven

From conversations with Annie, Charlotte is learning about poverty, sex, and the role of women. . . . *She promises to go on the next suffragette march.*

Feliks buys the necessary materials and makes a bomb.

Lydia thinks over her meeting with Feliks, suppressing for the moment her still-strong physical desire for him. She knows he was and doubtless still is an anarchist. Did he tell her the truth about why he wanted to see Oblomov? Perhaps he wants to murder Oblomov. It might even have been Feliks in the park that night! The more she thinks about it the more worried she is that she might have betrayed Oblomov to an assassin.

She tells Walden, "A man called this morning, a Russian whom I remembered vaguely from St. Petersburg, asking for Oblomov. . . . I told him the Savoy Hotel, I hope that was all right."

Walden says, "Don't worry about it."

Walden is concealing his anger. Things are getting on top of him. Oblomov is taking an unconscionably long time to reply to the British counterproposal. . . . Every day which passes makes a deal with the Russians more urgent. The unknown assassin seems incredibly daring and ingenious. Now once again he has located Oblomov. But perhaps Walden can turn this to advantage and actually *catch* the man.

During a political argument in the servants' hall, Annie makes a mistake: She declares that Mrs. Pankhurst is "a real lady"; she knows because Miss Charlotte said so. Marya reports to Lydia that Charlotte has met Mrs. Pankhurst. Charlotte is carpeted and forbidden to leave the house alone.

Feliks writes on an envelope: "Prince Oblomov, Savoy Hotel." He gives an urchin a penny to deliver it in fifteen minutes. By then Feliks is in the lobby of the hotel, reading a newspaper and apparently waiting for someone. The boy comes in and hands over the letter. Feliks watches carefully. His plan is to follow the envelope all the way to Oblomov. Suddenly the urchin is surrounded by plainclothes policemen who seem to have materialized out of the walls.

Walden is summoned from an office in the hotel. He questions the urchin. He opens the envelope and finds there is nothing in it. He begins to suspect what this is all about. He looks around.

But the lobby is empty.

Eight

. . . Walden moves Oblomov again. He tells his butler, "If 'Mr. Levin' should call again, you must admit him, but I want you to tell Pritchard immediately." He says to Pritchard, "If 'Mr. Levin' calls, follow him when he leaves."

Feliks tries following Walden around for a couple of days. The first day, Walden has lunch at his club, makes a couple of calls in the afternoon, dines at home, goes to the opera, and finishes up at a supper ball. Next day he leaves home early in his car. Feliks follows on his bicycle, but as soon as the car leaves Central London it picks up speed and Feliks is left behind.

There is nothing for it but to try Lydia again. . . .

Charlotte sneaks out of the house to join the suffragette march.

. . . Feliks sees his sister coming out of the Walden house. "Nadia!" he says. She gives him a puzzled look and walks on. Feliks realizes that he has not seen Nadia for twenty years, and although she looked like that when she was nineteen she doesn't anymore. This is presumably Charlotte, Lydia's daughter, whom Feliks has until now seen only from a distance. She might know where Oblomov is. Feliks follows her. . . .

He [Feliks] *sees Charlotte go down in a scuffle, rescues her and* takes her [Charlotte] to a cheap cafe and buys her a cup of tea. They talk. *So Lydia has a daughter who looks just like my sister.* . . . An incredible suspicion begins to dawn on Feliks. He asks Charlotte her exact date of birth. She tells him.

Then he knows; she is *his* daughter.

Nine

Walden is at Walden Hall, which is Oblomov's new hideout. Oblomov is in daily contact with the Czar, via the Russian Embassy, by messenger and coded cable. . . . Walden dashes back to London to consult with Churchill again.

Charlotte is fascinated by Feliks, for he has answers to the questions which trouble her: Why is there poverty? Why are there wars? Why is sex secret?

Feliks says that he knew Lydia in Russia long ago, and that Charlotte reminds him of his sister. "Maybe we're related," Charlotte says idly. Feliks catches his breath, hesitates, then says, "I doubt it."

They arrange to meet again.

Walden and Churchill come up with a new counterproposal. . . . Churchill says he must get Cabinet approval.

Feliks faces a dilemma. He has found a daughter he never knew he had—and she may know where Oblomov is. Should he use her?

He reads in the newspaper that the Archduke Franz-Ferdinand has been assassinated in Sarajevo.

He must use her.

They tour the National Gallery together. She talks knowledgeably about the pictures, opening a new world to Feliks. He feels so proud of her.

He tells her that the assassination in Sarajevo means war. He explains that Walden and Oblomov are trying to bring Russia into the war, and says that in order to stop them he must kill Oblomov.

Charlotte does not accept this easily, but after a long discussion she says, "You're right."

He asks her, "Where is Oblomov?"

She doesn't know.

But she will find out.

Ten

Charlotte asks Lydia where Oblomov is. She replies, "Ask your father." She asks Walden. He says, "It's better you shouldn't know."

. . . When he gets home *from a melancholy walk and a look from a distance at his ex-mistress,* Walden's house is in turmoil. Charlotte and two suffragettes have been arrested for setting fire to mailboxes. Walden has to go and get his daughter out of jail. He promises to send her out of London to keep her out of trouble.

The Cabinet approves his proposed counteroffer, so next day he drives to Walden Hall to put it to Oblomov. He takes Charlotte with him and leaves her there.

Feliks was due to meet Charlotte again. He waits all day for her but of course she does not turn up.

Eleven

. . . She [Bonnie] is now living on her savings, comfortable but a little lonely. They make love. Afterward she tells him that she knows (from experience) that he is infertile. He says, "But I've got a daughter." Bonnie says, "When was she born, dear . . . exactly?"

Meanwhile Feliks calls on Lydia and asks again where Oblomov is. Lydia says, "You're trying to use me to help you murder him!" Feliks says, "All these years I had a daughter . . . do you realize what you've stolen from me?" They quarrel like lovers who have betrayed one another. At the height of the row they kiss passionately. Lydia breaks away and runs out of the room. Feliks leaves.

Pritchard follows him.

When Walden gets home there are three messages.

One is from Churchill. Austria has sent Serbia a war ultimatum with a forty-eight-hour deadline.

The second one is from Oblomov, accepting the new deal. Walden notifies Churchill and proposes the papers should be signed Saturday at Walden Hall.

The third comes from the Red Lion pub in Stepney, from where Pritchard is watching the front door of the house where Feliks is lodging. It says, "I have tracked the lion to his den."

Walden sends another message to Churchill, then puts on a coat of Pritchard's and heads for the East End.

Twelve

When Feliks reached home there was a letter from Charlotte: "Oblomov is here at Walden Hall. Meet me any morning on the bridle path in the woods to the north of the house." Feliks is now methodically packing his bomb kit.

Feliks leaves before the police arrive at the Red Lion pub. Walden and Pritchard follow him to the railway station. Pritchard gets behind him in the queue and buys a ticket to the same destination, a market town near Walden Hall. Pritchard gets on the train, establishes where Feliks is sitting, then comes back and gives the ticket to Walden. Walden scribbles a note for Pritchard to take to Churchill, then gets on the train. The train pulls out.

Churchill gives orders for troops to stop the train and arrest everyone on board.

Pritchard rushes back to the house. He tells Lydia what is happening. Then he takes the Rolls and heads pell-mell for the place where the train is to be stopped.

Walden, on the train, is wondering why Lydia did not tell him that "Mr. Levin" had called again, and whether this has any connection with what Bonnie said this afternoon. The train slows to a halt on an uphill slope. Walden looks out and sees that the train is surrounded by soldiers. Then he sees Feliks go by, heading for the rear of the train. He gets up and follows.

Feliks gets into the guard's van, the last coach in the train. He releases the brake and dynamites the coupling. The coach begins to roll backward down the hill.

Walden leaps the gap and attacks Feliks. The fight is unequal, and Walden is thrown out of the coach.

The coach gathers speed and bursts through the cordon of soldiers.

Thirteen

Pritchard arrives. Walden is not seriously injured. The soldiers chase after the coach.

When it comes to a stop Feliks takes off over the fields. He has a good start on the soldiers. He reaches a main road. A car comes along. He stops it, throws the driver out, and takes the car.

The soldiers set up a roadblock. Feliks smashes through it.

Walden and Pritchard give chase in the Rolls.

Feliks has a puncture. He drives the stolen car off the road. He shatters the windshield and plants the shards of glass in the road. Then he heads across country.

Walden and Pritchard drive over the glass and get two punctures. They begin to walk, looking for somewhere to hire horses.

Feliks takes a horse from a field. He arrives in the vicinity of Walden Hall around 3:00 a.m. on Friday. There are a few police around, but the man who escaped from Siberia knows how to hide in the woods for a night.

Fourteen

Walden and Pritchard arrive just before dawn and organize a police dragnet in the area of Walden Hall.

Charlotte goes riding before breakfast and picks up Feliks in the woods. She gets him back to the stables, then leads him up over the roofs to her attic hiding place. She tells him that Oblomov's room is being guarded day and night, doors and windows. However, they are going to sign the treaty on Saturday at 3:00 p.m. in a room called the Octagon.

Lydia arrives from London. After what Pritchard told her last night she has deduced that Charlotte must be helping Feliks. She must tell Walden this, and in so doing she is obliged to reveal the secret of Charlotte's parentage. Walden was somewhat prepared for this by Bonnie. He and Lydia forgive one another and resolve to start afresh.

Meanwhile, Charlotte is confined to her room and the house is searched. Feliks evades the searchers by going out on to the roof.

In the night he creeps through the darkened house and plants a bomb in a flowerpot in the Octagon. He sets it to go off at 3:15.

Fifteen

. . . At three o'clock the secret treaty is signed by Walden and Oblomov in the presence of Churchill and the Russian ambassador. The four men drink a celebratory glass of champagne.

Charlotte is released from confinement. She goes straight to the attic and tells Feliks, "It's too late—they've signed it."

"It's not too late," he says. "They will all be blown up in . . . two minutes."

Charlotte says, "But you can't kill my father!"

"He's not your father," says Feliks. "I am. You see, Lydia and I were lovers, then—"

"It makes no difference!" says Charlotte—and runs off.

Feliks goes after her.

Charlotte runs into the Octagon at 3:14:30. She says, "Get out, everyone—"

Feliks comes in behind her and tries to drag her out. Walden and Oblomov jump him.

It is 3:14:50.

Feliks struggles. For an instant he gets free.

It is 3:14:59.

Feliks picks up the flowerpot containing the bomb. Clutching it to his chest, he throws himself through the window.

The bomb goes off before he hits the ground.

Charlotte runs to Walden. He puts his arms around her.

"Father," she says.

Postscript

In the first few months of the war, the Russian threat to Germany's eastern front, by drawing troops away from the west, played a crucial role in halting the German invasion of France. In 1915 the Russians were officially given Constantinople and the Bosporus. And in 1917 the Russian people did rise up and overthrow the Czarist regime. Of course Feliks was not alive to see the result of his life's work. But perhaps it was just as well.

The end.

Analysis of Fourth Outline

In this final outline, Follett starts his story in the present, 1914, and further tightens the emotional links between his major characters, thus creating possibilities for several moving scenes. He also introduces important physical actions with the mugging of the carriage driver on the Mall, the murder attempt at the Savoy, the chase on the train, and the

somewhat enlarged finale at Walden Hall. Of these, Feliks's dynamit-
ing a coupling between railway cars, then crashing with one through
a cordon of soldiers, rushing off and stealing an auto, losing it because
of a puncture and then sabotaging the road with shards of glass turn
out to have been a mistake and are not used in the book. The murder
attempt yet to come at Walden Hall must be the story's climax. The
scenes leading up to it, which these are, must be tense but not compara-
ble or greater in excitement. If you reread chapter thirteen of *The Man
From St. Petersburg*, you'll note how Follett maintains high tension but
tones down the melodrama.

The most important change in Outline Four is Follett's making
Feliks into Charlotte's biological father. Here is the potentially clichéd
improbability, a great risk for the author. But what Follett gains in
emotional power quite rightly outweighs what he risks losing in credibility. This change inflects the story with all sorts of new dynamics
and in many ways resolves weaknesses in the preceding outlines. The
personal stakes are now made incredibly high for all four characters. We
more easily identify with them, admire them, and become emotionally
involved with them. They and their dilemmas are now larger-than-life
in a highly contrived, high-concept situation, yet it is one that Follett
can trust his artistry as a writer to render credible.

Here are some of the specifics. Lydia, from her very first appearance,
now is endowed with a powerful thrust: to preserve her terrible secret
and make certain her daughter never gets herself into such a pickle.
And yet memories of Feliks pervade her being. She remembers her
wedding to Walden as the unhappiest day of her life. After the attack
in the carriage, Lydia doesn't recognize the intruder, but she dreams
about Feliks. Now when Feliks first calls on her, she is frightened, but
she also longs to touch him and he to kiss her. He almost forgets why
he came: to learn Oblomov's whereabouts. When he leaves, she feels
great relief that he hasn't guessed the rest of her story, about Charlotte.
Lydia in this draft is also given more presence of mind and greater
loyalty and love for her husband. All on her own she realizes Feliks
may be after Oblomov, and she warns Walden. Gone is the demeaning
business of her selling jewels and Walden's discovery of this. And although in the outline Pritchard still spies on her, in the book that
too is eliminated. This warmer relationship between husband and wife
resonates through almost every chapter, arriving finally at a more poignant reconciliation when she confesses to Walden about Charlotte. At

Feliks's second visit, when Lydia forcefully confronts him, "You're using me for murder," he even more strongly accuses her of having stolen his daughter. Then, amidst their anger and heartbreak, they kiss. Potent stuff.

From the very beginning of this draft, Feliks is made more vulnerable and human. Arriving in England, he's excited to be in the same country as the woman he loved. In his scenes with Lydia, he's more emotional and less coolly manipulative. Once he realizes that Charlotte is his daughter, he takes on a whole new softness. Gone is his seduction of her. He feels fatherly pride in her beauty and knowledge of art and suddenly has qualms about using her to further his deadly aims. No longer the single-minded assassin, he becomes torn in two directions and acquires a bit of humanity. If not for the Austrian Archduke having just been assassinated in Sarajevo and the sudden immediacy of a terrible war, the possibility is raised that he might even have backed off from involving her. And this feeling of love for a newfound daughter prepares well and begins to add credibility to his absorbing the explosion at the end to spare her.

Walden, in addition to being negotiator, father, husband, now is given actions that somewhat more solidly mark him rather than Charlotte as the protagonist, the principal adversary to Feliks, the other partner in the duel that is the spine of the book. Initially Follett sets Walden up as an arch-conservative who won't admit Churchill from the Liberal enemy camp to his home. But Walden is reasonable, patriotic, and agrees to undertake the mission, which is now the precipitating event of the novel. After warding off Feliks in the carriage outside the King's court, it is Walden who on the train to Surrey dares to leap the gap between separated cars and physically attack Feliks. But since this train episode is eliminated from the text, Follett in the book has Walden save the day by catching a bottle of nitroglycerine tossed at him by Feliks at the Savoy, an act that arouses great awe in everyone watching. Also in the book but not in this outline, Walden participates in a wild but fruitless shoot-out and chase after Feliks, who dashes over London rooftops. But it's Walden's tenderness toward Charlotte and Lydia in the closing scenes, again not in this outline but in the book, that do most to make him a wonderful character.

At the finale, it's Charlotte who saves Walden. Her already-strong character is further fortified in this outline. She, rather than Belinda, becomes the intrepid leader in the raid on the library to find out about sex. Not only is Charlotte shocked to discover a homeless Annie living in the street, but she now demands from her parents that the woman be hired as her maid, and she prevails. Under the influence of Feliks, Charlotte is no longer a character with whom he has to pussyfoot and to pretend that all he wants to do is kidnap Oblomov. Going along with his reasoning, she agrees to cooperate with the assassination and then takes a tremendous risk, bringing Feliks right into her house and hiding him there. But when she learns that Walden too is about to be blown up, nothing will stop her from trying to save him despite the terrible peril to herself.

The plotting changes should be clear to you, but a few are worth underlining. Note that as I pointed out earlier Feliks now operates alone (thus affording him richer attention and involvement as the sole antagonist) and that the drive toward the assassination now gets underway in the first chapter, virtually as soon as he appears. No need for a tepid scene with an unimportant character to lure him into a conspiracy. How much more suspenseful if, when first we meet him, he is already pushing toward his deadly objective.

The nonorganic prologue and epilogue are gone. Feliks's first assassination attempt is combined with the debutante presentation at the Royal Court, so that the palace episode now is not merely illustrative of the social mores of the period, but Follett integrates it into his ongoing action. Lydia now tells Walden about her having disclosed Oblomov's whereabouts to a "Russian visitor," which inspires Walden personally to take action, to set the trap at the Savoy. At the beginning of the outline Charlotte shows Belinda an attic hiding place and a way to get across several acres of roof that cover Walden Hall. All this then comes excitingly into play at the finale when Charlotte brings Feliks across the roof to sneak him into the house.

Depending on the level of your own experience as a novelist and writer of outlines, my analysis of these four snyopses may have seemed either overly brief and sketchy or glaringly self-evident and far too detailed. Those of you to whom much of this is new might now ask yourselves, What through the course of all four of these outlines has Follett most essentially done to transform a slender plot notion into a blueprint for a novel that became a huge success throughout the world?

To sum up, he began by giving us a fair bit of background but not much more of a dramatic premise than Feliks's seducing Charlotte as the assassin's way of getting to Oblomov, and Charlotte's undergoing

an adolescent rebellion that makes her vulnerable to Feliks. Two characters, and only a handful of scenes that portend high drama.

In the succeeding outlines, Follett adds more and more steps (and
then countersteps) to the assassination plot. By the last outline, he starts
it off in the very first chapter and carries it through to the last one.

Similarly, Charlotte and her rebellion little by little acquire an
entire suite of interlocking scenes, and some of her movements also
incur countermeasures.

Most crucially, perhaps, Follett transforms a story involving people
who are strangers to each other into one whose characters are most
intimately linked, thus creating the possibility for scenes of great poignancy and high emotion.

The action becomes focused more and more narrowly on his four
principal characters, with whom we can become more and more involved. At least one of them and usually more than one ultimately is
present in every scene. And all scenes that would have centered on
secondary characters are eliminated by the final outline.

A thriller needs an antagonist and a protagonist (and countervailing
characters are a sine qua non of all types of popular fiction). The first
outline presents Kell as a foil to Feliks through most of the story. Then
at the end it's Charlotte. But neither provides Feliks with a worthy
opponent who endures throughout the story. By the fourth outline,
Walden is amply developed to fulfill the role, and in the novel itself,
Follett takes him a step further and renders him heroic.

Vitally intersecting with the stories of Feliks, Charlotte and Walden is that of Lydia. In the first outline, she is little more than scenery.
By the final outline, however, she is developed as an influence on the
assassination intrigue and as a party to domestic dramas with her
daughter and husband, which stem of course from her youthful secret
relationship with Feliks. Her need to keep hidden the terrible secret of
her daughter's paternity now transforms her into someone who also has
a mission. This, coupled with the feelings that she still has for Feliks,
gives her an impetus to share in driving the plot.

The evolution of Feliks from a despicable German gun-for-hire, to
a cold-blooded Russian anarchist, to a man who begins to see some
beauty in life once he discovers he's a father should be clear by now.
But what Follett in the end does to make this character into a wonderful
villain is to give him self-doubt, to make him question the worthwhile-
ness of his holy mission, of his very role as a terrorist. Torn between

two paths, he becomes human, as do the other principals who also are given not dissimilar inner conflicts: Lydia torn between Feliks and her husband, Charlotte between her mentor-father and the man who raised her, and even Walden between his duty and his love for his family.

With these outlines, then, Follett establishes the characters and plot for the writing of a big book. Its other key components, you will see, become realized for the most part in the actual setting down of the text.

Toward the end of this book, you will come to a chapter on revision. Again I'll draw from this novel to explore and illustrate how an author goes about revising and improving the line-by-line writing of two specific scenes as well as rebuilding their overall structures. After that, I'll point up the salient ways in which the ending of the actual novel differs yet again from this final outline and discuss the principles of craft that impelled Follett to make these further improvements.

Now is a good time to ask yourself, What if Follett had written the book without developing all these outlines, using only the first— or none at all? There's no ready answer, but if you now go back and reread the first outline you will find it hard to imagine a number one best-seller deriving from it.

You may also ask, How does an author get beyond her original notion? Can she be objective enough all on her own to decide what needs changing and strengthening? I haven't taken a nationwide poll, but I suspect that a few authors can and many cannot. Still, if you put your outline aside and then reread it after a week has elapsed, and if you have firmly grasped the principles set forth all through this book, you ought to have acquired certain skills as well as enough distance from your original conception to be able on your own to spot at least some of its weaknesses. But as I point out in this book's final chapter, if you can get some intelligent feedback at each step from a knowledgeable agent, editor or novelist colleague, it could help immeasurably.

Then the question arises, How do you know when you've finished, when the last outline you've written should be your final one, and when it's time to start in on your text? The answer is you won't know that for sure any more than you'll know how wonderful your completed novel is. In the normal course, I would recommend at least three drafts for your outline. If, by then, each chapter contains some sort of climax and pushes your story ahead in some significant way, and if you have at least one character (and preferably two or three) with whom we can deeply empathize and whose fate gets resolved excitingly at the end, then you may have crafted a structure that you then can build into an exciting novel.

Chapter Five

LARGER-THAN-LIFE CHARACTERS

❧

DESPITE THE GREAT AND WELL-DESERVED SUCCESS of *Ordinary People* by Judith Guest, buyers of popular fiction are rarely content to be immersed in the lives of the nice little couple next door. Readers remember a wonderful book's characters long after they forget a story's exciting scenes or even its climax. Those characters who do stick in our minds over years and years appear in more than one way to be extraordinary. This chapter will explore how a few such representative characters are designed, built, shaped and brought alive.

When in our everyday lives we say that we know someone, know him well, intimately, what most elementally and specifically are the things about him that we take into account? Generally, we seize on the obvious externals: how he likes to dress, eat, spend or withhold money, and use his leisure time; how hard he works, plays or lusts; how likely he is to laugh and joke or be depressed and complain; to what degree he loves or hates his family members, friends, enemies, and others in his life, and how they in turn feel about him.

A novelist, in building a major character, needs to bring to bear many of these variables along with whole combinations of other possible habits, traits, idiosyncrasies and appetites. But the author must also dig deeper. He has to let us see and share the longings, hopes, carnal desires, ambitions, fears, loves and hates that reside privately within the soul of his character and that (much as in life) other characters may know little or nothing about. The writer must view the environment of the novel (both physical and human) through the eyes and sensibilities of the character. In so doing he achieves within himself and for the reader a closeness akin to love for the character.

MOTIVATION

Aristotle was perhaps the first to set down, in a work that survives, that a character in tragedy is defined by his actions. That, I believe, still holds true for characters in drama and in fiction, and indeed in life. But not only does Sophocles let us see what Oedipus and Antigone actually do, he first has them expose to us their motives. And therein lies the key to making the audience or the reader care, to cause her temporarily to abandon her own concerns and to empathize, pulsate with, become at one with the terrors, anxieties, longings, and joys of a fictional character. To cause this to happen, the author discloses what it is that the character wants more than anything, now, in this scene in the present, and also what it is that the character wants, dreams of for the future, for the rest of his life, or at least for the time span of the story. This illumining of a character's interior, whether revealed through dialogue or, more likely, through interior monologue or author narration, should bare the very soul of the character and in so doing draw the reader close.

If what your character wants, dreams of, longs for, is socially acceptable, something not shameful or bizarre or absurdly over the moon, something that won't cause your character to be thought of by the book's other characters as a nut case, a fiend or a laughingstock, then you can safely work his hope or goal into your dialogue. But if, as is more often the case, what your character desperately desires is too intimate, too fraught with danger, too kooky, too grandiose and over-the-top to reveal easily to others, then it's best to work this great wish through interior monologue or author narration. These techniques, as you'll soon see when we examine the development of Scarlett O'Hara, can be used both to vivify character depth and also to create line-by-line dramatic tension simply as a result of the contrast between what the character thinks on the one hand and what he says on the other.

Larger-than-life characters, the pillars of blockbuster novels, through one or another of these techniques reveal their hopes and goals as do all good principal literary characters. But the hidden desires and fantasies of the Scarletts and Meggies and Don Corleones are different. These characters aspire to and go after (within their social context) the impossible or nearly impossible. Feliks Kschessinski sets out to murder Prince Orlov and thereby deflect the Czar from joining Great Britain in a war against Germany—one puny individual singlehandedly trying to influence and even control mighty empires. Until almost the end of *Gone With the Wind*, Scarlett's barely controllable passion for Ashley Wilkes does not abate, despite his turning away from her and marrying Melanie and after that his continual rejections of her. In the second half of the book, her I-don't-give-a-damn-what-anyone-thinks lust for money and security is equally fervid. She is, in a word, irrepressible.

DON CORLEONE

To me, one of the wonders of modern fiction is how Mario Puzo contrives a gangster leader—a Mafia Don, a man who heads a mighty organization of killers, extortionists, loan sharks, crooked union officials, illegal bookmakers and other criminal types—and presents this character in such a way that he becomes memorable, admired if not beloved, and certainly the key figure in one of the most widely enjoyed novels of the last half-century. Let's now look closely at only some of the things that Puzo does to create an individual whom we might normally think of as a lowlife Sicilian hoodlum and to lead us to accept him as a revered Godfather.

The book begins with three men in the throes of painful and not easily surmountable predicaments. Amerigo Bonasera, the undertaker, fails to get justice in court for his daughter, who endured an attempted rape and was so badly beaten that her jaw had to be wired back together. Johnny Fontaine, the actor-singer, his career on the skids, is humiliated and thrown out by his trampy wife. Nazorine, the baker, must get U.S. citizenship for his Italian prisoner-of-war apprentice, or his plump and homely daughter may lose her only chance to get a husband. All three are invited to the wedding of Constanzia Corleone, daughter of the Don, and all three take the occasion to ask, even plead, for the Godfather's help. Their belief that one man, another human being, could right the wrongs of the judicial system, secure U.S. citizenship for an enemy alien, and compel a major Hollywood studio to cast an actor who has been summarily and strongly rejected establishes Vito Corleone within the opening pages as a personage of vast and mysterious power. With the actor he is a bit stern, with the undertaker much more so. But most importantly, in each instance he promises to put an end to their troubles, he asks for nothing except friendship in return, and he delivers. His desperate supplicants overflow with gratitude, and we the readers get caught up in the warm and admiring feelings these needy men have for so extraordinary a character.

LARGER-THAN-LIFE CHARACTERS

Then observe how Corleone puts into effect his kindness and generosity. Helping the baker involves a two-thousand-dollar bribe to a con-
gressman, which doesn't seem all that awful when the result smooths
the road for young love, especially when corrupting the legislator is
kept offstage, whereas the baker who pleads on behalf of his daughter
confronts us directly. Remember, what counts in determining character
for the reader is limited largely to what we actually see the character
do as opposed to what is said about him. The Don's satisfying the
undertaker leads to a hood's beating the two would-be rapists to jelly
with a specially made set of brass knuckles with one-sixteenth inch
iron spikes. The Godfather, though, comes out smelling almost like a
rose. Bonasera wants the youths killed, but no; Corleone orders the
revenge to be carried out by "people who will not be carried away by
blood. After all we're not murderers. . . ." Not only are these youths
who get battered themselves callous and brutal, but their parents are
hardly better, bribing a judge to grant their despicable sons a suspended
sentence. These parents, one might assume, love their sons and go to
extremes for them much as the undertaker does for his daughter. But
their desperation hardly registers, since in the book it never actually
confronts us. So Puzo's Don again and again in an evil world emerges
as much less evil than the corrupt institutions and people with whom
he must contend.

Acts of Power

The capstone of the novel's opening and the action that more than any
other establishes the Don as larger than life is Corleone's obtaining for
Johnny the motion picture role the actor so hungrily covets. Jack Woltz,
the all-powerful studio head, friend of J. Edgar Hoover and of the
President himself, initially tells a very polite Tom Hagen, the Don's
Consiglieri and emissary, to go to hell. Woltz hates Johnny's guts, calls
him a pinko punk, and promises to run him out of the movies. Woltz's
language is gross, openly insulting with his anti-Italian slurs. He's also
revealed to be a sadistic child molester. His love is his world-class
racing stable, and particularly Khartoum, the greatest racehorse in the
world, for which the movie mogul has paid the then-record sum of
$600,000. So, Corleone arranges for Woltz to wake up and find the
silky black head of the great horse severed from its body and placed at
the foot of his bed. The California executive who thought that the
immense power he wielded was greater than that of Don Corleone

discovers that, despite his great wealth and his connections with the FBI and the White House, he was wrong. The deed itself is revolting, but even more so it's awesome. To him and to us. Though in strict legal terms, Woltz clearly would be in the right, the awestruck reader's admiration and sympathy go to the Sicilian—for thinking of so ingenious a scheme, for having the guts and skill to carry it out, for making good on his promise to his godson Johnny, and most crucially for bringing low so cruel and distasteful a man as Jack Woltz. The "civilized" Don, by contrast, refrains from using foul language; he would never hurt a little girl or cultivate a protege who "could suck you out like a water pump."

Right after his daughter's wedding, Corleone is driven to French Hospital to visit Genco Abbandando, his old Consiglieri, who is about to die of cancer. Mrs. Abbandando calls him a saint for coming here on his daughter's wedding day. But what's truly startling is the dying man's feverish hope that the Godfather could still save him from death or, at the very least, that Corleone could have pulled a few strings to keep Genco from going to hell. This little scene does not prepare for or tie in with any subsequent plot development. Its purpose in appearing just prior to the episode in which the two would-be rapists get mauled is to demonstrate Corleone's capacity for kindness and tenderness, for taking charge of a painful situation. It notes how almost godlike people close to the Don consider him to be.

The episodes I've described above are all placed in the first 15 percent of the text, before the main thrust of the story, before the battle with Sollozzo and the rival crime families even begins. Puzo uses these pages to create the environment of the Corleone family, to set out briefly the characters of Sonny, Michael, Kay, Tom, Connie, Carlo, Johnnie and Lucy, but most importantly to endow his hero with enormous stature and put us solidly on his side. Having seen Don Vito so powerfully in action, we now can accept and believe in him as a benevolent despot, beholden to no man on earth. He is subject to no government or law other than the law he chooses to obey, devoted and generous to his friends and family, and ruthless when crossed, but never as low or evil as his opponents and enemies—in short, he is a unique character.

Almost everything we know about the Don we learn from what he says and does and from what the other characters say and think about him. Puzo uses a minimum of direct exposition of Corleone's thoughts and feelings and gives him only a few brief interior monologues. He keeps the Don at a slight remove from us and thus heightens his mysterious and almost godlike aura. Margaret Mitchell, to flesh out Scarlett, uses some of the same techniques as Puzo, but she also writes scene after scene in which what Scarlett says or does is immediately recognizable as different or even opposite from what she is thinking or feeling. What drama that contrast provides! What's more, Scarlett's interior is often revealed to be even more fiery than the outrageous things she says and does. Mitchell, unlike Puzo, by acquainting us with Scarlett's lusts and longings, her loves and hates, draws us into something of an intense intimacy with her.

SCARLETT O'HARA

From the book's very opening sentence, "Scarlett O'Hara was not beautiful, but men seldom realized it when caught by her charm as the Tarleton twins were," this sixteen-year-old girl is presented as someone out of the ordinary. Before the end of the first page, Mitchell tells us, "The green eyes and the carefully sweet face were turbulent, willful, lusty with life, distinctly at variance with her decorous behavior." We have not yet seen our heroine go into action, but the author is laying the groundwork, preparing us. Scarlett first makes her personality felt in refusing to let the twins talk about the "war." She does it with a smile—deepening her dimple, fluttering her lashes, enchanting the boys—but her motive, it's made clear, is narcissism. She cannot endure a conversation in which she is not the chief subject. Here is a character who aggressively asserts her will, but who nonetheless can incur delight rather than annoyance or anger.

Our first peek into Scarlett's driving passion comes with Brent Tarleton's announcement that Ashley Wilkes's engagement is to be announced at tomorrow's barbecue. Scarlett says nothing, but her lips go white. Then, speaking automatically, she agrees to do all the waltzes and eat supper with the twins, even though earlier she had told them that all her dances were already promised to others. Since in the past they have always had to beg and plead for even the slightest favors from her, they, unaware of what she's thinking and feeling, are jubilant.

Once the twins leave her and ride away, Mitchell expands on Scarlett's power and on her narcissism. Stewart and Brent, we learn, both have been deliberately bewitched by Scarlett, lured away from other quite suitable girls, not because she wants these boys, but because she cannot endure any young men friends of hers being in love with a woman other than herself. Although Scarlett has dazzled the twins with her dancing green eyes and merry laughter at their clever remarks, her success is not universal. The boys' mother openly dislikes Scarlett, calling her "a sly piece," a "two-faced little, green-eyed baggage." The story has hardly begun, and what contrary feelings this young woman already is arousing!

Sympathy for Scarlett

In chapter two, Mitchell substantively exposes and solidifies Scarlett's character in a number of ways. Not limiting herself with the earlier mention of Scarlett's unhappiness at the shocking news about Ashley, Mitchell now details the components of our heroine's pain: mouth hurting from her having stretched it unwillingly in smiles; heart swollen, feeling too big for her chest, beating with odd little jerks; hands feeling cold. With such vivid descriptions, it becomes easy—even natural—for the reader to actually share the character's distress.

Scarlett's earlier-mentioned indomitability is one key factor in establishing her larger-than-life stature, but equally crucial in arousing the reader's sympathy for this self-centered girl is the high intensity of her feelings, the ferocity of her passions. These come at us sometimes in dialogue and even more directly through interior monologue. After the above account of her pain, Scarlett bares her inner self: "not true, lies, a big joke, Ashley couldn't possibly love a mouse like Melanie. She, Scarlett, was the one he loved." What's most basic to her as a character is being forthrightly unbosomed. Later, when her father informs her that Melanie has indeed already arrived at the Wilkes's plantation, she feels her face growing red with annoyance and wishes she could shake him and tell him to shut his mouth. And then when he confirms the news of the engagement, a pain shakes "at her savagely as a wild animal's fangs." Her father berates her for moaning about a man who never intended more than friendship. Scarlett violently disagrees—but in her thoughts, which only we are privy to.

Another way that Mitchell causes us to care about so willful and selfish a creature as Scarlett is by adding a powerful positive side to her character. People we richly relate to in novels (as in life) have close ties with others. The isolated antiheroes of Kafka and Camus have virtually no place as lead characters in popular fiction. Scarlett's attachments to Mammy, Gerald, Ellen and to Tara itself are in the first three chapters pointedly presented. With her dear father she has a mutual suppression agreement. He may castigate her for acting like a tomboy, but to others, notably Mammy or Ellen, he says not a word against Scarlett. And she in turn keeps discreet about his jumping fences or losing at poker. Just being in his presence gives her comfort. And we learn, too, some of the specific things about him that she loves: his vitality, earthiness, and coarseness. She even loves his smells: bourbon mingled with a fragrance of mint, chewing tobacco, well-oiled leather and horses.

Mammy, whose eyes are unblinkered to all Scarlett's faults, who chastens her "lamb" continuously, accuses her of having no better manners than a field hand for failing to invite the twins to stay for dinner. Mammy's tirades all through the novel against Scarlett's outrageous acts never let up. Nevertheless, she goes on loving and rallying to the support of her young mistress, even when Scarlett, wholly beyond the bounds of decency, decides to woo Frank Kennedy, her sister's fiancé. Mammy's devotion is another factor that helps us feel for Scarlett. Scarlett never stops bargaining with Mammy, often outwitting her, about what to wear, eat, where to go or not to go, with whom to be seen. But she plainly respects and in some ways fears Mammy. At a time of great crisis, when Scarlett returns to a devastated Tara, it's on Mammy's broad sagging breasts that Scarlett lays her head. Later in the novel, during the Reconstruction period, when all of "Old Guard Atlanta" ostracizes Scarlett for her greed, her mannish ways, and her consorting with Yankees and carpetbaggers, it's Melanie's unswerving loyalty that similarly helps us maintain our sympathy for Scarlett. And as objectionable as Scarlett at times is, Mitchell, like Puzo, manages to build her up by favorably comparing her with others. For example, she is shown to be so much more caring and vital than her whining and treacherous sister, Suellen.

The adored godlike figure in Scarlett's world is her mother, Ellen. As Scarlett first expresses her love for Tara, we learn that she loves it as she does her mother's face under the lamp at prayer time. At Ellen's initial appearance in the book, as she's about to go off and try to help with Emmie Slattery's dying baby, she pats Scarlett's cheek with a mittened hand. Scarlett thrills to the never-failing magic of her mother's touch, to the faint fragrance of lemon verbena sachet that comes from her rustling silk dress. Ellen's little office is Scarlett's favorite room in all the house, where when aching about Ashley she longs to be, so she could put her head in her mother's lap. Scarlett as a child confused her mother with the Virgin Mary. And now the sight of her mother's serene face upturned praying to God brings her peace, a feeling of new hope, a belief that up in heaven Ellen's voice will be heard. Along with Scarlett's manipulative scheming, we also keep seeing her portrayed as a loving daughter.

Scarlett attempts the impossible or nearly impossible several times in the course of the novel. Given the confines of her sex, time, and social class, she can be perceived to be as gutsy and resourceful as Don Corleone. From the beginning Mitchell gives us glimmers of these qualities in Scarlett's dealings with the twins, Mammy and Gerald. But it's at the end of chapter four, less than 10 percent of the way into the book, that we have the first such display of her doggedness, when Scarlett decides that she simply cannot stand idly by and let Ashley marry Melanie. She, Scarlett, loves him too much, and she is positive that he feels the same toward her. She forms a plan. Tomorrow she'll be prideful, ignore him, flirt with every other man at the barbecue, keep them all swarming around her, impress him and make him sad with jealousy. And then she'll make him happy, modestly let him know that she prefers him to any other man in the world. And that of course will lead him to propose. Then they'll run off to Jonesboro and be married. Nothing, of course, works out as she hopes, but what counts in terms of building her character is our being awestruck by her determination and her audacity.

FELIKS KSCHESSINSKI

Scarlett and Don Vito are protagonists. Now let's take a close but brief look at how Feliks, a larger-than-life antagonist, is introduced and established. Not that differently, you'll find, except in one respect. When the book begins, whereas Scarlett and the Don are each integrated into their community and are literally surrounded by family and friends, Feliks has only casual relationships. He loves no one, and no one loves him. As the novel progresses, after his meetings with Lydia and then Charlotte, this of course changes. At the outset, however, the author concentrates on bringing to life Feliks's intelligence, humanity, and his extraordinary daring. His sophisticated political views reveal his thinking. Whereas his father, a priest, preached that God loves the Russian people, Feliks believes that, since God treats them so cruelly, He must hate them. Despite the surly narrow-mindedness of the peasants, Feliks sees in them a foolish generosity, spontaneous outbursts of sheer fun that suggest to him how humanely they might act in a better society. Among his anarchist colleagues, it's only he who recognizes that fiery newspaper articles will not burn down Czarist palaces. And when he matter-of-factly commits to his near-impossible course of action, we find that he won't take a step without first planning it carefully, including the tough job of teaching himself English.

We glimpse Feliks's humanity as we first meet him arriving in England, in his admiration for the orchards and hop fields of Kent; his shock at the beauty of Germany's neat green fields, picturesque villages, train stations garlanded with flower beds; his thrill at Switzerland's snow-covered mountains. In Geneva he attends concerts, works in a bookstore. Looking about London, he is fascinated by women's hats, enormous things "as broad across as the wheel of a dogcart, and decorated with ribbons, feathers, flowers and fruit." He may not love anyone in particular, but Follett does give him sentiments we can share.

Feliks, as first introduced, is also shown to be violent, determined and utterly fearless. If these were his only qualities, he would be just another brutal thug, a stock melodrama character, and would evoke little interest and probably no sympathy. But these traits combined with the gentler ones outlined above mark him as extraordinary. His anarchist colleagues fantasize about how wonderful it would be if someone could kill Prince Orlov, and sadly, how impossible. To their stunned surprise, Feliks says, "I know how, and I'll go and do it." In London, he eats at restaurants and walks out without paying, pilfers from food shops, knocks a man off his bicycle and steals it. From a flashback we learn that he's escaped slave labor in a Siberian mine; sneaked across a continent in a half-mad state; stole a pony, rode it to death, and then ate its liver; and near Omsk strangled a policeman to get the man's dinner. Given his awful deprivation, we can imagine that in Feliks's shoes we might have done much the same had we dared. And there's the point. What most essentially makes this antagonist larger than life is his willingness to attempt things that we in all likelihood would not dare. What makes Feliks interesting, compelling even, is Follett's gradually transforming him from a man ignorant of love to one who begins to feel it and then reaches out for it.

YOUR OWN LARGER-THAN-LIFE CHARACTERS

To sum up, Don Corleone, Scarlett and Feliks are three very different characters, at least superficially. But under the surfaces of their varying genders, ages and ethnicities, are they really so different? All three are schemers who, regardless of seemingly insurmountable obstacles, go after what they want with boundless energy. Their persistence, almost to the point of being possessed, is not typical of "normal" people. All have goals specific to themselves, but their context is often one where each desperately seeks relief from adversity. None of them are perceived as flawless. In fact, their faults may be seen to outweigh their virtues. Yet because we experience their worlds from within their sensibilities, and because these books contain supporting characters whom our three principals love and who in turn love and/or admire them, we are led at least to empathize with them, if not want what they want. In the end, it's this combination of their irrepressible determination and their humanity that causes us to remember them.

Your own book will probably need only one larger-than-life character. In fact, it's unlikely that it could easily accommodate more than one. Give him an aim, goal, longing or ambition with which you (and the reader) can empathize. It should be something that, if you were in his shoes, you too would desperately want and that you would do anything in your power to bring to fruition. Keep in mind, too, that this goal can be reactive as well as active. In most of the popular books by Mary Higgins Clark and in novels such as *Rosemary's Baby* by Ira Levin and, to some extent, in *The Godfather*, the main thrusts of their protagonists are attempts to achieve security, fight off outside threats, escape fearful dangers, or gain relief from adversity.

Each of your major characters, too (most of whom should not be larger-than-life), will also need to be given an inner desire of her own, a yearning for something or someone that motivates and defines her as a distinctive if not unique being. That drive may be tied totally into the main action, such as the sleuth's struggle to solve the crime in almost any mystery or Walden's efforts to negotiate his treaty and protect Orlov. If so, then to project your character's humanity, to make her into something more than simply a cog in your plot, you will need to give her at least one secondary problem or goal. This may or may not be tightly linked to her main thrust in the plot. With Walden, it's his problems with his wife and his daughter, his great need to keep their love. Your character could have to cope with a seriously ailing mother, a retarded sister, a semidelinquent, teenage son, a problematic but beloved dog or cat. These or a hundred other situations you might devise will complicate her life (and the plot), freeing her momentarily from the constraints of a fast-moving plot and illuminating her humanity. In Michael Crichton's *Rising Sun*, the hero's two-year-old daughter whom he is struggling to raise as a single parent serves exactly this function.

Introducing Your Characters

Once you have fixed upon the thrusts or goals of each of your main characters, you must decide how to introduce them and at what points in the story. Try to bring them on one at a time, separately, giving each at least a page before you introduce another character. That way you can solidly establish each one's identity, and the reader is more likely to remember and recognize him in subsequent scenes. Think of a cocktail party where you are introduced to five or ten people at once, and how difficult it is even to remember their names. In your novel, you don't want to subject your reader to this difficulty.

Your protagonist should be brought on in the first chapter and no later than the second. The reader wants to know whom the story essentially is about. If you keep your reader waiting longer than this, he may be disoriented, believing that the seemingly important character he first met is your chief subject. Avoid forcing the reader to make this awkward adjustment. It's good, too, to introduce all your major characters fairly early in your novel and to keep involving them all the way through, as opposed to bringing on a new character with each new plot complication or a new major character as you approach your ending. In Ken Follett's original outline for *Eye of the Needle*, Lucy, who as the novel comes to its climax meets and falls in love with Faber and then discovers he's a German spy, had no role whatsoever in the story until this point near the ending. But in the book, she is introduced in the third chapter. The ongoing subplot of her difficulties with her crippled husband develops our interest in her and prepares wonderfully for her eventual fateful encounter with the Needle.

Building Your Characters

Usually, it's best to create a protagonist who is loved, admired and respected, if not universally, then at least by one or two of the characters around him. And your hero in turn should give back some of that good feeling or love to one or more of the people with whom she's involved. This holds true, as we have seen, even with a terrorist like Feliks. Of course, there are always exceptions. Faber in *Eye of the Needle* is made larger than life by his strength, devilish cunning and ruthless daring, but he is given virtually no human connection until the last quarter or so of the novel.

Excellent books have been written exclusively about character depiction and construction, and the subject is as endlessly vast as the very diversity of human life. But for our purposes, to help you build a big commercial novel, I recommend two specific qualities over and above the ones already discussed: your principal characters' frailties or weaknesses and their levels of self-awareness. Think hard about them as you create your characters. People we think of as "perfect" we usually also think of as boring. The individuals we delight in are most often ones with some uncontrollable tendency, less-than-wonderful habit or off-key idiosyncrasy. As to self-awareness, in real life most of us are pretty blind to our shortcomings. So, the literary character to whom you give at least a glimmer of awareness of his own faults, and who deplores or feels guilty about them, takes on added stature in our estimation. Since you want to endow your characters with stature, cause them at least some of the time to do things that we'll admire and that may even take our breath away.

Chapter Six

POINT OF VIEW

IN ALMOST THIRTY YEARS AS AN AUTHOR'S REPRESENTA-
TIVE I have had a hand in the publication of seven hundred or so
novels, yet I have succeeded in placing only three for a professional
screenwriter, and he had been a novelist before getting into film. Dozens
of manuscripts have been submitted to me, many by accomplished
scriptwriters with major motion picture and television credits. Where
these Hollywood writers again and again fall short as novelists is point
of view. Watching a movie, the audience experiences the incidents of
the drama or comedy primarily from the point of view of the camera,
an outside observer rather than a participant in the story's goings-on.
A skillful director will, of course, set up a certain number of camera
shots, so that some of what the moviegoer sees and hears parallels what
we imagine the character in the film is seeing and hearing. But the
camera, which conveys its story only through visual images and dialogue and which to some degree must take a global view of the film's
action, is limited by its very exterior nature in exposing what a character
thinks, feels, hopes and longs for. In a good film, bits of interior life
are communicated with words and tones of dialogue, reaction shots,
the subtleties of the actors' performances and even the music score, but
the emphasis is always on what the camera shows us, what we see.
Fiction is quite different.

What we enjoy most in a novel are often things that can never be
physically seen. The authors about whom we become passionate delve
deeply into the minds and hearts of a book's characters. But externals
too, such as the landscape or the appearance of an individual—things
that can be seen—take on an added vibrancy in fiction when colored
with how a character also feels about the particular look of a place or

of a person. Marcel Proust in his great *Remembrance of Things Past* provides an extreme example, describing, anatomizing, dissecting, layer upon layer of feelings and emotions in such elaborate and exquisite detail that few readers these days have the patience to wade through this vast work. Best-selling authors to a lesser degree also do this. And my aim in this chapter is to show how most effectively they go about it.

When it comes to deciding upon point of view in a novel, you as an author have two main choices and many subchoices. First, and dating back to Homer and the Bible, is using the voice of the omniscient narrator, the author himself describing scenery, past events, present action and the exterior and interior of characters. Second, within a given scene or chapter, is the author's use of the tightly contained point of view of a single character. With this method, the reader participates in the story with the character. The relationship is exclusive. A particular piece of the novel unfolds through what the character himself experiences via physical sense images (seeing, hearing, feeling, smelling) or through inner expression of his thoughts, his feelings, his memories.

MANAGING POINT OF VIEW

Some writers are highly rigorous in how they go about controlling point of view. Others are more loose. *Gone With the Wind*, to cite a loose example, opens with a chapter from the point of view of the omniscient narrator. Chapter two then is written largely but not entirely from inside Scarlett. And this pattern continues throughout the book, with Scarlett's being the predominant point of view. But Mitchell also dips in and out of the hearts and sensibilities of all the major and many of the secondary characters and also steadily continues to inject her own all-knowing authorial voice. *The Man From St. Petersburg*, in contrast, contains a few bits of author narration, but point of view in this book is for the most part controlled with an iron hand. Chapter one is organized into four different units: one each from the point of view of Walden, Lydia, Charlotte and Feliks. Chapter two has three chunks: two from Feliks's point of view and one from Walden's. The third chapter again has one section from within each of the four principals. Through the rest of the work, Follett continues with this technique of illuminating only one character's interior in any given scene or chapter, causing us to experience the action as that character himself does, and all but eschewing the authorial voice.

To a writer aspiring to build her first best-seller, I strongly recommend Follett's method. Several kinds of richness can accrue from it,
some of them unsuspected. First and foremost, it forces the author to
forget about trying to tell the story in broad narrative strokes as an
outside observer might most readily imagine it. Instead, from the very
outset the author must burrow deep inside one character, then another,
and then another, focusing on the one character who at a particular
piece of the action has the largest emotional stake. By penetrating into
such a character's hopes, expectations and fears, usually from the time
the character is first introduced, the writer thus bonds both herself and
the reader to the character. Then, as the character progresses from scene
to scene, expressing doubts and fears to himself, reacting with pain or
joy to what others say or do to him, perhaps being prompted by the
present action to remember a warm or heartrending past event, we the
readers identify more and more with this character. We feel what he
feels, want what he wants, because we are experiencing the raptures
and terrors of the story solely through this one sensibility, this one
point-of-view character.

Disciplined managing of point of view in *The Man From St.
Petersburg* also has the effect of expanding one story into what almost
feels like four individual stories that intersect dramatically at key
points. We are exposed to one series of events, but through the sensibilities of four points of view, each with widely contrasting world views,
emotional makeups, and social and economic backgrounds. This adds
a breadth, scope and depth to this book that it would not otherwise
have. The fact that Follett chooses to enter the minds and hearts of
only four characters and no others also is important. Prince Aleks Orlov,
the Czar's nephew and emissary, is central to the plot. He's Walden's
negotiating counterpart, Feliks's prey, Lydia's cousin, and a potential
suitor to Charlotte. Besides being a target, however, he plays no role
in the main action, the assassination plot, nor does he pursue any agenda
that involves us emotionally. So Follett omits bringing in his point of
view, as well as those of the other important but secondary characters,
Basil Thomson, Belinda, Pritchard, Marya and Winston Churchill.

Involving the Reader

A key objective of a best-selling novelist is to involve us as closely as
possible with his characters. In a novel, as in life, we're inclined to
become more deeply involved with a few characters than with many,

especially when the author sustains them all in the action (as Follett does) from the opening chapter until the very end. Two of Follett's early novels still in print are *The Modigliani Scandal* and *Paper Money*. These are evocatively written, enjoyable books, but they each contain a dozen or so point-of-view characters, most of whom appear in one chapter and disappear in the next. The reader meets and develops an interest in a character, looks forward to spending more time with her, but instead keeps getting faced with new people. Between John Grisham's first book, *A Time to Kill*, and his blockbuster success *The Firm*, one can see a similar development. In both novels, Grisham freely mixes author narration with character point-of-view material, but in *The Firm*, he focuses tightly on a small cast, whereas in the earlier work, he enters into the interiors of almost every character he introduces, many more than we can relate to richly. Readers, once they develop an interest in a few key characters, find it bothersome, frustrating even, to be brought again and again into the interiors of brand-new or distinctly minor characters, such as some of those in *A Time to Kill*.

CONTROLLED POINT OF VIEW IN *GARDEN OF LIES*

Garden of Lies is written from the points of view of six characters. Rose and Rachel, the two babies switched at birth who grow up to love the same man, clearly have the lead roles, with Rose's point of view dominating in seventeen chapters and Rachel's in fourteen. Sylvie, the woman who substitutes another baby for her own and then must live a guilt-ridden life, is primary in nine chapters; and the two male leads, Brian and Max, control five chapters, with the villain, David Sloane, taking the lead only in one. Roughly 80 percent of the novel, then, is written from the points of view of three female characters. Their gender-colored longings, moods and emotions set the prevailing tone and make this into a book that appeals primarily to women. So why does the author bother writing even one chapter from the point of view of David, a heel who feigns loving Rachel, impregnates her, insists she have an abortion, and then later in the story tries to ruin Rachel and her medical career? The more obvious reason is that, by being admitted into his mindset and acquainted with past events that formed his personality, we can then at least minimally relate to him as a fellow human, real person, and not as a stock lowlife.

David's past is brought alive by the author's rigorously controlled

point of view. The opening to chapter five contains virtually no summary or narrative account of David's past life, his accomplishments or
failures. It's not uncommon for inexperienced writers and sometimes
experienced ones, too, to stop the action of a novel dead with a journalistic history of a character's prior life. What Goudge gives us in this
scene is David's own memory of a decisive past event in his own words
accompanied by the emotions he remembers feeling at the time. It's
an encounter with a rich country club girl who treated him like dirt.
The vivid details, he remembers, evoke the painful emotions that he
still feels. David, at other points, hears the voice and imprecations of
his now-dead, abusive, alcoholic father. Through memory and daydreams, he hears the old reprobate snarling at him. It takes only a few
well-chosen lines to vividly evoke the awful tenor of his childhood and
youth. No narrator intrudes, the momentum of the present action is
not allowed to slacken—the past is rendered as dramatically as the
action in the present.

A less apparent but perhaps more crucial reason for Goudge's structuring the chapter this way is David's vulnerability. Rachel is the strong
one and he, the weak. If he wants her embryo aborted, and he does,
then he, she insists, must personally perform the procedure. Being
confronted with a demand to kill, as it were, his own child, creates a
situation more terrible for him even than for Rachel. Since his emotions
are the most turbulent here and provide the richest drama, his character
becomes the better choice for point of view, although Rachel is also
given a few interior bits.

Most chapters in *Garden of Lies* are written in their entirety from
one character's point of view, but several are broken into two or three
units, each from a separate point of view. Studying why Goudge chooses
to do this will cast more light on the value of this technique. The final
scene of Rachel's malpractice trial is in a sense dominated by Rose, the
brilliant defense attorney, unleashing surprise attack after attack on the
crumbling David Sloane. But the point-of-view character, the one
whose interior opens to us here, is Rachel. It is she who has everything
at stake, not just money and her medical career but the possible baring
of what she feels is her shameful secret, how she once forced David to
abort his own child, and even worse, the likelihood of losing her beloved
Brian. Rachel, whose thoughts and feelings are at the center of the
action, speaks not one word aloud. The dialogue is all between Rose
and David, with a few bits from the opposing counsel and judge. But

then, to precipitate the climax, Goudge, as she should, activates her point-of-view character, Rachel. It's her giggling that prompts David to lose control and go berserk.

The trial is for all intents over, but the characters are still in the courtroom. Something cataclysmic is about to happen to Rose. For this, Goudge then shifts to Rose's point of view. Sylvie comes rushing up to Rachel, who has fainted. Rose thinks she recognizes the older woman and then realizes that this is the stranger who years ago appeared outside her schoolyard, thrust a diamond and ruby earring into her little-girl hand, and disappeared into a limousine. This unknown woman, connected to her in some mysterious way, is also Rachel's mother. Rose, all shook up, feels as if she's in a dream, and being inside her point of view, we can more easily share these weirdly troubling feelings with her.

POINT OF VIEW IN YOUR NOVEL

Having read all the above and, hopefully, the other example novels I've discussed, you may now be wondering if there is any optimum number of point-of-view characters. I would recommend the smallest number possible, taking into account the story you're telling, but no fewer than three or four. With only one or two points of view, it becomes quite difficult to work up the kind of plot complexity and interpersonal drama readers expect in a big novel. With more than six or seven, the emotional focus tends to become diffused, and reader involvement with your lead characters is likely to diminish. Determining which characters to select can be done at the very outset if you already have your story solidly in mind. In my experience, however, this choice is best made after an author is well into the outline process. Then you can ask yourself, Which characters most vigorously propel the action? Who has the greatest stake in its denouement? These are the characters, more than likely, through whose interiors you should write your novel.

Another factor to consider is your readership. Both contemporary and historical romances are usually written from only one point of view, a woman's, and almost all the buyers and readers of these books are women. Conversely, the same holds true for men with action-adventure novels and westerns. Authors who aim for a broad readership, one that comprises both men and women, and men and women of varying ages, tend to create point-of-view characters who epitomize these differences. In both *The Key to Rebecca* and *The Man From St. Petersburg*, Follett chooses two men and two women, and in *St. Petersburg*, three characters are middle-aged and one is young. Readers of varying ages and genders can each find a character in this novel with whom they most strongly identify. At the same time, the contrasts between these characters' world views deriving from their sexes and stages of life contribute vitally to the book's tension and drama.

But if you are not deeply interested in men or their concerns, or if you feel hostile toward them, it would be a mistake to include a male point-of-view character in your novel simply as a ploy to attract a wider readership. For a reader to become engrossed in your character, be it your hero or heroine or even your antagonist or villain, you must love each of them or at least feel deeply with and for them. If that isn't happening for you with any one of them, then you are better advised to avoid that character's point of view and to limit your choices for points of view to those characters with whom you can richly and comfortably empathize. Character variety is a definite plus, but never at the expense of emotional power.

Chapter Seven

TIGHTENING CHARACTER RELATIONSHIPS

⊶

WHEN ONE PERSON KILLS ANOTHER, and they are strangers to each other, we see such an act as frightening, terrible, maybe even shocking. But when a child murders a parent or vice versa, or a brother slays a brother, such a deed strikes us as much more horrific. Conflict of any kind, from the most trivial to the most serious, between characters who have close ties by blood and/or intense relationships through friendship, marriage or love, magnifies what's at stake for the parties on both sides. They may have violent feelings about what's at issue between them, but a second and usually more potent dimension is added when they care personally (positively and/or negatively) about each other. Such personal conflict, too, bridges easily to the emotions of the reader, whose strong feelings about his own parents, children, friends, lovers or spouse, then lead him to empathize all the more with the feelings of the fictional characters.

An example can be seen in an actual crime committed in a New York City subway station in 1990. A group of young thugs ganged up on a Utah family en route to the championship tennis matches at Flushing Meadow. The young man of the family stepped forward to protect his mother and her purse and got stabbed to death. The hoodlums, who ran off and used the stolen money for admission to a dance hall, were quickly apprehended, and the story generated an enormous hubbub in the media. Books based on highly publicized true crimes have for years been a popular genre, and two of my agency's clients (one of whom was personally acquainted with the murdered youth and his family) put together a solid proposal for a book on this tragedy. No publisher was interested. The work could have dug deeply into the characters on both sides and into the social phenomena that gave rise to the incident. But no editor thought that these elements would make for a salable book. The story was rejected. It lacked a strong interpersonal connection between perpetrator and victim.

FAMILY RELATIONSHIPS

I cannot recall who first said that all great stories are family stories, but as you'll see, it's certainly true of the five novels on which I have been focusing, as well as of such diverse and towering works as Tolstoy's *War and Peace*, Balzac's incredible series of interlocking novels, *The Human Comedy*, or Thomas Wolfe's *Look Homeward Angel*. We don't normally think of *Hamlet* or *Oedipus* as family dramas, but at their cores that's just what they are. Hamlet is betrayed not by strangers but by his father's brother and by his own mother. The main person sent to spy on him is his beloved fiancée. Oedipus must glean, not from Creon or the chorus, but from his own wife the first clue that she actually may be his mother, that he may be the one responsible for the plague and the one who killed Laius, his own father.

In chapter four, I pointed out how Follett began with an impersonal assassination plot and then, by knitting together a tight web of relationships between the main characters, juiced up the emotional voltage of *The Man From St. Petersburg*. Margaret Mitchell, as far as I know, has left no outline for *Gone With the Wind*, but a fast look at this aspect of her text will show that she, too, was organizing her work along these lines.

Family Ties in Gone With the Wind

No sooner has Scarlett lost Ashley then she rebounds into marriage with, of all men, Charles Hamilton, the brother of her despised rival, Melanie, thus becoming a sister-in-law both to Melanie and to Ashley. When Scarlett goes off to Atlanta, who can she stay with but her freshly acquired and only relatives in that city, Aunt Pitty and Melanie, the one woman whose presence at Scarlett's side chafes constantly on the wounds of her obsession with Ashley? Ashley returns on furlough, and of course it's to this house he comes. Scarlett is beside herself with frustration because at night he goes to Melanie's room and by day he's surrounded by others. Not until he's about to return to the front can Scarlett get even a moment alone with him. The point here is that when a man marries, his ex-girlfriend usually drifts out of his immediate sphere and eventually out of his life altogether. By contriving this new familial bond for Scarlett, Mitchell additionally sets up Scarlett's flight with Melanie and her newborn to Tara, Ashley's return there after the war so that Scarlett can once again try to get him to run off with her, and Melanie's insistence that Ashley take on running one of Scarlett's Atlanta sawmills, which yet again keeps Scarlett and Ashley in heatedly tinderbox proximity.

Frank Kennedy, the man Mitchell selects for Scarlett's second husband, produces lesser but nonetheless interesting complications. First, he is not just any well-to-do businessman who could come up with the money Scarlett desperately wants to save Tara from a tax sale; he is her sister Suellen's intended. Scarlett doesn't just lure a man for whom she has no feelings, but she lures this one away from her own sister. This seduction, then, acquires more bite and novelty than it otherwise might have had.

Suellen, who is portrayed as even more self-involved and petty than Scarlett, returns to the novel at Gerald's death. He doesn't die in the war or from illness. Mitchell has Suellen, his own daughter, get him drunk while trying to induce him to sign a Union loyalty oath. He then goes tearing off on a horse and breaks his neck. This sets the stage for a funeral at which two outspoken longtime neighbors are prepared publicly to condemn Suellen. Mitchell deftly returns the focus to where it belongs, on Scarlett, with the angry Mrs. Tarleton and Grandma Fontaine escorting our pregnant heroine out of the hot sun and back to the house. There Scarlett is warmly praised for being democratic and practical because she approves of her sister's impending marriage to Will, a lowly cracker. The climax, though, brings us back to the book's main theme, Grandma's accurate appraisal of Ashley as an incompetent, an assessment that upsets Scarlett and the truth of which she cannot hear or recognize.

As Suellen is an indirect cause of her own father's death, Mitchell uses the same ironic stroke with Scarlett and Frank Kennedy. Frank clearly must be disposed of to make way for Scarlett's long-awaited marriage to Rhett. But Frank, too, isn't allowed to die of natural causes or in some random Ku Klux Klan raid. Scarlett, who again and again has been urged to stay home, has been attacked in her carriage. To avenge her (and presumably to frighten the shanty-town vagrants from trying any more such attacks), Frank goes off with the Klan and gets shot. Scarlett doesn't grieve for this husband, but she feels guilty as hell.

Family Ties in Other Blockbusters

The Godfather appears superficially to be a novel about warring gangsters, but in its heart, it too is a family story. The main characters are all related either by blood or by long and close ties: the Don and his three sons and daughter; his son-in-law and daughter-in-law; his caporegimes, Clemenza and Tessio, lifelong associates; Consiglieri Hagen, an orphan who was taken in and grew up in the Corleone house; and his godson Johnny Fontaine. The initial assassination attempt on the Don is business related, but then through the bulk of the novel the thrust of the plot derives almost entirely from personal motives. Michael, who had no intention of going into his father's business, gets savagely punched by a crooked police officer while standing guard outside the hospital where the Don lies critically wounded. We are led to infer that anger at a corrupt world whose officials are evil combines with deep family loyalty and spurs Michael to redirect the course of his life. He goes on to daringly avenge the attacks on his father and himself, then he flees to Sicily. Upon his return, he arranges the deaths of three men: his wife-beating, traitorous brother-in-law for having sold out Michael's older brother, Sonny; the man who killed Michael's young Sicilian bride and who almost killed him, too; and Barzini, the engineer of Sonny's murder. The territories Michael regains for the Corleone bookmaking, horserace-fixing and shylocking seem almost incidental in comparison with the ferocious intensity of his familial concerns.

The Thorn Birds appears to be nothing other than the family story it is. But the power of the links McCullough forges between her characters is exceptional. The love story begins with Meggie, only ten years old, and Ralph, the man enchanted by her, a handsome Catholic priest eighteen years her senior. It's not enough that their love is doomed by his celibacy vows and love of holiness, but they also are physically driven apart by another woman who also loves Ralph. She's no stranger to the Cleary family; she's Meggie's own imperious, sixty-five-year-old aunt. Rather than bequeath her vast fortune to Meggie's father, who is her brother and closest relation, Mary Carson, jealous of Meggie, wills it to the Church under Ralph's guardianship, knowing that this will torture his moral sense and also elevate him in the hierarchy and impel him to leave Meggie and move away to a metropolitan center. Separation fails to diminish the two mismatched lovers' feelings for each other, however.

Highlights of the book become Ralph and Meggie's infrequent comings together. One such meeting occurs after her father's funeral, when she gives him an ash rose that he carries with him all his life. Another is on Matlock Island where, though still married to a man she gave herself to because he resembles Ralph, she and the priest finally consummate their love and she conceives his child. Their final and most moving meeting is close to the end of the book. He's never known that he, now a Cardinal in Rome, is the biological father of her son Dane. Of all the possible careers the young man might have chosen, Dane has become Ralph's beloved protegé in the church, gifted with a spirituality that Ralph admires and even envies. When Dane later dies in a drowning accident and is hastily buried in Crete, Meggie flies from Australia to Rome and demands that Ralph drop everything to help her find the body and take it back home with her. He'll help, but he cannot get away. With a Holy Congress in progress, the Pope needs him. Then Meggie, fifty-three years old to Ralph's seventy-one, drops her bomb. He was your son. He had all your features, and you were too blind ever to recognize him. Ralph must deal with the shocker that this young man, who was closer to him than anyone else, was in fact his child and he had failed to see it. Her bitterness and his guilt over the loss of a whole lifetime of love that they might have shared poignantly crown their encounter.

Early in the book, before the Meggie-Ralph story begins to dominate, the character who generates the most drama is Meggie's oldest brother, Frank. His relationships with his mother, Fee, whom he adores, and his father, Paddy, whom he hates, are plainly Oedipal. In scene after scene, the passion of these characters for and against each other generates constant heat. Frank is little Meggie's refuge in a family too large, overworked and distracted to show her much affection. Frank's prevailing emotion, however, is seething anger—at his father for what he perceives to be Paddy's mistreatment of his mother, primarily by burdening her with more and more children, and at his mother, too, for patiently enduring this so-called mistreatment. With the outbreak of World War I, Frank runs away to enlist, but Paddy gets him dragged back home. At a country fair, after the family moves from New Zealand to Australia, Frank goes into the ring and successfully pummels some professional boxers. Paddy merely jeers. Frank grows incensed, and Paddy in a fit of temper reveals that Frank is not his son. (McCullough may have been influenced here by Mitchell, since Fiona Cleary and

Scarlett's mother, Ellen, both were raised in top-drawer families, loved men they couldn't have, and then agreed to wed the first available candidates, decent lower-class men, whom they never could wholly love.) Frank, for the first time, understands why he's always felt so out of place. He abandons his family to go off with the boxing troupe. Fee, for years mourning his leaving, is less able than before to love her husband or children. Then she's devastated by the news that he's been sentenced to life imprisonment for killing a man. Thirty years later, who but Ralph, Frank's illegitimate brother-in-law as it were, arranges for his release. Frank's reunion with his mother and with Meggie, the two people in the world he cares about, becomes another of this book's heartrending scenes.

NONFAMILY RELATIONSHIPS

You may ask, But what about the blockbuster novels that do not include families or family relationships? There are lots of them: spy thrillers, major mysteries, big action stories, and other genres, too. Let's look briefly at two novels in which there are no blood ties or in which these appear to play a minimal role. Here, too, relationships between characters are established in such a way that there is a resonance of personal closeness in the action without which these books would not be nearly so successful.

Triple by Ken Follett is about a Jewish spy in the late 1960s trying to hijack a shipload of uranium for Israel. The agents bent on thwarting him, his antagonists, are an Arab and a Russian. In real life, men from such disparate backgrounds in all likelihood would be total strangers. But fiction is art, not life. So twenty years earlier, all three are introduced in a prologue at a professor's sherry party at Oxford where they are students together. As youths, they are already at odds about whether or not there should be a Jewish state, and the Jew and Russian are presented as fierce chess rivals. The young Palestinian, Hassan, is observed in the garden making love to the professor's wife, a young beauty with whom from a distance the Jew, Dickstein, is madly in love. But Dickstein is the favorite of Suza, the professor's little daughter. Twenty years later, when Dickstein returns to this house seeking information about Hassan, Suza now looks like her gorgeous mother did. Dickstein is smitten, and she, warmly recalling his playing with her and her cat, bounds into a relationship with him.

The fifteen-page prologue establishes interpersonal connections and tensions between these characters that play a key role all through the novel and transform a purely political struggle between these characters into a fiercely personal one. There is one family element in the novel: Suza discovers that her father, the professor, is in league with Hassan in trying to find and kill Dickstein, the man she loves. Bitter, she is compelled to face the fact that her father has never really loved her. She is then galvanized into trying to save Dickstein. Her experience of betrayal at the hands of her own father, of course, gives her decision special power.

The Firm by John Grisham is about Mitch McDeere, a brilliant young lawyer who accepts a lucrative job with a Memphis law firm. Mitch discovers that the firm is a money-laundering front for a Mafia family, gets enlisted by the FBI to help bring the firm and its criminal clients to justice, and then has to run for his life with hordes of both Federal agents and gangsters hotly pursuing him. He and his antagonists start off as total strangers, then develop some acquaintanceship with each other over time, but the struggles Mitch has with his deadly opponents become only minimally personal. This is in no way a family story.

Bonds of familial closeness, however, are a secondary but crucial part of the book. Mitch is deeply attached to his wife, Abby, and it's his feeling and concern for her that exposes the tender and human side of his character. Without his having her as a confidante and ally, we would see him almost exclusively as a cold-blooded and aggressive lawyer. We would be disinclined to feel much sympathy for him and might even be turned off by the book as a whole. Grisham also gives Mitch a convict brother, Ray, to whom Mitch is devoted—so much so that he won't make a deal with the FBI unless they agree to spring his brother from prison. The close tie Mitch feels with his brother serves to bond us more closely to him. Ray's controlled violence and Abby's intelligence both play important roles in the climactic chase and escape. The story then becomes not of one man alone trying to outwit his enemies, but of a family group making desperate efforts to save themselves and each other.

CHARACTER RELATIONSHIPS IN YOUR NOVEL

In your own novel you presumably have set up or are thinking of setting up a central conflict between two characters. Can you tie these two together by making them into two brothers, two sisters, father and son, mother and daughter? If your story won't lend itself to so intimate a familial relationship, you might consider other ways of establishing closeness. Could they have been dear friends, and could one have provided an invaluable service to the other as a college roommate, a soldier in Vietnam, a mentor and savior in some do-or-die job assignment? Could they have been deadly rivals in some past endeavor? Or could your two characters be unknown to each other but then discover intriguing and plot-influencing connections through a mutual relative, friend, teacher, lover?

If you think it works against your story to link your protagonist and antagonist in any of these ways, then what about tightly connecting your principals with minor characters, giving them spouses, lovers, children, parents, beloved friends (one or two of these, of course, but not all)? What your main characters have at stake then becomes more momentous as it affects the secondary characters who love them. And then, too, you might find a way to associate, if not the two opposite lead characters with each other, then perhaps a few of the lesser personages on both sides. The relationship of these secondary characters to each other combined with their links to the principals could then be used interestingly to twist your plot. As examples, consider Lydia's relationships in *The Man From St. Petersburg* and Brian's in *Garden of Lies*.

It is easier, remember, to establish these sorts of ties between your characters while your novel is still in outline form. Once you have completed a draft manuscript, or more than one, the identities of your characters and the relationships between them are usually so solidified in your mind that making changes to bring them somehow closer together may feel almost impossible. If it does, don't worry; you hopefully have a lot more than one book in you.

Chapter Eight

SETTING UP SCENES

THE OVERARCHING DRAMATIC QUESTION, the one that knits together the many individual scenes of *The Man from St. Petersburg*, is posed in the first chapter: Will Feliks succeed in assassinating Orlov, thereby disrupting an impending Anglo-Russian alliance and keeping Russia out of Britain and France's imminent war with Germany? It is, in essence, the foundation of suspense upon which the novel's forward-thrusting action is built. In *Gone With the Wind*, *Garden of Lies* and *The Thorn Birds*, the equivalent structural spines are the unsettled, unresolved relationships between heroine and hero—Meggie and Ralph, Rhett and Scarlett, Rose and Brian. Will each of these pairs be able to come happily together?

This setting up of a dominant, unresolved issue around which the novel's characters have a huge stake is central to the plotting of a book as a whole. A similar technique in miniature can be vital to most individual scenes, the novel's building blocks. In a blockbuster novel, a scene is almost always more than merely a well-written account in description and dialogue of an episode between characters. Popular authors intuitively or deliberately *build* their scenes. Somewhere in the first few lines or paragraphs (or carried over from an earlier scene) a question is subtly (or not so subtly) raised that could be anything from, Will Michael Corleone succeed in killing Sollozzo? to, Will Feliks manage to find out from Lydia where Prince Orlov is hidden? By informing the reader early, either before the scene actually begins or just as it starts, of what a character wants and is trying to accomplish, or of what danger (or pleasure) lies ahead, about which the character involved knows little or nothing, the author sets up suspense for the oncoming scene. We become hooked, wondering how the particular issue will be resolved. Our attention can then remain engaged through pages and pages of relatively nondramatic material (backstory of the characters, general history of the place and period, dreams and fantasies of major and secondary characters, cultural mores of the world of the book) until the issue is joined and the scene's dramatic question, if not answered, is at least dealt with.

TWO TECHNIQUES

Puzo is especially interesting in this regard, using as he does in *The Godfather* two quite different techniques to set up his scenes. One method is to begin with a sudden shock. Almost out of the blue, something happens that profoundly affects one or more of his characters. The question becomes, How did, how *could* this terrible thing have happened? Then Puzo backtracks in time and follows this initial but short-lived shock with the fearsome scene whose outcome we already know, but which we nonetheless read toward with excitement and dread much as we become drawn into the mounting horror in a foreordained Greek tragedy. His second method is more traditional: He introduces the issue in question early in the scene through interior monologue, dialogue or author narration. But as we'll see from a close look at a few such scenes, whichever variant Puzo chooses, he generates a solidly suspenseful effect.

Tom Hagen is working quietly in his office when he picks up the phone. Suddenly he hears Jack Woltz screaming curses and threats at him. Why, we ask? What's happened? What will happen? Then Puzo backtracks, has Woltz wake up in his bed, see the severed head of his prize horse stuck in a cake of blood, and realize he must yield to Don Corleone. But it is this preparatory phone call that sets up what becomes, until this point, the book's most startling and powerful scene.

Later in the same chapter, Michael reads in the newspaper about his father's being shot. Michael is filled with rage but also feels weak in the knees and sick with guilt that he was enjoying himself while his father was, and perhaps still is, close to dying. His brother Sonny is frantic, not only about their father, but also because Tom Hagen has been kidnapped and because the family key's enforcer, Luca Brasi, cannot be located. The display of emotions with Michael is deeper, more sustained here than in the scene with the Woltz phone call to Tom. Our curiosity, fearfulness and awe about the attempted murder that is dramatized in the following scene (as again Puzo backtracks in time) are thus set up as with the Woltz scene. More importantly, this somewhat straightforward and hardly extraordinary scene of the Don being shot acquires great impact due to its already having so powerfully affected Michael, the character we like most.

Puzo's most substantial use of this technique is brought to bear with the killing of Sonny. An entire small chapter, one built around the lifestyle, work habits, hopes and fears of Amerigo Bonasera, the undertaker, a strict chaperone to death, is devoted to creating a preparatory mood of grim foreboding. The Don arrives following the corpse, pleads for a restorative cosmetic job, and displays the bullet-smashed face of his eldest son. Making us witness to Bonasera's fear, the Don's grief and the gruesome corpse, Puzo sets us up to become intensely involved. Only then does he goes back in time to dramatize the outcome of Sonny's war against the crime families, culminating in Sonny's being shot to death.

With the reader knowing the climactic shootout is coming, looking forward to it, perhaps worrying about how awful its details will turn out, Puzo can afford now to seemingly digress. In general terms, he brings us up to date on the status of the conflict between the five families and follows this with an ugly scene in which a drunken Carlo brutalizes his wife Connie. But the scene turns out to be no digression. A badly mauled Connie calls and asks to be taken home to her parents, triggering her brother Sonny's rage, who then races off to help and falls into the ambush that has been set for him. Puzo then quickly tops the climax of Sonny's assassination with a bigger one—the Don, for the first time since he's been shot, unexpectedly appears and takes command of his lieutenants and of the perilous situation. Without, however, the little preparatory scene at the funeral parlor, Sonny's being killed would have affected us far less than it does.

Puzo's altering chronology in these three instances is also a way to quickly move his story forward with big, highly dramatic scenes while preparing for these with maximum economy and effectiveness. For example, the Don's planning the decapitation of a beautiful and innocent horse would revolt the reader rather than create suspense. So what the book delivers instead is the effect of this action—slight on Hagen, whom we like, and great on Woltz, a character we dislike. To set up suspense for the shooting of the Don in a traditional way, Puzo would have to put us into the point of view of the Godfather's would-be assassins, either bosses or button-men, for whom we have absolutely no feeling. How much better to begin with its effect on Michael!

Most of the big scenes in *The Godfather*, unlike those discussed above, are prepared for in a straightforward time sequence. Look at how Puzo sets up suspense for the scene in which Michael avenges his father against Sollozzo and McCluskey.

With the Don out of his reach, at least for the time being, Sollozzo has offered to present a so-called peaceful settlement if he can have a meeting alone with Michael. At a Corleone gathering, the pros and cons of this probably phony offer are being kicked around when Michael abruptly comes forward and states, to the amazement of everyone present, that they should accept the offer, that he'll go and he'll "take both of them." Can the civilian in the family, the noncriminal, possibly succeed? Will he fail? Either way, what will happen to him, to the whole tightly knit Corleone family? These are the unspoken, unformulated questions that stick in our minds as we keep turning pages, which first deal with the Corleone group's putting together their plans, with Captain McCluskey and his career history, then with Michael being trained, being driven back and forth across the George Washington Bridge, with his tensely trying to listen to Sollozzo's proposal until, some eighteen pages after the issue was first broached, he pulls the trigger. The expectancy that has been raised in us sets up the suspense and elevates the shooting in the restaurant into a thrilling event.

PLANTING QUESTIONS

The examples I've given so far might lead you to think that setting up a scene to be suspenseful requires a violent or even murderous climax. But that's not the case at all, as should become clear as we look closely at chapter one of *Garden of Lies*.

"Bless me, Father, for I have sinned," is its opening line. These few words immediately raise questions. Who is the sinner? What is the sin? The first is quickly answered. The sinner is sixteen-year-old Rose Santini, who feels flushed and hot, as if she's coming down with the flu. But worse, she thinks she's doomed forever, and that when she actually reveals her awful sin, the shock might cause old Father Donahue to have a heart attack. Then, instead of having Rose continue with her confession, and speak about her sin, Goudge leaves the presumably forbidding details, the suspenseful question, hanging. While we readers are hooked, wondering exactly what this girl could have done, the novelist can now afford to sidestep, as it were, and begin to fill us in on Rose as a character.

The author first dips back into Rose's childhood and shows how, when Rose was in fifth grade, a nun's exhibiting a bit of burnt flesh from a Catholic martyr triggers guilt in the little girl. If she hadn't been born on the night she was, her mother would not have died in the hospital fire.

Goudge then returns us to the confessional. The question of the sin is reemphasized. Now it's so overwhelming to Rose that she dares speak it only by working up to it, by starting first with lesser sins. These lead into more memories that bring alive Rose's bitter home life: her grandmother, who emotionally abuses her and curses her out as "bad blood"; her bossy older sister, who's always telling Rose to fix up her hair and clean up her half of the room. The priest then brings Rose back to the present. Others are waiting to confess. She takes a deep breath and blurts in a hot rush, "Father, I fornicated." The question that has held us in suspense appears to have been answered. Or has it? The sin, or what Rose believes was her sin, has been revealed but with no details. So now we are expectant about the particulars. With whom did Rose commit this act? Under what circumstances? Why? What will happen to her as a result?

Having implanted these new questions in us, Goudge can again temporarily change direction. She's given herself fresh breathing space to focus on this chapter's primary function: introducing and developing Rose and her world. In another high-tension memory scene, Marie, the older sister, announces in their smelly, stagnant kitchen that she's getting married. Nonnie, the vicious grandmother, realizing the girl is pregnant, slaps her full across the face and calls her a filthy whore. Clare, the goody-goody middle sister who plans to become a Holy Sister, flees in tears. Rose, at her wits' end between the flaring tempers of her sister and grandmother, is suddenly thrown an emotional wallop. Nonnie spits out that she, like Marie's unborn child, is a bastard. Rose cannot be a child of Nonnie's son Dom; his now-dead wife, Nonnie says, had been playing around while he was off in the war. Now it's Rose, crushed, who flees.

Where? To whom? Brian, of course, the boy in the apartment upstairs whom she adores. Now, some fifteen pages after the first few words of her confession, we are brought to the McClanahan apartment, cluttered with kids, empty baby bottles, couch cushions on the floor, home to Brian with whom she has played cards, smoked and talked in a makeshift "fort" on the roof of their tenement since she was seven and he eight-and-a-half, and who over the years she's learned is the one person on whom she can rely. Now he leads the way up to the roof to try to comfort her. She tearfully tells him her grandmother's accusation, which she fears may be true. A tender and poignant scene of teenage uncertainty, jealousy, sex and love ensues, culminating in Rose's asking Brian to kiss her, some heavy petting between them, and his ejaculating with his clothes still on. In her innocence, she thinks that anything that felt this good had to be a sin, had to be fornicating. The question raised by "Bless me, Father, for I have sinned," has, after twenty-five pages, been answered, but the important point is not this seeming resolution in itself. Instead, note the framework of suspense this question provides and how it makes it possible for Goudge dramatically to sketch in Rose's physical and human environment, life history and current problems.

Then, setting up the suspense that will overarch the forty or so chapters yet to come, Goudge ends her fumbling, teenage love scene with Rose imagining awful punishments for her sin. Fear takes hold of her when she realizes what the worst of all these would be: losing Brian. Thus, a new dramatic question is posed. The chapter concludes, bringing us back into the church in the present, Rose completing her penance, going home to her grim apartment, and taking comfort from the ruby earring mysteriously given to her seven years before in the schoolyard by an elegant lady in a mink coat. Here Goudge is beginning the setup for Rose's climactic confrontation with Sylvie toward the end of the book. Finally, Rose, looking hard at the ruby teardrop dangling from a tiny gold and diamond stud and longing for some magic, whispers the chapter's closing lines to herself, "Don't leave me, Bri. . . . Please don't ever leave me." The question (which in effect can also be called a cliffhanger, placed as it is at the chapter's end) gets firmly implanted in the reader's mind. Will he or won't he leave her? And what will happen to Rose if Brian does leave her?

BUILDING ANTICIPATION

The question posed by Rose's sin provides the suspense spine of a chapter that runs almost thirty pages. In *Gone With the Wind*, Margaret Mitchell's preparations for the first face-to-face encounter between Scarlett and Ashley span more than a hundred pages and constitute one of the most prolonged and skillful buildups leading to an individual scene (one that is not the climax of an entire book) in any modern novel. This structuring, of course, goes largely unnoticed by the average reader, who experiences this grand flow of characters and episodes as having the natural inevitability of the flow of a mighty river.

Mitchell begins just a few pages into the first chapter. The news of Ashley's engagement, to be announced at tomorrow's Wilkes ball, is leaked by Brent Tarleton to a stunned Scarlett. In the next five chapters, before Scarlett finally confronts Ashley, the author accomplishes two tasks. On one hand, she brilliantly uses this space to introduce most of the story's colorful major and minor characters as well as the physical and social environment, including political and numerous familial issues. On the other hand, she emphasizes and reemphasizes subtly and broadly Scarlett's feverish longing to somehow head off this engagement announcement and to marry Ashley herself. To see how this works, we'll look at the repeated accentuations of this theme and examine how they heighten the suspense and increase our anticipation for this yet-to-come scene.

Chapter two begins with Scarlett alone. The Tarleton twins, puzzled at their not having been invited by Scarlett to stay for dinner, have left. Scarlett returns to her chair like a sleepwalker. Her face and mouth hurt, her heart feels swollen and too large for her bosom. In an interior monologue she insists this news has to be a mistake, because she is, must be, the one he loves. Mammy approaches. Scarlett quickly gets rid of her on a phony errand. She cannot bear a lecture on her being inhospitable to the Tarletons while her heart is breaking. But maybe, she tells herself, this awful story isn't true. She'll catch her father alone at the end of the driveway when he returns from the Wilkes's and try to find out from him.

Having solidly implanted the dramatic question in us, Mitchell now backtracks and in a few pages sketches in Scarlett's rosy but largely nonspecific memories of her prior dealings with Ashley. Next, she introduces her whiskey-loving, fence-jumping, Irish father, Gerald O'Hara. Scarlett struggles to find a way to raise the subject without his catching on to her desperation. Seeing through her ploy, he confirms the engagement and berates his daughter for running after a man who doesn't want her. If she marries one of the twins, he'll even build her a fine house. But she, "pain slashing at her heart as savagely as a wild animal's fangs," wants only Ashley. Gerald cogently argues that bookish Ashley would be the wrong husband for her. He points out how different he and she are, but Scarlett will not be deterred. If she were to marry Ashley, she'd change him.

Having made us intensely curious as to what lengths this strong-willed girl will go, how she'll fare, whether she'll succeed, with chapter three Mitchell can again backtrack, this time recounting the stories of Scarlett's parents: Gerald, the rough-hewn but determined immigrant Irishman, and Ellen Robillard, the jilted daughter of Savannah aristo-crats who married Gerald on the rebound, gave him three daughters, and brought order, dignity and grace to his household. But even this chapter cannot end without a re-echoing of the dramatic question. Scarlett longs to be just, truthful, tender and unselfish like her mother—but not right away. There would be time for that after she was married to Ashley.

Chapter four begins at supper with Scarlett longing for her mother's comforting presence while she is enduring the first tragedy she's ever known. She cannot understand how her father can fulminate about the forthcoming war and the damn Yankees while her heart is breaking. Ellen returns from assisting at a stillborn birth at the Slattery's, and the family then kneels to pray. A new idea, shining like a comet, comes to Scarlet. Ashley has no idea that she's in love with him. He must be brokenhearted, thinking she's in love with Brent or Stuart or Cade. Suddenly she's overflowing with happiness. The engagement has not yet been announced, so she need only come up with a way to let him know how she feels. By the time she gets to bed, she's come up with a detailed plan. At tomorrow's barbecue she'll be gay, flirt with every man in sight and let Ashley yearn for her. Then she'll get him alone somewhere, and if he doesn't make the first move, she will. By evening they will have eloped to Jonesboro and she'll be Mrs. Ashley Wilkes. Defeat to her is an impossibility. As readers, we implicity ask ourselves, With such fiery determination, how can she not succeed?

The anticipation builds in chapter five as Scarlett dresses and gets ready and then is en route in the carriage with her father and sisters. First we see her worrying over what to wear to best show off her charms, to make her look as youthful as Melanie, and as grown up. Mammy is dead-set against the low-cut green-sprigged muslin. It's unsuitable for morning wear, too revealing. But Scarlett foxily prevails by agreeing to eat the breakfast Mammy has brought her. Thinking about the im-pending party, she decides she'll faint, pretend to faint, simper, do anything it takes to make Ashley succumb to her. As she rides to Twelve Oaks, the spring glory of the countryside with flowering crab trees bursting their buds inspires her to fantasize about how beautiful a day she might be having for her wedding. She imagines a ceremony by moonlight, and she'll tell her children and grandchildren what a great day this was. Mrs. Tarleton's carriage meets the O'Hara's at an intersection, and Mitchell deftly introduces the horse-loving Beatrice Tarleton, who not only reconfirms Ashley's engagement but adds that everyone has known about it for years. Scarlett is devastated, but only briefly. Her courage flows back. She knows Ashley loves her. Again we ask ourselves, does he or doesn't he? How much longer before we find out?

Chapter six finally brings Scarlett to the Wilkes plantation. She's surrounded by greeters, everyone but Ashley. Where is he? Learning Rhett Butler's background, how he compromised a young lady in Charleston, Scarlett wishes she'd got Ashley to compromise her. At the barbecue her plan is not working. She's surrounded by beaux, but no Ashley. She's the belle of the occasion, but watching Ashley sitting quietly with Melanie, she's miserable. She hatches a new plan. She'll catch him alone while all the girls are upstairs napping. Overhearing Melanie tell Ashley why she prefers Dickens to Thackeray, Scarlett gains new courage. Melanie, she decides, is clearly a bluestocking, hardly the type to interest a man. Mitchell then brings on an old veteran of the Seminole and Mexican Wars and Rhett Butler, who, to the fury of the hotheaded young men, begin to foreshadow the horrors of war and the ultimate defeat of the South. And then Scarlett is on the landing, peering over the bannister, her heart in her throat. She sneaks to the semidark library but cannot remember a word of what she planned to say to Ashley. With that, Mitchell's far-reaching buildup for Scarlett's meeting with Ashley finally is complete. The crescendo has been orchestrated in such a way that we now can barely wait to see what will happen.

SETTING UP YOUR SCENES

Now pull out your own manuscript. It could be a short story, novella or novel—it doesn't matter. Pick out two or three substantial scenes and read them over. Does anything in the text of their first or second pages raise a question that sets up suspense that is then dealt with or resolved in the scene's climax? Does the scene have a climax? If your answer to these questions is negative, then get back to work. First, determine what your climax should be, write it, and then find a way to prepare for it. If you already have a climax that pleases you, figure out which set-up strategy works better for you: Puzo's technique of abruptly starting with the climax and then going back in time and rebuilding toward it, or the traditional procedure of moving ahead chronologically, posing what's at issue at the scene's opening with interior monologue or dialogue and then slowly or swiftly moving ahead to your high point. To evaluate how well you've done the work, you might compare the structure of your finished scene or scenes with one of those discussed in this chapter.

Chapter Nine

BIG SCENES

IN BLOCKBUSTER NOVELS, NOT ONLY ARE THE IMPOR-
TANT SCENES prepared for and set up, but they are built to be big
in themselves, built in such a way that they excite and move us a lot.
Each of the five novels we've been analyzing contains from ten to twenty
individual chapters or episodes in which the lives and destinies of their
major characters are profoundly affected. As readers we participate vicariously in murders, attempted murders, deaths from natural causes,
marriage proposals, declarations of love, betrayals, seductions, last-ditch
rescues, births, abortions—all weighty acts. But an author's merely
depicting such life-transforming events in themselves doesn't necessarily give us big scenes.

   To generate the kind of power that places it into the "big" category,
a scene often contains a startling surprise, is built around a powerful
conflict, substantially alters the situation, plans, hopes, dreams of one
or more major characters, and extends over a goodly number of pages.
More often than not, too, its core action stems from one or both characters' desperately wanting something from the other. Of these elements,
perhaps the most crucial is maintaining intense action and/or high
emotion within a scene for a sustained period. Such a scene keeps ex-
tending; the physical action and/or emotions of a character can rise,
fall, and rise again to higher and higher peaks. The tension and excitement grow, becoming almost unbearable, and what happens in the
scene impacts more and more forcefully on the reader.

BIG SCENES IN *GONE WITH THE WIND*

Scarlett's initial meeting with Ashley, which is climaxed by her unex-
pected encounter with eavesdropping Rhett Butler and followed by her

on-the-rebound eliciting of a marriage proposal from Charles Hamilton, embodies quite wonderfully most of the elements I've pinpointed above as integral to a big scene. Now let's look closely at how Mitchell has built this memorable minidrama.

First, as I pointed out in the last chapter, our expectations have been primed. Will our desperate and undaunted heroine manage to hook the man of her dreams? Here at last comes the event that obsesses Scarlett and that we've been set up to anticipate. Now note the emotional progression. Optimism, happiness at the outset—Scarlett at the touch of Ashley's hand feels that her dream is going to happen. Pride and even greater joy surge through her as she dares openly to confess her love. He, pained, tries to let her down gently. Her joy fades, an emotional downswing. Scarlett realizes something is wrong, all wrong! But not one to give up, she pushes hard and gets him to admit that he does care for her. She then struggles heroically with all her willpower to transform this admission into a commitment to marry her. Ashley, echoing Gerald's words in an earlier chapter, tries to explain why they wouldn't be suited to each other. To Scarlett, Ashley's admission that he cares but is unwilling to marry her make him a liar and a cad. Rage, a more intense emotion, begins to grow in her. When a bit later he defends Melanie from Scarlett's vicious putdown, her anger has now grown to the point where it consumes her. She rails; she'll hate him till he dies; she can't think of a word bad enough to describe him; and then, in a climactic moment, she slaps him with all her strength, after which we have a diminuendo. Her rage subsides and she's desolate. He kisses her hand and slips away. She's miserable. She's lost him forever. Now he'll hate her, she thinks, and she hates herself. She has to do something or she'll go mad, and in a burst of passion she abruptly smashes a china bowl against the marble mantle.

Partaking of her up-and-down emotions in this scene might be likened to a ride on a lengthy and treacherous roller coaster, with some shocking twists and turns yet to come. First is the sudden appearance of Rhett, who, stretched out on the couch and out of sight, has heard everything. Not only must Scarlett suffer the pain of Ashley's rejection, but now Mitchell elevates her anger to new heights as Scarlett feels she's been humiliated, figuratively stripped naked, before a total stranger. Rhett, who admires how honestly and boldly she's acted with Ashley, says he takes his hat off to her and assures her she's too good for Wilkes. But his saying this only infuriates her all the more. Rhett, she shouts, isn't fit to wipe Ashley's boots. She wishes she could kill this rude interloper.

Heightening the Drama

Many writers, having created a scene as powerful as this one between Scarlett and Ashley, would feel satisfied that they had created drama enough. Not Mitchell, who develops a strong situation and here tops it with a stronger one. What a startling and provocative first meeting she contrives for Scarlett with Rhett Butler, who then goes on to pursue her and strives to win her love through the years of Civil War and Reconstruction, through most of the rest of the novel!

Back upstairs, after leaving the depressing library, about to loose her stays and try, in her misery, to rest, Scarlett overhears the girls gossiping about her. Honey Wilkes calls her "fast." Scarlett's heart begins to race madly. Melanie, of all people and to Scarlett's dismay, defends her. Honey proclaims that the one person Scarlett does care about is Ashley. Scarlett is mortified. She'll become a laughingstock. She decides to flee, go home and cry to her mother. But no, she can't. That would give these catty girls even more ammunition against her. No, she'll stay. Somehow she'll get her revenge and make them sorry.

Using Devices

Note how first Scarlett is eavesdropped upon, and then she becomes the eavesdropper. To some, this may seem a corny device, especially when used twice and, indeed, twice sequentially. But such devices are often most useful in making possible a big scene's surprises and shocks, which then affect the characters deeply and impel them to do things, make decisions, which otherwise would be difficult to motivate. And when these devices are set up by their author to seem "natural," as is the case here, the reader experiences the electrification in the story and almost never perceives the device. Rhett here is carefully set up. Prior to his encounter with Scarlett, he is seen by her and much noticed almost as soon as she arrives at Twelve Oaks. Later, she is disconcerted to find that he has observed her teasing Charles Hamilton, whereupon she learns in detail from Cathleen Calvert how he once ruined a girl in Charleston. Outside at the barbecue, he outrages the assembled company by daring to tell of the North's military superiority and then excuses himself to visit the Wilkes library. So, when he rises from the couch after nearly being struck by Scarlett's flying china bowl, he is someone whom we and she already know about. We are interested in him because he's so different from all the other men at the barbecue. And he is, after all, where he said he was going to be. Honey's malice is equally well prepared for. Unattractive and jealous of Scarlett's charms, it's she who, we learned earlier, has an unspoken understanding of marriage with Charles Hamilton, the very fellow with whom Scarlett has been brazenly flirting to pique Ashley's jealousy.

Coincidence, yet another device, is crucial to what comes next, the scene's finale. As Scarlett braces herself to slip into another bedroom to rest, who should enter the house but the same Charles Hamilton who moonily proposed to her while she was readying herself to confront Ashley and whom she politely, almost absentmindedly, brushed off. Now with the news that has just arrived of Lincoln's calling up troops (a second timely coincidence), the South, including all the able-bodied men here at the barbecue, is mobilizing. Charles blurts that he's joining up and timorously asks if she would wait for him. Charles's initial proposal, which at the time seemed irrelevant to the story line except to punctuate the devastating effect Scarlett has on the young men at the party, now becomes important. It's the preparation, the foundation, for her now being able to accept him. Scarlett thinks of his money, of getting back at Honey, and of showing Ashley that she couldn't care less. No, no waiting, she responds, she'll marry him now. Thrilled, he rushes off to ask her father, and she asks herself, "Oh Ashley, what on earth have I done?" Her victory is Pyrrhic. It's more a defeat.

In the space of a dozen or so pages, Scarlett is kept solidly center-stage and is painfully buffeted by, in order, Ashley, Rhett and Honey. All three affect her in different ways, and with each she feels beaten down. But somehow each time she picks herself up, reasserts herself. Finally, with Charles Hamilton, it's she who takes control, though foolishly and impetuously. The scene that began with her determination to get married ends with her sought-for goal, but not with the man she had wanted and still wants. Observing her and participating with her in this one scene, we are surprised, shocked, moved and amused. We see her life transformed.

THE OBLIGATORY SCENE

Playwrighting texts often refer to something called the obligatory scene, which derives from the French expression *la scene a faire*. Literally translated, it means the scene that must happen or must be made. In a traditionally structured play and in a blockbuster novel, it is the coming together near or at the end of the work of the two main opposing characters or forces who in a scene of great power, resolve the issue between them. Much of the plot has been built around this issue, and its outcome becomes more and more crucial to these characters as the novel approaches its conclusion. Another and perhaps more commonly used term for such a scene is the climax or the climactic scene, but to me this is not as apt a term as obligatory.

Climax in The Godfather

In most big novels, this resolution takes place between major characters, usually protagonist and antagonist, but not always. In *The Godfather*, for example, Sollozzo is disposed of fairly early in the book. Thereafter the forces opposing the Corleones are offstage crime families whose names are mentioned from time to time, mostly Tattaglia and Barzini. In the body of the novel, they actually appear in only one scene, and only briefly: the peace conference held in a small commercial bank after Sonny's ambush. Given what's at issue in the book, the survival and triumph of the Corleones over their enemies, the obligatory scene can be nothing other than an act of victory or defeat against these enemies. Interestingly, the extension Puzo provides for this big scene is more in the preparatory phase—in establishing Albert Neri, the Corleone's new cold-blooded enforcer—than in the quick, individual killings of the relatively anonymous Tattaglia and Barzini, of the traitors Tessio and Carlo Rizzi, and the completely anonymous pizza counterman who in Sicily once tried to kill Michael and ended up killing his young wife.

Two surprises in this sequence are Tessio and Carlo. Puzo keeps obscure that they had turned against the Corleones. Note that the very first chapter begins with Constanza's marriage to Carlo, and the last man murdered is Carlo, a family member, Michael's brother-in-law. Although Michael himself does not yank the garotte around this betrayer's throat, for this victim and this one only, Michael, the protagonist, does personally confront his antagonist, deceitfully interrogating and sucking out Carlo's confession.

Five onstage killings, the Corleone enemies all vanquished, and Puzo still isn't quite finished with us. Michael, with consummate skill and daring, has settled all accounts and set his house of crime in order. What episode could Puzo now devise that would top all this? Quite simply, a lie. A blatant lie by Michael to his beloved and devoted wife,

Kay. A hysterical Connie lunges at Michael for having killed Carlo.
Kay asks if it's true. Michael, looking directly into her eyes, says that
it's not. With this scene, we have seen him transformed both profession-
ally and personally. He has shown himself to be as tough, as shrewd,
and as ruthless as his father. With Kay, his role as boss takes precedence
over that of husband, father or human being. A moment later, his
retainers enter and pay homage to a new man, Don Michael. And then
Puzo lets us see that the cost of Michael's triumph is his wife's trust
and his own humanity.

Finally, note the organization and emotional intensification of this
entire climactic chapter. Its first two units prepare for the killings of
Carlo (subtly) and Tessio (openly), which then take place toward the
end of the chapter. The first person actually killed is the anonymous
pizza counterman, and second, the little-known Philip Tattaglia. Some
excitement, but only a little. Next, Albert Neri's assassination of Barzini derives from an elaborate ruse that is intriguing in itself but develops only moderate emotional power because neither we nor Michael are
involved with Barzini as a person. More emotion comes into play when
Tom Hagen orchestrates the abduction (and soon murder) of Tessio,
who all through the novel has been a friend and loyal caporegime.
When Michael comes onstage and confronts Carlo, the intensity esca-
lates. Carlo is a despicable wife-beater and philanderer, but nonetheless
his wife, Michael's sister, still loves the man. At issue now is something
more than mere business-related bloodiness. Carlo has to answer for the
murder of Michael's brother Sonny. By promising clemency, Michael
extracts a confession from his terrified brother-in-law and then surprises
us. In true Sicilian Mafia style, he reneges. Carlo's plea for mercy and
his strangling have the biggest impact in the chapter so far. But then
Michael has to deal with two characters who are dearer to him than
any of the others: his bereaved, hysterical sister and Kay, the woman
he loves and who loves him. With Carlo, we've just been prepared for
how smoothly Michael can lie. But because of the closeness between
him and Kay, his lying to her and her disillusionment with him hit us
harder than all the previous mayhem.

Climax in Garden of Lies

The obligatory scene in *Garden of Lies*, and its most powerful one, has
its roots in the book's prologue, its principal falsehood, Sylvie's lying
and hanging onto another woman's baby amidst the confusion of a

hospital fire, which leads her to abandon her own infant. Though she then becomes a devoted mother to Rachel, she's racked with guilt and tormented with longing for thirty years for her real child. Rose, Sylvie's blood child, is raised in a Brooklyn tenement by a vicious grandmother who despises and persecutes the girl. Rose never feels she's a part of the family with whom she's living, and her life is a misery. She and Rachel grow up, and the bulk of the novel is then taken up with their love stories (they both fall in love with the same man) and with Sylvie's too. But the themes of Sylvie's guilt and longing and of Rose's feelings of displacement and abandonment are subtly and at times boldly woven through scene after scene—most importantly when Sylvie appears at Rose's schoolyard and impulsively gives the girl a ruby earring. The questions implicitly planted in the reader as to how this issue will be dealt with overarch thirty-eight chapters. Will Sylvie ever acknowledge her own blood child? Will Rose ever find she does have a mother? If Sylvie's dread secret is ever revealed, will Rose hate her? Or is there a possibility of reconciliation, friendship, even love between them? These are the questions that provide the buildup at the end of chapter thirty-eight to Rose's arriving at Sylvie's door.

The entire novel, to some degree, is a preparation for this confrontation, when Sylvie at last comes face to face with this young woman, this child of hers whom she abandoned practically at birth, and is forced to reveal the shameful thing she's done. And for Rose—lonely, unhappy, confused—the scene brings an astonishing and shattering discovery. Her awful childhood fears are confirmed. She did not belong to the family in which she was raised. Her real mother, this woman, Sylvie Rosenthal, committed an unspeakable act against her but is now struggling to reach out to her. Even in brief summary, these actions appear powerful. A look at some of the details of this scene's construction will illuminate the techniques Goudge uses to maximize this climax's impact.

The final preparations for this scene are begun four chapters earlier, in the courtroom where Rose has been acting as Rachel's lawyer. Rose recognizes (or imagines she does) an elegant, older woman coming forward toward Rachel (who has just collapsed) as the same woman who in the schoolyard years ago gave her the ruby teardrop earring. Rose is mystified, confused and then stunned to hear Rachel cry out to this woman, "Mama." Two chapters later, after Nonnie's funeral, Rose goes home with Marie, hoping her sister may know something about why Sylvie Rosenthal once gave Rose the precious earring. Rose questions her sister. When Marie vehemently denies there's any substance to her questions, Rose grows suspicious. Pushing hard, relentlessly, Rose all but compels the guilt-ridden Marie to break down and tell about the $25,000 someone had anonymously given for Rose as a child back in 1954. The scene is one of conflict and high drama between two somewhat estranged sisters, but the plot at the same time is pushed forward with Rose now having obtained proof that her ancestry is different from Marie's and that somebody did actually care about her. Now she must find out how that somebody is connected to Sylvie Rosenthal.

In the next chapter, Goudge switches us to Sylvie alone, contemplating her accounts, all in order, all debts paid, except one. Sylvie berates herself for having exposed herself to Rose in the courtroom. She feels pride in her secret daughter Rose and her brilliant accomplishment and then feels overwhelmed with regret and guilt. Nothing can ever make up for what she has done. She has never stopped grieving for Rose and longs to be forgiven. Can Rose ever forgive her? She hears the door buzzer and, though frightened, goes to answer it without asking, Who's there? Because in her heart somehow she knows.

The setup is now complete. We have been led to experience the fierce desires and ineffable longings that both women feel about what is to them this almost life-and-death issue. Now they're about to collide, to commence after thirty or so years their obligatory scene.

As Rose enters, Goudge initially makes Sylvie the point-of-view character. She is the threatened one, the character desperate to preserve her awful secret, to keep her guilt forever hidden. She lets loose a surface stream of innocent-sounding chatter, which Goudge neatly counterpoints with Sylvie's inner pain and self-hatred. Before long Rose forthrightly asks if Sylvie is that same woman who once gave her the earring. Sylvie longs to answer truthfully but at the same time feels that the secret is so much a part of her that revealing it would be like killing some part of herself. Sylvie lies and ushers Rose to the door, while feeling so bad that she wants to lie down and die. This first movement of the scene is clearly down. Failure, as it were, for both characters. For the action to progress, a reversal is needed. Note how Goudge provides one.

While Sylvie is fetching her coat, Rose (and we are now moved into her point of view) glances about and spies a portrait. It's Sylvie as a young woman, with "a bit of red shining below her ear, a ruby set in gold, and shaped like a teardrop." Rose, so shaken that she's barely able to squeeze out the words, calls Sylvie on her lie. Sylvie stumbles. When Rose fingers the single ruby earring that she is wearing, Sylvie flinches as if struck. Rose, now dead certain that Sylvie has lied, asks who she is, and Sylvie, trapped, her back to the wall, must answer, "I am your mother." This is a stunning moment but not yet the high point of the scene. The drama continues to grow more and more intense as Sylvie half reveals her story and half pleads for forgiveness, while Rose becomes more and more furious, condemning Sylvie, gripping her at one point. She rails at Sylvie for having left her at the hospital fire as though she were a stray dog or kitten. Their differences seem irreconcilable as Rose starts to storm out the door.

The awful truth is out. Rose has vented great anger, and both characters are even more miserable than they were earlier. What's needed to keep building the scene is yet another reversal, and observe how Goudge fashions this one. Sylvie pleads for Rose to wait. Rose knows she should leave, but part of her still longs for what she could never have, a mother's love. Sylvie plunges outside, with no coat or sweater, into the snowy garden, oblivious to the freezing weather, and claws bare-handed at one of the bricks in the wall. Rose, watching Sylvie who is blue with cold, broken and weeping, drops to her knees trying to make her stop. Then the brick yields to Sylvie's tugging: "Here," and Sylvie offers her the matching ruby earring. A surprise, but again one that's been well prepared for. Rose feels her heart tumble over and over. Her anger has been deflected. A turning point of sorts, a hint of peace, is thus obtained, and the two go back inside.

The emotional climate now progresses from momentary acceptance to partial reconciliation—not a complete reversal this time but an upward movement with only one stumbling block menacing their further coming together. Sylvie pleads for Rose to keep their relationship secret from Rachel. Initially Rose is resentful and angry, but she eventually comes to see that Rachel, after all, is a wholly innocent party, though Rose knows she'll go on resenting her. But more importantly, Rose wants what Sylvie offers—friendship, possibly closeness one day, and even love. After its down and up and down movements, this scene fulfills its objective. Lives are transformed. Long-separated mother and daughter have been excitingly and movingly, albeit tenuously, reunited.

Obligatory Scenes in Other Blockbusters

A sampling of just a few other big scenes worth your careful study but that we lack the space to analyze in this book are the following: the encounter between Scarlett and Rhett that takes up the final chapter of *Gone With the Wind*; chapter seven of *The Thorn Birds*, which focuses on the death of Mary Carson and the temptation of Ralph de Bricassart; and chapters twenty and twenty-one of *Garden of Lies*, in which for the first time after Brian has married Rachel, Rose and Brian come together. Check particularly for how these scenes are prepared for, for the surprise or surprises they contain, for their intense conflict, for what their characters desperately want from each other, for how their characters' lives are transformed, and for their extension.

YOUR BIG SCENES

Now take a look at your manuscript or the one that you're planning. Does it contain a good number of big scenes, episodes that radically alter the destiny of an individual character or the dynamics between your characters? If it doesn't, then set about reworking your outline or draft to include more such scenes. These, of course, can encompass just about any activity affecting human beings, ranging from births to marriage proposals to weddings to deaths by normal causes to murders.

Next, check to see if at least some of the scenes you have contrived have extension. Is the main conflict and/or prevailing emotion of these scenes sustained over enough pages to generate a powerful effect on the reader? Don't take this as an invitation to pad a scene with extra dialogue or description simply to stretch it out. Instead, see about what you can do to build in fresh twists, complications, revelations, reversals, surprises, some or all of which can help generate greater excitement and additional highs and lows of emotion. If ideas along these lines don't come easily to you, go back and reread and analyze the construction of the big scenes referred to earlier in this chapter, and then try to apply the techniques used by these authors to your own characters and story. Or you might even try to use one of these as a model, tracing its emotional dynamics but at the same time filling it in with your own situation and characters.

The previous chapter dealt with "setting up" individual scenes in general. For your big scenes, it's crucial that you plan out and set up preparations earlier in your novel, well before the reader gets to your climactic encounters. Scrutinize your outline or manuscript. Have you planted the seeds that will raise questions in the reader's mind and cause her to look ahead, look forward to the stunning confrontations that you will then deliver? Keep in mind, too, that your big scenes will often depend to some extent on surprise, coincidence, something or someone coming in from out of the blue. But for your story to retain credibility, these surprises and coincidences should be subtly or not-so-subtly prepared for. Remember Rhett's sudden appearance after Scarlett smashes the china bowl. If Mitchell had not introduced him earlier in the chapter, this would not have worked nearly so well.

Finally, take a close look at your story's ending. Does it have a big scene, one in which your principal opposing characters face off against each other and stingingly or touchingly resolve the main issue between them? But your story, you feel, doesn't lend itself to or doesn't contain two distinctly adverse entities. What then? Well, your finale may not need as violent a climax as the rescue of Charlotte and the death of Feliks in *The Man From St. Petersburg*, but if you're serious about trying to produce a blockbuster, your story line will have to be reconfigured to build to an obligatory scene with great emotional power, as in the desperate resolution we find in Scarlett's final meeting with Rhett.

Chapter Ten

WEAVING PLOT STRANDS

⌘

PLOTTING A BLOCKBUSTER NOVEL, in addition to the outlining and scene-building techniques already discussed, usually requires other strategies as well. One such strategy is to start a story not at a beginning when its characters first meet or when some other precipitating event takes place, but instead at a point where the action is well underway and already moving toward a climax. These "beginning events," which took place before (sometimes long before) what happens on the first few pages or even the first few chapters, are called backstory. Such past happenings, often secret or unknown to at least one character, may become revelations that jolt the present action and sometimes transform a moderately exciting plot into a thrilling one. Even in a story whose action is almost totally in the present, the injection of a plot-twisting complication arising from the past can significantly heighten the drama.

BACKSTORY

You as author, in an outline only for yourself, should create your story from its initiating crucial event, going as far back in time as seems interesting or helpful, more or less as Follett did in Outline Three for *The Man From St. Petersburg.* Give your main characters life histories that set out how and why they have become who they are. Establish clearly the major actions that have gone on between these characters. Then decide at what later point in their lives the novel will begin, how much of the backstory, if any, will actually be dramatized in the novel, and where and how it will be presented—as author narration, a character's memory, dramatic flashback, or some combination of these.

Backstory in The Man From St. Petersburg

In *The Man From St. Petersburg*, the youthful love affair between Feliks and Lydia nineteen years before the novel begins serves as a springboard to several key turning points in the plot. It also imbues the novel as a whole with an emotional tension and resonance rarely found in a thriller whose main action is an assassination attempt. To highlight and analyze all Follett accomplishes with this one brief episode of backstory (but one that profoundly affects all four major characters) might take twenty or thirty pages. Instead, I'll show how he uses this only in the first four chapters. If you're interested enough, you can continue this study on your own through the rest of the book.

After the scene between Walden and Churchill in chapter one, the first few paragraphs in Lydia's point of view continue as in the previous scene to set her in the present. Follett then quickly and smoothly segues into her anticipating seeing Aleks, which makes "her think of another young Russian, a man she had not married." To create a vivid account of her past, the author uses a mix of author narration, Lydia's memory and her interior monologue. We get telling sense-image details about the young man ("his skin was white, the hair of his body soft, dark, and adolescent; and he had clever, clever hands"). More importantly, Follett lets us know that this middle-aged married countess still lusts for the wild and hungry love she knew as a student. She feels guilty that she does and prays to God that she'll be able to keep her secrets—but we are pointedly not yet told what these are. Here at the outset, Follett reveals only a glimmer of what happened in the past, just enough to show Lydia's fear, to portend danger to her, and to hook us into wanting to know, What are these secrets? And, indeed, Will she be able to keep them?

Feliks is introduced in the present on the train between Dover and London. A scene in the immediate past with anarchists in Geneva explains why he's come to England and begins to establish his character. In chapter two, he knocks a man off a bicycle and steals it. Observing to himself that he has no fear, Feliks conjures up an eleven-year-old memory of the episode that taught him that a man who has no fear can do anything. Follett writes a flashback of less than two pages in which a freezing and starving Feliks steals a policeman's dinner, strangles him to prevent the food from being taken away, and then makes off with the dead man's precious boots and clothing. Note the economy.

Nothing about Feliks's parents, childhood, schooling, political involve-
ments. Just enough to establish that he's escaped from a chain gang.
Though hungry and in rags, he has managed to traverse a thousand
miles, and if provoked, he's capable of literally anything. He clearly
emerges as formidable, someone to reckon with, and we absorb all this
about his formation in the context of a dramatic scene.

Midway into the swirl of present action in chapter two, Walden,
after making love to his wife, remembers how he first met her at a
reception in St. Petersburg, became fascinated by her wildly passionate
piano playing, learned that very night of his father's death, decided
that as the new Lord Walden he would need a wife, the next day asked
Lydia's father for permission to call on her, and then married her six
weeks later. Now, after nineteen years, he's still helplessly, hopelessly
in love with her. Not quite four pages of memory and flashback, yet
more than enough to delineate Stephen's origins, upbringing, his relationship with his father, pastimes as a young man, decisiveness, and
capacity for love. Note, too, that among hundreds of possible scenes of
Walden's early life, Follett keeps a narrow focus. He contrives that we
learn everything that we do about Walden in and around his encounter-
ing and courting Lydia. This, of course, sets us up for the irony of
Walden's situation when later we learn about the love affair that she
at the time was having with Feliks. But Follett holds off on dramatizing
this until chapter four. In establishing Walden's great love for Lydia,
the scene becomes a building block in enhancing the emotional impact
when, toward the end of the story, Walden finds she has betrayed him.
Interesting, too, is how Follett has us experience this episode exclusively
from Walden's limited point of view. Later, by bringing us back to it
with a whole new perspective, the author renders it even more momentous.

The three intrusions from the past I've so far discussed are illustrative. These scenes are presented more or less dramatically, but their
primary structural function has been to enrich character, to deepen our
knowledge of Lydia, Feliks and Stephen, and secondarily to prepare for
some of the big actions to come. The first such big action, one in which
the past event now actually drives the plot in the present, is Feliks's
flinging open the Walden coach, hearing a startlingly familiar woman's
cry, then losing all his momentum as he recognizes Lydia, his Lydia,
remembering how she used to look lying naked beneath him, whereupon Walden bites into his hand with a sword, then thrusts it into

Feliks's shoulder. The anarchist, his arm hanging limply, must flee. The main focus of the novel through this first quarter of the book has been building inexorably toward this attack by Feliks on Orlov. It goes awry because the assassin hears a voice and sees a face from his past. Feliks's failure is crucial. Had he succeeded, the novel would have been over before it had hardly begun.

Henceforth the plotting gains a double intensity. Walden knows that he and Orlov are in mortal danger, and he sets in motion a counter-movement against the mysterious would-be killer who, of course, will also persevere relentlessly to get at the Russian Prince. Follett could have had Feliks fail for any one of a hundred reasons. His choice of Feliks's momentary paralysis on recognizing his past love is a master-stroke. What a powerful way to bring back into his life the great passion of his youth! When Feliks arrives from the botched attempt to the safety of his furnished room, we at last get the backstory of the love affair and of Feliks's imprisonment and torture, the memory of which caused him to freeze when he meant to shoot. Although the aborted love affair took place nineteen years earlier, note the similarity in technique here with Puzo's having something big happen, and then going back into the immediate past and dramatizing the preceding episode. In the remainder of the novel, Follett continues to draw from the same well, using this episode of what happened years ago to butt up against and to twist and drive the present action.

Backstory Techniques

In lengthy novels, such as *Gone With the Wind* and *The Godfather*, in which no past secret impacts mightily on the present action, the backstory is straightforwardly presented within a dedicated chapter or two, as opposed to being woven in small units through several chapters that are set primarily in the present. But in *Gone With the Wind*, note that the book does not begin with Scarlett first meeting Ashley and then falling in love with him. When Mitchell first presents her, Scarlett is already mad for Ashley, head-over-heels in love. The day or moment when she discovered this about herself is not described or dramatized. There's no need. Her passion in the present is more than enough. It's the past of Scarlett's parents, Gerald and Ellen, that is given a twenty-page chapter, which illuminates such character traits as the determination of her father and the managerial ability of her mother, traits that Scarlett inherits or absorbs. The chapter establishes the history of Scarlett's family and of Tara within the context of their North Georgia neighbors. It also grounds the entire novel in an environment of folkways, mores, political and social attitudes. The backstory here provides a foundation both for Scarlett's mercurial character and for the richly portrayed world she inhabits.

Note that in both *The Man From St. Petersburg* and *Gone With the Wind*, the authors solidly establish the ongoing present action before bringing in any substantial backstory. This is important. Inexperienced writers will sometimes dive into the past almost immediately after introducing a character and before solidly engaging the reader with what is at stake for the character in the present. This is not a good tactic. The author should first establish the character within the context of his present problem or dilemma. After that, we're more likely to be interested enough in him to want to learn about his past.

In *The Godfather*, the book is almost half over before Puzo brings on a thirty-two-page backstory. As in *Gone With the Wind*, this lays down a foundation of sorts, but it also serves a special and unique purpose. Vito Corleone is the head of an organization that extorts, robs and murders. Yet he's a hero of the novel, someone in whom we are meant to be interested and for whom we are meant to feel sympathy and even admiration. The story of the boy of twelve who had to flee from his father's murderers, who couldn't feed his family after losing his grocery store job to the nephew of a murderous criminal, who had to steal to get by and was preyed upon by that same murderous criminal, establishes the Don as a persecuted soul, as a man who tries to live and behave decently, but who, when oppressed, has the guts to fight back. We then understand how he became the man he is, and how, if we were in his shoes, we conceivably might have acted similarly.

To sum up, in all three books the backstory is kept brief compared to the present action. Generally, it's a good practice to bring in the past (in flashback or memory) when it has a direct bearing on what's happening in the present. Note that it's only right after the failed assassination in the carriage that Follett dramatizes the Lydia-Feliks youthful love affair. Now we can understand why Feliks became momentarily paralyzed, but we gain this understanding within a context of intense action.

A similar and equally good technique is to bring a character to a moment of decision, slip back into the past, and then use this past event as the influencing or triggering factor for how the character chooses to act. Sylvie, in the prologue of *Garden of Lies*, is in labor and en route to nearby Lenox Hill hospital. Remembering her wedding night, her rich husband to whom she is grateful but whose body is repellent to her, and then her lover Nikos, she tells the cabdriver to go instead to St. Pius Hospital in the Bronx, a place where presumably her husband won't find her. In instances like this one, backstory provides not only some foundation for the novel and enrichment of character but also becomes the motivating spur to a present action.

Mysteries, of course, are about nothing if not unraveling the back-story, which the author has no choice but to work out beforehand. But many books in the genre bring in the key past elements only with the solution in the final chapter or two, so that these elements don't neces-sarily impact upon or enhance the novel as a whole. On the other hand, in such works as *Presumed Innocent* and *Burden of Proof* by Scott Turow, backstory is pervasive and crucial to the present action in virtually every chapter. Both books are wonderful examples of novels built on top of a series of past events quite as fascinating as those in the present, and it's these past doings that thrust again and again into the present ones.

Finally, I should mention that some blockbusters (like most films) have little or no backstory. *The Firm* by John Grisham, for example, takes place entirely in the present. Some past events are discussed and even lightly investigated: the prior FBI investigation; the unexplained deaths of two associates before the young lawyer hero joined the firm; and the imprisonment of the hero's brother. There are, however, no scenes set in the past. What the author gives up by way of character deepening, he regains with this novel's breakneck pace.

In writing your book, too, it will help you to compose a detailed backstory. Write short biographies of each of your main characters in which at least some of their lives in the past have intersected. But at the same time, keep in mind that it may not be necessary to bring much or any of this onstage or actually include it in your text. You may get more mileage out of keeping your action in the present and letting the characters' pasts add to their depth and resonate in small conflicts, joys, veiled barbs. Or what might contribute most to strengthen your work would be to select a few critical scenes from your characters' pasts and dramatize only those. Ideally, these should be events that were turning points—high or low—in their lives. Addition-ally, when recalled in memory or flashback by a character in the present, these scenes can also serve to help with a crucial decision that a character must now make, and thus you can weave such a flashback neatly into your story in the present. A history of your character's life told in straight narrative form may halt the forward motion of your novel dead in its tracks, whereas one or two well-dramatized scenes can powerfully represent that past life and at the same time keep your action moving.

TIGHTENING CHARACTER FOCUS

A second element in plotting worth giving close attention to is organizing the thrusts (the short- and long-term goals) of each of the principal characters in such a way that the action keeps turning in on itself. In other words, the big scenes again and again are arranged so as to be primarily between these key personages and to minimally involve new or secondary characters in whom the reader has developed little or no interest. Conversely, scenes in which these main characters are enmeshed are the ones most likely to get us excited and to evoke our empathy.

Feliks, for example, has scenes with landladies, fellow anarchists, people who along the way he robs and even kills, but his big scenes are all separately or together with Lydia, Charlotte and Walden, and only with them. He never has a verbal confrontation with Walden, but in the carriage it's Walden who strikes him with a sword. In the bombing attempt at the Savoy, it's Walden who catches the nitroglycerine. And when Feliks is chased over rooftops by the police, Walden is right there, and it's through his intensely involved point of view (mixed with Feliks's) that we experience this episode. Charlotte's thrust to free herself from the shackles of her constrained upbringing, to become a liberated woman, impels her to sneak off and join the suffragette march. Feliks, who's watching the house for another chance to get at Orlov, follows her and rescues her. Before long he realizes she's his biological daughter. Eventually he manages even to enlist her into his conspiracy. But the point here is that Charlotte, too, though she has scenes with Belinda, Mrs. Pankhurst, Annie the "fallen" housemaid and others, has her big scenes only with her mother, Walden and Feliks. The same holds true for Lydia and Stephen. Follett's continual turning in of these characters on each other is a plotting tour de force.

Controlling the Number of Characters

Another facet of the same technique is the elimination of unnecessary characters, or at the very least eliminating them as point-of-view characters. This makes it possible for an author to concentrate more on the ones who count. In Follett's Outline Three, Dieter Hartmann or Andre Barre participate in eight scenes. It's Hartmann who buys and tests the dueling pistols, and he also accompanies Feliks to the ball where the assassination is meant to take place. But is Hartmann really needed? Wouldn't he be a distraction at the murder attempt? And wouldn't it be more interesting if we as readers were to participate with Feliks alone when he acquires his weapons? Follett plainly comes to this conclusion, and in *The Man From St. Petersburg* discards both the German and the French Bolshevik so as to focus more intensely on Feliks.

Bonnie, the woman with whom Walden years ago had an affair, which he now resumes, appears in all the outlines but the first. In Outline Four she is given an important function. It's she who reveals to Walden that he's infertile, that he could not be Charlotte's father. But how much more poignantly and dramatically this is handled in the book itself where he learns this from Lydia, his wife, the woman he loves and whom he loves more passionately than in any of the outlines! Bonnie's elimination from the book not only tightens the focus but also adds to Walden's stature. With the first whiff of marital adversity, he no longer goes running off to another woman for consolation. Instead, he struggles manfully to sort things out with the wife to whom he is so deeply devoted.

Gone With the Wind, when you first read it, appears to be panoramic and to disregard such strictures of tight plot focus. Scarlett has important and sometimes big scenes with Gerald, Mammy, Charles Hamilton, Prissy, Frank Kennedy, Johnny Gallegher, the thieving Yankee cavalrymen, Melanie, Jonas Wilkerson, and perhaps a dozen others. Although this novel may seem to flow like a mighty river with its detailed presentation of whole eras of peace, murderous war, and devastating Reconstruction, and with its portrayals of dozens of intertwined characters and relationships, this immense flow actually is contained and driven by only two relationships, those of Scarlett with Ashley and Scarlett with Rhett. Except for one section of somewhat more than a hundred pages in roughly the middle of the book when Scarlett is back at Tara slaving to feed her household and restore the ruined plantation, during which period both Ashley and Rhett are away soldiering, Mitchell contrives for one of these two men either to dominate Scarlett's thoughts or to be physically present with her, often in a situation of intense conflict and in virtually every chapter. The author can and does twist the plot so that again and again it turns back into scenes between these very same emotionally involved characters, scenes that may contain some repetitious elements but that are for the most part fresh and different. For me to analyze each of these scenes and their actions would take far more space than this chapter allows, but it would be exceedingly worth your while to thumb through *Gone With the Wind* with this plotting process in mind and concentrate on the progression of only these scenes and their content.

It often seems easier to an author and also closer to what we perceive as "realism" to bring on a new character to cope with a new plot development. But if an already existing point-of-view character can somehow be worked into the same scene, the author gains an opportunity to enrich the character and imbue the scene with more emotion. For example, in *The Man From St. Petersburg*, Basil Thomson and his police have located Feliks's hideout and are about to flush him out. Thomson or an officer of his who is leading the raid would appear to be the expected focus for such an action. Instead, Follett wisely has Thomson summon Walden to the scene, something that in real life probably wouldn't happen. In the excitement, the reader doesn't notice this. The reader does, however, care about Walden much more than about Thomson or some faceless policeman, and Walden cares desperately that Feliks be caught. It's Walden's frenetic hope and ultimate disappointment coupled with Feliks's fury that endow the scene with a power far above and beyond its daredevil physical chasing around.

WEAVING YOUR PLOT STRANDS

If all the above is clear to you, it's time to go back through your outline or draft manuscript and evaluate or reevaluate each scene in terms of its impact or emotional weight. If you've put together scenes that do not center on a point-of-view character, then chances are their emotional weight is slight or nonexistent. Probably you now need to rethink, reorganize, and either cut these scenes or rebuild by focusing each scene on one of your point-of-view characters.

This approach can work as long as your point-of-view character—even an antagonist—is at least somewhat sympathetically portrayed. If, however, your scene's main character is thoroughly villainous, and the secondary character or characters are also unlikeable, you have a problem. The reader then is left with no one to root for. She can make no investment in the outcome of the scene, and your writing is likely to turn her off. So again, either cut away such scenes or restructure them around a personage toward whom you (and the reader) can generate at least some warmth or understanding.

Finally, look over your work and ascertain how much of its drama is generated in scenes between major and minor players. If most of your high-fever action is generated by goings-on between and among your point-of-view people, then your story is probably in good shape. But if a lot of your scenes involve point-of-view characters butting up only against secondary characters, then you need to reexamine what you have written. Can your story in general, and these scenes involving primarily minor characters in particular, be replotted to focus on and create excitement between more of your major characters? If you can do this, you'll have a seriously better chance of compelling the reader to keep turning your pages.

Chapter Eleven

RHYTHM IN PLOTTING

───────────────────── ∽ ─────────────────────

PLOTTING A POPULAR NOVEL IS ALSO AN EXERCISE IN AL-
TERNATIONS, in laying out somewhat rhythmically ups and downs,
scenes in which the protagonist comes out ahead or wins outright, and
scenes in which the hero or heroine is battered or decisively beaten. A
useful image is a football game, where two more or less equal teams
regularly or sporadically push each other up and down the field, with
the team you're rooting for sometimes gaining ground, sometimes falling back, but in blockbuster novels usually winning in the end.

SUBPLOTS

At a football match, both the players and the audience from time to
time crave relief from the relentless pounding the contestants inflict
on each other. In blockbuster novels, too, one aspect of a plot's rhythm
is relief of some kind from the story's intensity and from its lead characters' main struggles. Such relief in fiction often takes the form of a
diverting subplot or plots that sometimes have the added value of also
being comic.

As an example of rhythm, let's look now at how Puzo sets out the
ups and downs of the Corleones, and also how and when he diverts us
from their bloody story.

The first movement is up. The requests made to the Don at the
wedding are all fulfilled, culminating in Jack Woltz's hiring of Johnny
Fontaine. In each instance, on behalf of his supplicants, the Godfather
gets what he's after; he seems virtually omnipotent. But no sooner does
he meet Sollozzo than he senses danger and sends for Luca Brasi. Then
Hagen is abducted, Don Vito is shot and almost killed, and Luca, his
ferocious protector, is strangled. The Corleones have been badly mauled.

But in a third movement their fortunes partially recover as young Michael comes to the rescue, first by warding off outside the hospital a further attempt on his father, and then by killing rogue cop McCluskey and Sollozzo.

Puzo then relates in a few lines that the Five Families War of 1946 had begun, after which the novel immediately changes tack. Having given us eleven chapters of illicit schemings, beatings and killings, the author estimates the reader is ready for a breather and introduces a thirty-six page mini-roman à clef (a story based loosely on real people) focusing on the sexual, domestic and professional life of unhappy Johnny Fontaine, a fictionalized Frank Sinatra. The appeal of these pages is to the readers' interest in behind-the-scenes celebrity gossip and in Hollywood's notorious sexual mores. As the pages relate to the main plot, however, with their scenes of domesticity, Hollywood party-going and deal-making, they do provide a relief from the grim ferocity of the gangster goings-on.

Now that I've pointed the way, you may find it helpful to continue with this type of analysis through the rest of the Corleones' story and/ or to chart the ups and downs of Feliks or Meggie. Then reexamine the novel you are writing and see if you've plotted enough powerful high and low points for your own protagonist.

Some of the best subplots, such as that of Charlotte in *The Man From St. Petersburg*, with her adolescent attempt at understanding sex, her presentation at court, her attendance at a big coming-out party, her awakening to the plight of the poor and to the second-class status of women, are written seemingly as diversions from the main plot and in fact for a time serve that purpose. But then Follett takes hold of this almost frivolous story line and gradually and integrally weaves it into a key pillar of the main action, thus getting double-duty, as it were, out of this element. This approach is one you, too, should aim for. A subplot that ties into and affects the main action will generally lead to a stonger book than a subplot that stands independently from your story's central characters and climax.

COMIC RELIEF

Another approach an author may take to offer relief from high intensity is through an oddball or comic character, one who serves no significant plot function other than to distract or lighten the mood. In tragedy, two of the best-known examples are the Gravedigger in *Hamlet* and the

Gatekeeper in *Macbeth*, taking the stage as they both do just prior to scenes of overwhelming power. These famous comic scenes relax the audience, lightening its mood and causing it to be more open and receptive, more shocked by the jolting events that follow.

Mason Gold appears in chapters two, eight, and thirty-two of *Garden of Lies*. He is the son of Sylvie's best friend, a contemporary of Rachel's. He's part of no ongoing subplot, nor does he figure in the main plot. What he does, in addition to enriching the texture of the novel, is provide Rachel with some lighthearted companionship, something she gets from no other character, and he does this within the context of fairly humorous scenes: a comedy of errors deflowering, a hippie vegetarian wedding, some years later a nostalgic reunion in an oyster bar. And the reader gets a breather from Rachel's almost constant *sturm und drang*.

A more prominent example of diversionary comic characters are the delightfully portrayed Uncle Peter and Aunt Pittypat in *Gone With the Wind*. For much of the novel, Scarlett resides not only with her secret rival Melanie, but also with Melanie's helpless, flibbertigibbet aunt, a childlike overweight woman in love with gossip and given to fainting spells. Pitty is as unlike Scarlet as it is possible to be, someone sweet and kindly who cannot make up her mind about a single thing and depends totally on her bossy but utterly devoted black slave houseman, Peter. Mitchell brilliantly uses these two again and again to lighten the atmosphere of their tense home, fraught with Scarlet's jealousy and with the terrors of war and Reconstruction. She particularly highlights Pitty's naivete, vanity and gullibility as characteristics Rhett can play upon as a means of ingratiating himself into the household and guaranteeing contact with Scarlett, who often very much wishes to avoid him. So Pittypat and Peter are fun in themselves, but here, too, they are made to serve the plot.

Diversionary subplots and characters such as those I've just described can be wonderful enrichments to a novel, but it is also possible to get by without them. You won't, for example, find these in *The Firm*. But every Big Book does require a plot with some alternation of ups and downs.

YOUR PLOT RHYTHMS

Looking at your project, do the fortunes of its protagonist have enough ups and downs? These should more or less permeate your entire story.

If they do not, then it might be wise to go back to the drawing board and replot your scenes so that they end up with distinct, albeit sometimes subtle, defeats and victories, failures and successes, satisfactions and woes.

A diversionary subplot or a character who provides comic relief may or may not benefit your book, depending on its genre and scale and depending, too, of course, on your skill at handling this kind of material. If your story is one of unrelenting tension, with frightening events in chapter after chapter, then it might make sense to weave between these chapters a secondary plot strand that is lighter in tone and that also contains a bit of comedy. Just as we can do more running, swimming, push-ups after a bit of rest, your reader will be better primed to absorb the full impact of a powerful scene if you give him a breather between it and your previous knock-down-drag-out episode.

Ideally, these diversionary characters and scenes should in their own limited way be as dramatic as the core portions of your book. Charlotte's raiding her father's locked bookcase for reading matter to help her figure out how children come into this world may seem like light stuff compared to Feliks's life-and-death maneuverings, but to her at that moment, her girlish quest has paramount importance.

Novels differ, so I hesitate to give general advice about when a reader may need diversion, where exactly you should place it, or how long or short you should make it. I would suggest, though, that you avoid having one scene of unbearably high emotion or violence directly follow another and that you intersperse such scenes with other kinds, some of which could be diversionary and/or humorous. Between the shootings, stranglings and maulings of *The Godfather*, Puzo writes love scenes, sex scenes, attempts at conciliation, strategy sessions, and then after the climaxes of his subsections brings on the Johnny Fontaine and Lucy Mancini subplots. Follett diverts from his assassination plot with a Walden negotiation or a Charlotte adventure in almost every chapter. If you can weave the equivalent of a Charlotte or an Aunt Pittypat into your story and then develop scenes around that character, you may be giving your novel a wonderful leavening.

Chapter Twelve

STORY POINTS

———————————— ∽ ————————————

THE ONE ASPECT OF A BLOCKBUSTER NOVEL'S STRUCTURE
that usually keeps the reader turning the pages more than any other is
pace—storytelling that moves relentlessly forward, constantly reposi-
tioning the characters and posing ever new dramatic question in the
reader's mind. The author of the Big Novel must, with each scene and
each chapter, take care to keep developing the plot, twisting it, spin-
ning it in fresh directions and thus advancing the action. And on a
lesser scale, he must develop and twist and spin even within each scene
in small units of actions that endure for a page or two or even less.

You may now ask, What exactly does advancing the action mean
in concrete terms? In a word, the answer is change. In the course of a
page or a scene or a chapter, characters do things, learn things, and have
things done to them. These actions, while interesting or compelling in
themselves, also alter (improve or worsen) the status of a character or
the dynamics of a relationship between characters, raise new questions
in the reader's mind about the story's possible developments or out-
comes, and prepare for and foreshadow events yet to come. *Gone With
the Wind* contains here and there a few consecutive pages of general
historical background, and in *The Thorn Birds* scenic descriptions occasionally are lengthy, but these elements, when they last more than a
page or so, are exceptional. In all five of our example novels, the stream
of action for the most part keeps pounding ahead and never lets up.
Chapter forty-five of *Gone With the Wind* (which I chose at random)
runs twenty-one pages and contains twenty-six or so story points—
small events, rhythmic beats if you will, that subtly or not so subtly

shift, stir, change the situation of a character or characters or of a vehicle, epidemic, environment, city or nation. In a word, a change of some kind occurs.

BOLD STROKES

Before we dig into the nitty-gritty and microscopically examine some step-by-step movement of story points within a chapter or a scene, let's first look at a few bold strokes, changes that are larger than story points. These big actions are created to cap a given chapter and propel the readers into the next. Examples, of course, abound, and I'll point to some. But for you to fully benefit from this chapter, examine the novel you are now reading, or the one you are writing. Note how every chapter (usually every scene) is built around a happy or unhappy event, decision, discovery, all actions that change (slightly or radically) how things were and that imply more change to come.

Chapter one of *The Man From St. Petersburg* is full of riches, deftly and excitingly introducing all four major characters and bringing alive the environment of the book with color and verve. Yet it builds up to only one main action: Feliks's decision to go to London and kill Orlov. Chapter two, similar in structure, picks up and continues Lydia's and Walden's subplots and again Follett orchestrates to a main action crescendo that is unmistakable. Feliks is reading the newspaper, figures out a way to get to Orlov, and then steals a gun to put his plan into effect and kill him. In chapter one we witness a decision to assassinate, which makes Feliks seem brave but also maybe a bit out of his depth. In chapter two, Feliks's brazen theft of a pistol causes his plan now to feel real, concrete, imminent. Each chapter ending embodies an event that is momentous, a big change, and that promises further effects not only on Feliks but on every key character in the novel.

Garden of Lies begins with Sylvie trying on a new hat in a department store. By the prologue's end, she has given birth, rescued another woman's baby from a hospital going up in flames, and decided to abandon her child, keep this other woman's baby, and pretend it's her own. This mind-boggling decision is a main action for the chapter that changes not only Sylvie's life but even more profoundly those of the two babies who become the book's heroines. Not every chapter in every blockbuster novel has a main action that so irrevocably alters the lives of its characters, but if you thumb through the rest of *Garden of Lies*, searching out main actions, you'll find that every chapter contains one, and it's an action that possesses distinct size and scale.

STORY POINTS

A chapter's main action, you will have found out by now, is usually easy to spot. Planning a main action for each chapter of your own book should not overly tax your creative powers. But laying out the ten to thirty story points within a chapter—small and middling actions that ideally should mount in intensity and lead inexorably to your climax—can be difficult. In a first draft there's usually no way to write a scene other than in your head, to imagine the characters living it and at the same time to set it down as you envision it. It's in the rewriting of the second, third and tenth drafts that you gradually work in all the story points you deem necessary to maintain the pace (while taking out excess dialogue, description, digression and other flab) and build and tighten the linkage between the page-by-page actions and the chapter's main action.

Story Points in Gone With the Wind

For an examination of story points—what they are, and how they work—let's look closely at Mitchell's pacing and plot moves in chapter forty-five. To fully appreciate these, though, we need a bit of background from the previous chapter that ends with Scarlett's being assaulted, her bodice ripped open by vagabond thieves, and her providential rescue by Big Sam, a former slave from Tara. Her misfortune, however, is to some extent brought on by herself; she has, after all, insisted on driving her carriage alone through an area that she has been warned is dangerous.

Forty-five begins that night with Scarlett arriving at Melanie's, and her flashing back to her panicked homecoming that afternoon, her longing for consolation and then her fury at Frank's calmly abandoning her to go to what he claims is a political meeting. Note how this very first action, her angry little scene with him, is already ironically preparing for the chapter's finale: Scarlett's stunned discovery that her meek and mild husband has secretly gone off to avenge her and will never return because he's been killed.

At Melanie's, Scarlett tries to talk about the terrifying experience she's had, but Melanie keeps steering the conversation to other subjects.

This second action, in which Scarlett's distress is ignored, is a sort of repetition of what just happened with Frank, except that now oddly it's Melanie who subtly frustrates her.

Scarlett then notices odd behavior, unusual tension. Archie, who most evenings sleeps on the sofa, tonight violently spews tobacco juice on the fire. Melanie, who is invariably kind, snaps at her aunt and takes overlarge stitches in her sewing. India directs hateful looks at Scarlett. Until now, Scarlett has been too preoccupied with her own distress to take notice of others'. The new action is her becoming aware.

Next, Scarlett rouses herself and demands to know why India's been staring at her all evening. India lashes out, accusing Scarlett of having gotten (in being assaulted) only what she deserves. They snarl furiously at each other. India is on the verge of revealing how Scarlett has endangered the lives of their menfolk when Archie orders them to shut up. He hears someone coming. Conflict has been constant in the chapter so far, but for the most part implicit and understated. Now it flares up excitingly and also poses the new question to the reader and to Scarlett, How might their men's lives be in danger?

Before she can inveigle an answer, Rhett arrives, desperate. Where are the men? He's heard of a Yankee trap. It's life or death. The scene shifts from a spat between two feuding women to a confirmation of India's accusation and an alert to real and terrifying peril.

Archie and India distrust Rhett and are against Melanie's telling him anything. But she decides to put her faith in him and reveals the location of the meeting place; he rushes off. Another change. Now maybe Rhett can save the endangered menfolk. Even more important, Rhett's brief appearance prepares for and makes possible his later or-chestrating the onstage salvation of Ashley by Rhett's leading Ashley to pretend, with a Yankee officer looking on, to be drunk from having spent the evening at Belle's brothel.

After Rhett hurries off, the next three beats are blows against Scar-lett, each one more powerful. First, India, continuing where she left off before Rhett appeared, lashes out at Scarlett as responsible for what could turn out to be the deaths of Ashley and Frank. Scarlett, frantic, almost hysterical, is next stunned to learn from Melanie that their men are off raiding with the Klan. Scarlett now is scared stiff that she'll lose her mills and store, and she wants to rush downtown to find out. Archie, ferociously stopping her, accuses her. If the men don't make it back, the blood is on her hands. The plot advances with a changed situation.

Scarlett finally understands what she's done and feels horrified, screaming to herself that she's killed Ashley. Melanie rises to her defense but
is cut off by the sound of horses trotting up to the house.

The long-promised threat to these women and to their men now
physically materializes with the arrival of Captain Jaffery and his troop,
seeking Frank and Ashley, who the Captain grimly confirms are not
meeting at Frank's store where Melanie claims they are. The Yankees
then position themselves around the house to lie in wait for the men's
return. The danger that until now was only talked about and therefore
speculative and remote, is now inescapable. It confronts Scarlett directly.

The next beat dramatizes fear-stricken reactions. While Melanie
tries to maintain calm by reading aloud from *Les Misérables*, Scarlett,
to herself, decries Frank for breaking his promise and joining the Klan.
She worries about the ruin of her business, about Frank and Ashley
who may be hanged; she berates herself as the guilty one, the cause of
all this trouble, and at the same time defends herself. She needed money
and couldn't have done otherwise. The change in this unit is more in
intensity, greater fear and self-blame, than in new story material. Also
this mini-scene provides a necessary interval between the arrival of the
feared Yankees and the soon-to-come feigned drunken return of Rhett
and Ashley.

At this point we are roughly halfway through the chapter. Note
how little that is truly momentous has happened, and yet how many
distinct, story-advancing actions we've witnessed in only twelve pages.
As intense as these have been, they seem mild compared with what
follows: Rhett and Ashley play act to convince Captain Jaffery that they
were at a whorehouse and not out on a Klan raid; Ashley nearly bleeds
to death; Scarlett learns of Frank's having been killed. The thirteen or
so actions that charge the second half of the chapter are strong and clear.
If you feel it's useful, pinpoint and analyze these actions for yourself.

Worth noting too about chapter forty-five is how Mitchell chooses
to focus this piece of her story. A less-talented and less-shrewd author
might well have taken the reader off with the men on their raid, dramatized their meeting, planning, donning their Klan robes, attacking,
being beaten back, being rescued by Rhett and escorted to Belle's
brothel. But the real drama in this chapter (and throughout the novel)
resides not in the male characters, in what they themselves do or don't
do, but in the effects they have on the women and most especially on

Scarlett. The most thrilling physical actions in this part of the story, the shooting and killing, wisely are kept offstage. Scarlett, however, is placed before us in this chapter from beginning to end. In terms of her taking the lead and aggressively pushing the story, she does very little, although others desperately exert themselves. Yet the dramatic high points are hers for the most part. It's her deeply felt but often unspoken reactions, discoveries, new awarenesses, denials and self-recriminations that mark and climax many of this tense chapter's individual beats.

Not every chapter in our example novels or in other blockbuster novels will always exhibit such a narrowly directed character focus. But they all contain (if you look), punctuated through every chapter, distinct units of action, beats, story points, usually at least a dozen and often many more. These keep the novel dynamically in flux and in movement toward ever-new situations.

YOUR STORY POINTS

Now turn to a chapter you have written. Mark its units of action, its story points. Do you have a few or a goodly number? Do they provide some alternating ups and downs for your scene's point-of-view character? If you have a fifteen-page chapter and can find only two or three shifts in the dynamics between your characters, your writing is probably flabby. More than likely it would benefit either from substantial cutting or from your working in new elements, as in our *Gone With the Wind* chapter, that would alter again and again the situation of the characters vis-à-vis one another.

Finally, take a close look at how your scene's sequence of actions builds to and impacts upon its climax. As in the scene we've just analyzed, most of your minute-by-minute actions should serve this function but not necessarily all. You should be constantly preparing for happenings in future scenes and chapters; to accomplish this, you will at times have to insert material that at first glance may appear to the reader as a digression. But if, at the outset of a scene, you set up what is at issue and clearly raise its dramatic question, as with Frank Kennedy's mysteriously going off into the night, then you can afford to go off briefly on what seems to be a tangent, plant the seed or seeds that will germinate later in your story, and then push ahead beat by beat to your climax.

Chapter Thirteen

REVISION

YOU HAVE DILIGENTLY STUDIED ALL THE TECHNIQUES presented in this book so far, developed a number of outlines for your own book, finished one outline that feels rock solid, and written a complete draft of your novel. What now? Put it aside for a week or two. Reread it with all the cool objectivity you can muster. Try to consider it as if someone else wrote it. Be ruthless in pinpointing its weaknesses. Then figure out how you're going to eliminate them. It's time for a second draft, and you may well have to repeat the process with a third or fourth. Although Dick Francis and Harold Robbins are reputed to write their books only one time through, most popular authors do at least two completed scripts followed by a final polish. Sidney Sheldon is said to do a dozen complete rewrites, and for Saul Bellow ten times is not unusual.

The point is that the likelihood of your novel being terrific in every respect the first time you set it down is from slight to nonexistent. Liken yourself to a sculptor fashioning a complex figure or set of figures from a great block of stone. On a first go-round, you chisel the stone down to roughly the shape you seek, but overall it lacks precise definition. On a second try, you manage to carve some portions finely, but others still resist the form you feel they should have. Finally, after what feels like an infinite amount of tedious and laborious chopping, shaping and smoothing, the sculpture emerges as you imagined it.

Difficult as this work may seem, it should be the most enjoyable part of the job. And for most writers, it is. Creating from nothing, with a blank piece of paper in front of you and the choices open to you seeming almost infinite, is generally considered the toughest part of writing a novel. Once your story and characters have begun to take shape, to achieve enough reality so that you can at least start to believe in them and what they do, then you have real concrete stuff in front of you: words, lines, pages, the raw material of fiction on which you can bring to bear your innate artistic feel for character and storytelling as well as the craft you hopefully have acquired from this book.

Authors who, because they've had some success, think that whatever they set down needs no further work and should be published as is do so at their peril. For a few years in the mid-1980s, I represented a gifted novelist who had achieved enormous popularity in Britain but whose books had never caught on in the United States. I was hired to launch him here, and I made some modestly attractive deals for him for already completed works. Then he sent me a new manuscript that had patches of brilliance but also some important structural flaws. I carefully analyzed the novel and wrote him a ten- or twelve-page letter, pointing out how he might improve his book. By return mail, he fired me. His British publisher had loved the book. What did I know? He wanted enthusiasm from his agent, not advice. Since then, he has written eight or more novels, none of which have brought him recognition in the United States.

REVISION OF *THE MAN FROM ST. PETERSBURG*

Ken Follett, on the other hand, as you perhaps have already concluded after reading chapter four, is a perfectionist, an author who'll keep working for as long as it takes to get it right—adding a line, a scene, a chapter, a character's makeup, a new twist to ignite the plot, a sense image to convey a bit of local color. For you vicariously to participate in the revision process, we shall now look at successive drafts of two scenes from *The Man From St. Petersburg*. After you read the first draft material, try to imagine what changes you might make to improve it. Or better yet, rewrite your own improved version. Then read Follett's final draft and compare the changes you envisioned or actually wrote with those made by the author.

For you to get the full benefit of what follows, to discern all the changes and to arrive at an understanding of the reasons behind them, not only a close reading of both texts but probably two or three readings of each will be required. But your effort should prove rewarding.

Early Draft of Opening Scene

"Churchill? Winston Churchill?" said Walden. "Here?"

"Yes, my lord," the butler said.

"Send the blighter away," Walden said. "I'm not at home."

The Earl of Walden was profoundly irritated. On Thursday Churchill had sent him a note which he had ignored. On Friday Churchill had called on him in London, and Walden had refused to see him. Today, Saturday, Churchill had followed him into the country and knocked on the door of Walden Hall.

Churchill was First Lord of the Admiralty in the Liberal government—a government whose attack on the traditional English way of life had become so savage that Society, that is to say Walden and his friends, would no longer have Liberal politicians in their homes.

Privately Walden thought this was a shame, for political life in London was usually so civilized—an example to the world, he liked to say. But somehow the quarrels normally confined to the Houses of Parliament had escaped and made their way across to St. James's Park and into the drawing-rooms of Belgravia. Society had begun by not inviting the Prime Minister and his crowd to the smaller, more intimate dinner parties; then they had been excluded from the larger gatherings; and the process had gone on until now Walden could not raise his hat to a Liberal back-bencher without feeling disloyal.

He regretted this mainly because he was a courteous man, and his courtesy was not a superficial social habit but sprang from a gentleness which was probably his deepest instinct. If a gentleman did not behave decently, he felt, then these socialist johnnies were right and he was nothing more than a self-indulgent parasite. He also thought the Conservatives were making a strategic error in allowing a political dispute to become personal, for it is hard for a man savagely to attack your traditional way of life when he is pleasantly full of your roast beef and vintage port.

Walden was therefore doubly irritated: firstly, by Churchill's oafish refusal to be snubbed, and secondly by his own feeling that he was not entirely in the right in snubbing him.

The butler, Brittan, also looked uneasy. He was not used to turning away Cabinet Ministers. The old butler, Thomson, would have done it without turning a hair; but Thomson was sixty-five, retired, and growing roses in the garden of a little cottage on the estate, and Brittan, who had been here as a footman for a mere twenty years, had yet to acquire the unassailable dignity of his predecessor.

"This is becoming awfully boring," said Lydia, Walden's wife.

She was not bored at all. In fact, she found it rather exciting, he thought; but she said that because it was the kind of thing an

Englishwoman of her class would say, and since she was not English but Russian she liked to say typically English things, the way a man speaking French will say *alors* and *hein?* a lot.

Brittan coughed.

Walden said: "Are you still here?"

"Mr. Churchill told me you'd be not at home, my lord, and said I must give you this."

Walden realized that the butler was carrying a letter on a tray. He decided not to read it. "Give it back to him—"

Then he saw the seal on the envelope, and for once the Earl of Walden was intimidated.

"No, wait," he said. He picked up the letter, broke the seal, and took out a single sheet of heavy paper, folded once.

He read:

> *Buckingham Palace*
> *2nd May 1914*
>
> *My dear Walden,*
>   *You will see young Winston.*
> *George R.*

Walden recognized the handwriting. It was the King's.

He was so embarrassed that he flushed. It was *frightfully* bad form to drag the King into something like this. He felt like a schoolboy who is told to stop quarreling and get on with his prep. For a moment he was tempted to defy the King. But the consequences . . . His wife would no longer be received by the Queen, his daughter would not be presented at court, people would be unable to invite him to parties at which a member of the Royal Family would be present, the Waldens would gradually be crossed off more and more invitation lists . . . It would be worse than what the Conservatives were doing to the Liberals. The Waldens might as well go and live in another country. No, there was no question of disobeying the King.

He gave a defeated sigh, but it was also a sigh of relief, for now he could break ranks and no one could blame him. "Letter from the King, old boy; nothing to be done, you know."

Brittan was still waiting. Walden said, "Ask Mr. Churchill to come in."

Lydia raised her eyebrows. Walden handed her the letter, then walked across the polished floor to the tall window. He looked out on to a broad, level lawn dotted with mature trees: a Scots pine, a couple of mighty oaks, a willow, some chestnuts. Peering to his left he could see, on the gravel drive in front of the South Portico, the large motor car in which Churchill had arrived. The dust had settled but the machine was still rattling and smoking. A driver in helmet, goggles and heavy motoring coat stood beside it, with one hand on the door, as if he had to hold it like a horse to stop it wandering away. A few gardeners and stablehands were gazing at it from a safe distance.

More and more visitors came to Walden Hall by motor. In the summer they were a terrible nuisance to the village, sending up clouds of dust from the unpaved road as they roared through. Walden was thinking of putting down a couple of hundred yards of tarmacadam in the village. Ordinarily he would not have hesitated, but roads had not been his responsibility since 1909 when Lloyd George set up the Roads Boards. That had been a characteristic Liberal decision: They took money from Walden in order to do themselves what he would have done anyway, then they failed to do it. Which brought him back to Churchill.

Lydia handed him the King's letter and said, "How odd."

The Liberals really did not understand how the monarchy was supposed to work, Walden reflected. He said, "George is just not firm enough with these people." This touch of disrespect was the dying flicker of his impulse to defiance, and now he prepared himself to be icily polite.

Brittan came in and said, "Mr. Winston Churchill."

Churchill was forty, exactly ten years younger than Walden. He was a short, slender man who dressed in a way Walden thought was a shade too elegant to be quite gentlemanly. His hair was receding rapidly, leaving at the temples two curls which, together with his short nose and the permanent sardonic twinkle in his eye, gave him a mischievous look. Walden had liked him, in the old days: he was dreadfully theatrical, of course, but never dull.

Churchill shook hands and said, "Good afternoon, my lord," without a trace of deference. He bowed to Lydia. "Lady Walden, how do you do."

Walden told him to sit down and Lydia poured him a cup of tea. He seemed quite unembarrassed. He said, "First of all, my apologies, together with the King's, for imposing myself on you."

Walden nodded.

Churchill said, "I might add that I should not have done so, other than for the most compelling reasons."

"You had better tell me what you want."

"I want Russia."

It was a promising beginning, Walden thought. One of the few things which Liberals and Conservatives had in common was their attitude toward the Russian government. The Czar's regime was incompetent, undemocratic and brutal; which was embarrassing, for the British needed the Russians as allies against Germany. The German army was the best in Europe, and to make it even better the government had imposed a special tax to raise a billion marks. By Walden's reckoning this was the biggest levy in European history, and in his opinion such a tax was created for one purpose only: war. However, Britain could and did overlook superior armies on the European continent; but rival navies were another matter. Churchill, as First Lord of the Admiralty, had adopted with enthusiasm the policy of his Liberal and Conservative predecessors, which was that the Royal Navy should be bigger than the combined navies of the two next biggest sea powers, to protect Britain's vital trading arteries. Now Gemany was catching up, and refused point-blank to negotiate an arms limitation treaty. So Britain needed allies. Germany's weakness was—as always—her vulnerability to war on two fronts: against France in the west and Russia in the east. For this reason the aim of German diplomacy was to neutralize Russia. And for the same reason British policy, conducted for the last eight years by the patient, devious Sir Edward Grey, was to form a Triple Entente between Britain, Russia and France.

So Walden knew exactly what Churchill meant when he said that he wanted Russia. Walden said, "There is an alliance between France and Russia."

"But consider its wording," Churchill replied. "Russia is obliged to fight if France is the victim of aggression. It is left to Russia to decide whether France is the victim or the aggressor in a particular case. When war breaks out both sides always claim to be the victim. Therefore the alliance obliges Russia to do no more than fight if she wants to."

"You could say that of all defence treaties," Walden said.

"I agree. Everything depends upon whether the will to fight is there. Take England and France. We have no alliance, not even an agreement; but the atmosphere generated by these military talks over the years is such that, if and when the crisis arises, we shall feel obliged to fight together. Of course I have to say the opposite in public."

Walden could not restrain a smile. Churchill's thinking was remarkably similar to his own.

Churchill went on. "The third side of the triangle is the relationship between England and Russia."

"I should have thought there was no likelihood of you chaps forming an alliance there," Walden said.

"Then you misjudge us. If the national interest is at stake, we'll deal with tyrants."

"Your supporters won't like it."

"They won't know."

Now Walden was intrigued. He was beginning to see where all this was leading, and the prospect was exciting. He said, "What have you in mind? A secret treaty? Or an unwritten understanding?"

"Both."

Walden looked at Churchill through narrowed eyes. This young demagogue might have a brain, too, he thought; and that brain might not be working in my interest. So the Liberals want to do a secret deal with the Czar, despite public opinion—but why tell me? They want to rope me in somehow, that much is clear. Why? So that if it all goes wrong they'll have a Conservative on whom to put the blame? It will take a plotter more subtle than this one to lead me into a trap like that.

Walden said, "Go on."

"I've initiated naval talks with the Russians, along the lines of our military talks with the French. They've been going on for a while at a rather low level, and now they're about to get serious. A young Russian admiral is coming to London. His name is Prince Alexei Andreivitch Oblomov." Churchill looked at Lydia. "I believe he is related to you, Lady Walden."

"Yes," Lydia said, and for some reason Walden could not even guess at she looked uneasy. "He is the son of my cousin, which makes him . . ."

"Second cousin," Walden supplied.

"He is young to be an admiral," Lydia added. She was her usual, prefectly composed self, and Walden decided he had imagined that moment of unease.

"He's thirty," Churchill said promptly. Walden recalled that Churchill, at forty, was very young to be in charge of the entire Royal Navy. Churchill's expression seemed to say, The world belongs to brilliant, radical young men like me and Oblomov.

But you need me for something, Walden thought.

"In addition," Churchill went on, "Oblomov is nephew to the Czar and, more importantly, one of the few people other than Rasputin whom the Czar likes and trusts. If anyone in the Russian naval establishment can swing the Czar on to our side, Oblomov can."

Walden asked the question that was on his mind. "And my part in all this?"

"You know the Czar personally. You know Russia and speak Russian fluently. You have in the past brought off at least one great diplomatic coup in St. Petersburg." Churchill paused. "Nevertheless you were not our first choice to represent Britain in these negotiations. The way things are at Westminster . . ."

"Yes, yes." Walden did not want to start discussing that. "However, something changed your mind."

"In a nutshell, you were the Czar's choice. It seems you are the only Englishman in whom he has any faith. Anyway, he sent a telegram to his cousin, His Majesty King George the Fifth, insisting that Oblomov deal with you."

Walden could imagine the consternation among the radicals when they learned they would have to involve a reactionary old Tory peer in such an underhand scheme. "I should think you were horrified," he said.

"Not at all. In foreign affairs our policies are not so very different from yours. And I have always felt that domestic political disagreements were no reason why your talents, sir, should have been lost to His Majesty's Government."

Pompous ass, Walden thought. Aloud he said, "How is all this to be kept secret?"

"It will seem like a social visit. If you agree, Oblomov will stay at your London house for the season. You will introduce him to society. Am I right in thinking your daughter comes out this year?" He looked at Lydia.

"That's right," she said.

"So you'll be going about a good deal anyway. Oblomov is a bachelor, by the way, and obviously very eligible, so we can noise it abroad that he's looking for an English wife. He may even find one."

"Good idea." Suddenly Walden realized he was enjoying himself. He had used to be a kind of semi-offical diplomat under the Conservative governments of Salisbury and Balfour, but for the last eight years he had taken no part in international politics. Now he was about to go back onstage, and he began to remember how absorbing and fascinating the whole business was: the secrecy, the gambler's art of negotiation, the conflict of personalities, the cautious use of persuasion, bullying, or the threat of war. And the more he thought about his new task, the more important it seemed. The German army was stronger, better-equipped, more modern and better-led than the French. Any help from England would be niggardly and late. France would fight, but she could not win. However, if the Russians could be relied upon to attack Germany from the east, the Germans would have to switch forces out of the west to defend her rear, and the picture would alter. If Russia would fight, Germany could not win, in Walden's opinion. And it was his job to make Russia fight.

Churchill said, "May I take it, then, that you'll do it?"

"Of course," said Walden.

Final Draft of Opening Scene

It was a slow Sunday afternoon, the kind Walden loved. He stood at an open window and looked across the park. The broad, level lawn was dotted with mature trees: a Scotch pine, a pair of mighty oaks, several chestnuts and a willow like a head of girlish curls. The sun was high and the trees cast dark, cool shadows. The birds were silent, but a hum of contented bees came from the flowering creeper beside the window. The house was still, too. Most of the servants had the afternoon off. The only weekend guests were Walden's brother George, George's wife, Clarissa, and their children. George had gone for a walk, Clarissa was lying down and the children were out of sight. Walden was comfortable: he had worn a frock coat to church, of course, and in an hour or two he would put on his white tie and tails for dinner, but in the meantime he was at ease in a tweed suit and a soft-collared shirt. Now, he thought, if only Lydia will play the piano tonight, it will have been a perfect day.

He turned to his wife. "Will you play, after dinner?"

Lydia smiled. "If you like."

Walden heard a noise and turned back to the window. At the far end of the drive, a quarter of a mile away, a motor car appeared. Walden felt a twinge of irritation, like the sly stab of pain in his right leg before a rainstorm. Why should a car annoy me? he thought. He was not against motor cars—he owned a Lanchester and used it regularly to travel to and from London—although in the summer they were a terrible nuisance to the village, sending up clouds of dust from the unpaved road as they roared through. He was thinking of putting down a couple of hundred yards of tarmacadam along the street. Ordinarily he would not have hesitated, but the roads had not been his responsibility since 1909 when Lloyd George had set up the Roads Boards—and that, he realized, was the source of his irritation. It had been a characteristic piece of Liberal legislation: they took money from Walden in order to do themselves what he would have done anyway; then they failed to do it. I suppose I'll pave the road myself in the end, he thought; it's just annoying to pay for it twice.

The motor car turned into the gravel forecourt and came to a noisy, shuddering halt opposite the south door. Exhaust fumes drifted in the window, and Walden held his breath. The driver got out, wearing helmet, goggles and a heavy motoring coat, and opened the door for the passenger. A short man in a black coat and black felt hat stepped down from the car. Walden recognized the man and his heart sank: the peaceful summer afternoon was over.

"It's Winston Churchill," he said.

Lydia said: "How embarassing."

The man just refused to be snubbed. On Thursday he had sent a note which Walden had ignored. On Friday he had called on Walden at his London house and had been told that the Earl was not at home. Now he had driven all the way to Norfolk on a Sunday. He would be turned away again. Does he think his stubbornness is impressive? Walden wondered.

He hated to be rude to people, but Churchill deserved it. The Liberal government in which Churhchill was a minister was engaged in a vicious attack on the very foundations of English society—taxing landed property, undermining the House of Lords, trying to give Ireland away to the Catholics, emasculating the Royal Navy and yielding to the blackmail of trade unions and damned socialists. Walden and his friends would not shake hands with such people.

The door opened and Pritchard came into the room. He was a tall Cockney with brilliantined black hair and an air of gravity which was transparently fake. He had run away to sea as a boy and had jumped ship in East Africa. Walden, there on safari, had hired him to supervise the native porters, and they had been together ever since. Now Pritchard was Walden's majordomo, traveling with him from one house to another, and as much a friend as a servant could be.

"The First Lord of the Admiralty is here, my lord," Pritchard said.

"I'm not at home," Walden said.

Pritchard looked uncomfortable. He was not used to throwing out Cabinet ministers. My father's butler would have done it without turning a hair, Walden thought, but old Thomson is graciously retired, growing roses in the garden of that little cottage in the village, and somehow Pritchard has never acquired that unassailable dignity.

Pritchard began to drop his aitches, a sign that he was either very relaxed or very tense. "Mr. Churchill said you'd say not at 'ome, my lord, and 'e said to give you this letter." He proffered an envelope on a tray.

Walden did *not* like to be pushed. He said crossly: "Give it back to him—" Then he stopped and looked again at the handwriting on the envelope. There was something familiar about the large, clear, sloping letters.

"Oh, dear," said Walden.

He took the envelope, opened it and drew out a single sheet of heavy white paper, folded once. At the top was the royal crest, printed in red. Walden read:

> *Buckingham Palace*
> *May 1st, 1914*

My dear Walden
> *You will see young Winston.*
George R.I

"It's from the King," Walden said to Lydia.

He was so embarrassed that he flushed. It was *frightfully* bad form to drag the King into something like this. Walden felt like a schoolboy who is told to stop quarreling and get on with his prep. For a moment he was tempted to defy the King. But the consequences . . . Lydia would no longer be received by the Queen, people would be unable to invite the Waldens to parties at which a member of the Royal Family would be present and—worst of all—Walden's daughter, Charlotte,

could not be presented at court as a debutante. The family's social life
would be wrecked. They might as well go and live in another country.
No, there was no question of disobeying the King.

Walden sighed. Churchill had defeated him. In a way it was a relief,
for now he could break ranks and no one could blame him. *Letter from
the King, old boy*, he would say in explanation; *nothing to be done,
you know.*

"Ask Mr. Churchill to come in," he said to Pritchard.

He handed the letter to Lydia. The Liberals really did not understand how the monarchy was supposed to work, he reflected. He mur-
mured: "The King is just not firm enough with these people."

Lydia said: "This is becoming awfully boring."

She was not bored at all, Walden thought; in fact, she probably
found it all quite exciting; but she said that because it was the kind of
thing an English countess would say, and since she was not English
but Russian, she liked to say typically English things, the way a man
speaking French would say *alors* and *hein?* a lot.

Walden went to the window. Churchill's motor car was still rattling and smoking in the forecourt. The driver stood beside it, with
one hand on the door, as if he had to hold it like a horse to stop it from
wandering away. A few servants were gazing at it from a safe distance.

Pritchard came in and said: "Mr. Winston Churchill."

Churchill was forty, exactly ten years younger than Walden. He
was a short, slender man who dressed in a way Walden thought was a
shade too elegant to be quite gentlemanly. His hair was receding rapidly, leaving a peak at the forehead and two curls at the temples which,
together with his short nose and the permanent sardonic twinkle in his
eye, gave him a mischievous look. It was easy to see why the cartoonists
regularly portrayed him as a malign cherub.

Churchill shook hands and said cheerfully: "Good afternoon, Lord
Walden." He bowed to Lydia. "Lady Walden, how do you do."

Walden thought: What is it about him that grates so on my nerves?

Lydia offered him tea and Walden told him to sit down. Walden
would not make small talk: he was impatient to know what all the fuss
was about.

Churchill began: "First of all my apologies, together with the
King's, for imposing myself on you."

Walden nodded. He was not going to say it was perfectly all right.

Churchill said: "I might add that I should not have done so, other than for the most compelling reasons."

"You'd better tell me what they are."

"Do you know what has been happening in the money market?"

"Yes. The discount rate has gone up."

"From one and three quarters to just under three percent. It's an enormous rise, and it has come about in a few weeks."

"I presume you know why."

Churchill nodded. "German companies have been factoring debts on a vast scale, collecting cash and buying gold. A few more weeks of this and Germany will have got in everything owing to her from other countries, while leaving her debts to them outstanding—and her gold reserves will be higher than they have ever been before."

"They are preparing for war."

"In this and other ways. They have raised a levy of one billion marks, over and above normal taxation, to improve an army that is already the strongest in Europe. You will remember that in 1909, when Lloyd George increased British taxation by fifteen million pounds sterling, there was almost a revolution. Well, a billion marks is equivalent to *fifty* million pounds. It's the biggest levy in European history—"

"Yes, indeed," Walden interrupted. Churchill was threatening to become histrionic: Walden did not want him making speeches. "We Conservatives have been worried about German militarism for some time. Now, at the eleventh hour, you're telling me that we were right."

Churchill was unperturbed. "Germany will attack France, almost certainly. The question is, will we come to the aid of France?"

"No," Walden said in surprise. "The Foreign Secretary has assured us that we have no obligations to France—"

"Sir Edward is sincere, of course," Churchill said. "But he is mistaken. Our understanding with France is such that we could not possibly stand aside and watch her be defeated by Germany."

Walden was shocked. The Liberals had convinced everyone, him included, that they would not lead England into war; and now one of their leading ministers was saying the opposite. The duplicity of the politicians was infuriating, but Walden forgot that as he began to contemplate the consequences of war. He thought of the young men he knew who would have to fight: the patient gardeners in his park, the cheeky footmen, the brown-faced farm boys, the hell-raising undergraduates, the languid idlers in the clubs of St. James's . . . then that

thought was overtaken by another, much more chilling, and he said:
"But can we win?"

Churchill looked grave. "I think not."

Walden stared at him. "Dear God, what have you people done?"

Churchill became defensive. "Our policy has been to avoid war,
and you can't do that and arm yourself to the teeth at the same time."

"But you have failed to avoid war."

"We're still trying."

"But you think you will fail."

Churchill looked belligerent for a moment, then swallowed his
pride. "Yes."

"So what will happen?"

"If England and France together cannot defeat Germany, then we
must have another ally, a third country on our side: Russia. If Germany
is divided, fighting on two fronts, we can win. The Russian army is
incompetent and corrupt, of course—like everything else in that country—but it doesn't matter so long as they draw off part of Germany's
strength."

Churchill knew perfectly well that Lydia was Russian, and it was
characteristically tactless of him to disparage her country in her presence, but Walden let it pass, for he was highly intrigued by what
Churchill was saying. "Russia already has an alliance with France,"
he said.

"It's not enough," Churchill said. "Russia is obliged to fight if
France is the victim of aggression. It is left to Russia to decide whether
France is the victim or the aggressor in a particular case. When war
breaks out, both sides always claim to be the victim. Therefore the
alliance obliges Russia to do no more than fight if she wants to. We
need Russia to be freshly and firmly committed to our side."

"I can't imagine you chaps joining hands with the Czar."

"Then you misjudge us. To save England, we'll deal with the devil."

"Your supporters won't like it."

"They won't know."

Walden could see where all this was leading, and the prospect was
exciting. "What have you in mind? A secret treaty? Or an unwritten
understanding?"

"Both."

Walden looked at Churchill through narrowed eyes. This young
demagogue might have a brain, he thought, and that brain might not

be working in my interest. So the Liberals want to do a secret deal with the Czar, despite the hatred which the English people have for the brutal Russian regime—but why tell me? They want to rope me in somehow, that much is clear. For what purpose? So that if it all goes wrong they will have a Conservative on whom to put the blame? It will take a plotter more subtle than Churchill to lead me into such a trap.

Walden said: "Go on."

"I have initiated naval talks with the Russians, along the lines of our military talks with the French. They've been going on for a while at a rather low level, and now they are about to get serious. A young Russian admiral is coming to London. His name is Prince Aleksey Andreyevich Orlov."

Lydia said: "Aleks!"

Churchill looked at her. "I believe he is related to you, Lady Walden."

"Yes," Lydia said, and, for some reason Walden could not even guess at, she looked uneasy. "He is the son of my elder sister, which makes him my . . . cousin?"

"Nephew," Walden said.

"I didn't know he had become an admiral," Lydia added. "It must be a recent promotion." She was her usual, perfectly composed self, and Walden decided he had imagined that moment of unease. He was pleased that Aleks would be coming to London: he was very fond of the lad. Lydia said: "He is young to have so much authority."

"He's thirty," Churchill said to Lydia, and Walden recalled that Churchill, at forty, was very young to be in charge of the entire Royal Navy. Churchill's expression seemed to say: The world belongs to brilliant young men like me and Orlov.

But you need me for something, Walden thought.

"In addition," Churchill went on, "Orlov is nephew to the Czar, through his father, the late Prince, and—more importantly—he is one of the few people other than Rasputin whom the Czar likes and trusts. If anyone in the Russian naval establishment can swing the Czar on to our side, Orlov can."

Walden asked the question that was on his mind. "And my part in all this?"

"I want you to represent England in these talks—and I want you to bring me Russia on a plate."

The fellow could never resist the temptation to be melodramatic, Walden thought. "You want Aleks and me to negotiate an Anglo-Russian military alliance?"

"Yes."

Walden saw immediately how difficult, challenging and rewarding the task would be. He concealed his excitement and resisted the temptation to get up and pace about.

Churchill was saying: "You know the Czar personally. You know Russia and speak Russian fluently. You're Orlov's uncle by marriage. Once before you have persuaded the Czar to side with England rather than with Germany—in 1906, when you intervened to prevent ratification of the Treaty of Bjorko." Churchill paused. "Nevertheless, you were not our first choice to represent Britain at these negotiations. The way things are at Westminster . . ."

"Yes, yes." Walden did not want to start discussing *that*. "However, something changed your mind."

"In a nutshell, you were the Czar's choice. It seems you are the only Englishman in whom he has any faith. Anyway, he sent a telegram to his cousin, His Majesty King George the Fifth, insisting that Orlov deal with you."

Walden could imagine the consternation among the Radicals when they learned they would have to involve a reactionary old Tory peer in such a clandestine scheme. "I should think you were horrified," he said.

"Not at all. In foreign affairs our policies are not so much at odds with yours. And I have always felt that domestic political disagreements were no reason why your talents should be lost to His Majesty's Government."

Flattery now, Walden thought. They want me badly. Aloud he said: "How would all this be kept secret?"

"It will seem like a social visit. If you agree, Orlov will stay with you for the London season. You will introduce him to society. Am I right in thinking that your daughter is due to come out this year?" He looked at Lydia.

"That's right," she said.

"So you'll be going about a good deal anyway. Orlov is a bachelor, as you know, and obviously very eligible, so we can noise it abroad that he's looking for an English wife. He may even find one."

"Good idea." Suddenly Walden realized that he was enjoying himself. He had used to be a kind of semi-official diplomat under the

Conservative governments of Salisbury and Balfour, but for the last eight years he had taken no part in international politics. Now he had a chance to go back onstage, and he began to remember how absorbing and fascinating the whole business was: the secrecy; the gambler's art of negotiation; the conflicts of personalities; the cautious use of persuasion, bullying or the threat of war. The Russians were not easy to deal with, he recalled; they tended to be capricious, obstinate and arrogant. But Aleks would be manageable. When Walden married Lydia, Aleks had been at the wedding, a ten-year-old in a sailor suit: later Aleks had spent a couple of years at Oxford University and had visited Walden Hall in the vacations. The boy's father was dead, so Walden gave him rather more time than he might normally have spent with an adolescent, and was delightfully rewarded by a friendship with a lively young mind.

It was a splendid foundation for a negotiation. I believe I might be able to bring it off, he thought. What a triumph that would be!

Churchill said: "May I take it, then, that you'll do it?"

"Of course," said Walden.

Analysis of the Two Versions

Here are two versions in which the large and small actions are essentially similar if not identical, and yet these drafts differ in scores of major and minor ways. Without pointing up every minute change, which would take up pages and pages, and would be more helpful if you do it yourself, the question is, What can be learned about the process of building a blockbuster novel from what Follett has done here?

First impressions of a character are crucial. How a literary personage is introduced may determine how a reader feels about him all through a book. Walden, our novel's protagonist, in the first draft is peremptory, contemptuous, somewhat stuffy, and a man who has no apparent close relationships with anyone else. In the final version, no longer referred to as distancingly as the Earl of Walden, we meet a man who is in love with the beauty of his Sunday afternoon, whose brother and family have come to visit, whose sense of what would make a perfect day would be to hear his wife play the piano after dinner, and whose major-domo Pritchard is as much a friend as a servant. On meeting Churchill, Walden asks himself, What is it about him that so grates on my nerves? Indeed, Walden's feelings and emotions, the qualities that bring out his humanity, are given fresh emphasis all through the scene with Churchill, including his feeling badly for his wife when Churchill tactlessly disparages the Russians. When war appears to be imminent, Walden sees it not just as a sort of grand chess game as in the first draft, but he fears what will become of the young men to whom he's attached. And when he learns that his Russian counterpart is Aleksey Orlov, he's excited. Aleks is not only Lydia's nephew, but a young man who often came to visit while at Oxford and with whom Walden feels a strong friendship. To sum up, Walden is made more sensitive, responsive, closer emotionally to the people in his life, and more adventurous in his eagerness to take on this challenging task.

Readers want to be "right there" with a book's characters, to see, hear, smell what they do, to be plunged into their environment. The first draft starts with Churchill's arrival, whereas the final one first sets the scene. Note Follett's economy. We see a park with mature trees; a Scotch pine, a pair of mighty oaks, learn that Walden wore a frock coat to church, will wear a white tie and tails for dinner and is now in tweeds with a soft-collared shirt. The ambience of Walden's home is in a page deftly established. The reader is given a sense of place. Later, as the story unfolds and requires them, more and more of the features of this palatial house and vast estate are made vivid.

Factual details appropriately chosen and placed persuade us to suspend disbelief and to give credence to characters and events we know are fictional. In the first draft, for example, we learn that Churchill's Liberal government's attack on the traditional English way of life has become so savage that Liberal politicians have been banned from Society. But the basis or components of that so-called attack, without which it remains abstract and not tangible to the reader, are lacking. In version two, Follett provides its vital underpinning. The attack includes "taxing landed property, undermining the House of Lords, trying to give Ireland away to the Catholics, emasculating the Royal Navy and yielding to the blackmail of trade unions and damned socialists."

Along the same lines, a foundation of this novel is the crucial nature of the negotiations between Walden and Aleks. The stakes in a thriller must be huge, and in this book they can be so only if England is perceived to be in dire peril. In the first draft, Walden anticipates war with Germany but appears hardly concerned that he personally or England could be harmed. The dialogue with Churchill in the final draft, by contrast, is fraught with emotion, surprise, conflict, and considerably more factual detail. Walden is shocked to learn that England will be required to come to the aid of the French and even more stunned when Churchill admits that even the French and British together couldn't beat the Germans. Now there is only one way to save England: to join hands with the Czar. And the whole responsibility for making that happen falls on Walden.

Follett also makes lots of other kinds of changes, such as setting up Churchill's arrival, characterizing Pritchard, refining lines of dialogue, enhancing descriptions, transposing material from inner monologue or author narration into active dialogue, and moving text from one part of the scene to another. One tiny change I'd like to point out is Lydia's reaction to Churchill's first mention of the Russian prince. In draft one, Churchill says,

> *"His name is Prince Alexei Andreivitch Oblomov." Churchill looked at Lydia. "I believe he is related to you, Lady Walden."*
>
> *"Yes," Lydia said, and for some reason Walden could not even guess at she looked uneasy. "He is the son of my cousin, which makes him . . ."*
>
> *"Second cousin," Walden supplied.*
>
> *"He is young to be an admiral," Lydia added. She was her usual, perfectly composed self, and Walden decided he had imagined that moment of unease.*

In the final version, Churchill says,

> *"His name is Prince Aleksey Andreyevich Orlov."*
> *Lydia said: "Aleks!"*
> *Churchill looked at her. "I believe he is related to you, Lady Walden."*
> *"Yes," Lydia said, and, for some reason Walden could not even guess at, she looked uneasy. "He is the son of my elder sister, which makes him my . . . cousin?"*
> *"Nephew," Walden said.*
> *"I didn't know he had become an admiral," Lydia added. "It must be a recent promotion." She was her usual, perfectly composed self, and Walden decided he had imagined that moment of unease.*

In both versions, Lydia is meant to be distraught about the arrival of this relative who reminds her of a prior life in St. Petersburg that she is trying to bury and forget. In the first draft Churchill mentions his name and at the same time asks about a relationship. Lydia's response is an unaccented, "Yes." In the second, Churchill mentions only his name. Lydia says, "Aleks!" clearly an excited or startled reaction. Only then does Churchill ask about the relationship. Thus a basis is established for Walden's thinking her to be uneasy. Note, too, that Oblomov is changed to Orlov, from a cousin to a nephew and that Lydia's speech is slightly Russified with, "I didn't know he had become an admiral," and with her failing to come up with the word nephew. The changes between these two bits of dialogue are miniscule and minor, but it's hundreds of tiny changes such as these that in the aggregate culminate in first-class writing.

First Draft of Last Section of Chapter One

Feliks Murontsiv looked out of the window of the railway carriage as the sun rose over the orchards and hop fields of Kent. He had arrived at Dover in the dark, so this was his first sight of England. He could remember when, in his youth, he and other Russian extremists had upheld England's constitutional monarchy as the ideal form of government. That had been before they realized that more drastic changes were necessary.

Political stability must be easy to achieve, he thought, in a country as lush and green as England. He never ceased to be astonished at how *pretty* Europe was, with its neat fields, its dainty houses, its fat animals and its fat, smiling people. When he first saw it he had suffered a profound shock, for he like any Russian peasant had been incapable of imagining that the world could look like this. These people must be happy, he had thought; and soft.

He recalled dawn in his home village: a grey, boiling sky and a bitter wind; a frozen swampy field with puddles of ice and tufts of coarse grass rimed with frost; himself in a worn canvas smock, his feet already numb in felt socks and wooden shoes; his father striding along beside him, wearing the threadbare robes of an impoverished country priest, arguing that God was good.

His father had loved the Russian people because God loved them. It had always been perfectly obvious to Feliks that God hated the people, for He treated them so cruelly. From realizing that God was not good it was a small step to realizing that he was not even there. Logically then Feliks should no longer have cared about the Russian people, but he found that he still did, and ultimately he realized that a human being was the *only* thing worth caring about. And still he went to church, for he had no other faith.

That had changed, ironically, when he went to the school in St.

Petersburg to be trained for the priesthood. He had befriended secular students from the University, and had been invited to their lodgings, and had listened to wild talk of republicanism, and democracy, and finally anarchism. Slogans like "All property is theft" had been at first incomprehensible and then revelatory. Anarchism had answered his questions. Why did the nobleman own the land? Answer: He did not own it, he had stolen it from the people. By what right did the Czar govern? Answer: He had no right to govern, he was a tyrant. These notions burst upon Feliks with the impact of truths which, once they have been formulated, are self-evident.

It had taken him longer to shake off his father's philosophy of nonviolence. Back in 1894 he had refused to have anything to do with plans to assassinate Czar Alexander III, although he knew and in a way admired the people who were making those plans. They succeeded in killing the Czar, but they were caught. Feliks had stood in the crowd of eighty thousand people and watched the hanging of the assassins. It was a scene of barbarity full worthy of the Russian nobility. One of the condemned was a woman, Perovskaya; another, Rysakov, was a boy, eighteen years old, younger than Feliks. The hangman was drunk. The stools which the hangman kicked away were too low, so that none of them died instantly; and the noose around Mikhailov's neck was improperly tied, and slipped, so that he had to be lifted up and hung again, not once but twice.

Feliks had very nearly changed his mind about the necessity for violence. He had thought: This is a war, we are forced to kill. But he had gone on turning the other cheek. In the following year he was arrested by the secret police and tortured, and still he did not believe in violence. When they released him he began to tramp the Russian countryside, dressed as a monk, preaching the anarchist gospel. He told the peasants that the land was theirs because they tilled it; that the wood in the forest belonged to anyone who felled a tree; that nobody had a right to govern them except themselves, and because self-government was no government at all it was called anarchy. He was a wonderful preacher and he made many converts. If a fraction of the peasantry now had the beginnings of a political education, he could take some of the credit.

This had been his life for almost ten years. Now, looking back on that period while a railway train sped him through the Garden of England, he could see how like his father he had been. It was a different gospel, to be sure; but he had still been preaching, still trying to give the people wisdom and a better life by talking to them and living among them.

The phase had ended when he was arrested again. This time they sent him to Siberia. His years of wandering had inured him to cold, hunger and pain; but now, working in a chain gang, using wooden tools to dig out gold in a mine, laboring on when the man chained to his side had fallen dead, seeing boys and women flogged, he came to know darkness, bitterness, despair, and finally hatred. In Siberia he had learned the facts of life: steal or starve, hide or be beaten, fight or die. There he had acquired cunning and ruthlessness; there he had killed a man. He had learned the ultimate truth about oppression: that it works by turning its victims against each other instead of against their oppressors. He had learned the ultimate truth about himself: that he was capable of being as savage as the most brutish half-mad peasant.

His escape had been brilliant, for the camp officials thought he was dead—he had even provided them with an unidentifiable corpse—so there was no chase. But getting out of the camp had been easy compared with getting out of Siberia. Sometimes he had ridden, in railcars loaded with ore or wagons full of pelts; but most of the way he had walked. It had taken him two years. During that time he had become half-human, skirting the fringes of civilization, robbing its garbage. He had slept with animals and eaten their feed, he had ridden an open railcar in a blizzard, one time he had stolen a pony, ridden it to death, then eaten some of it. He had come perilously close to madness; perhaps he had been mad some of the time.

Then, when at last he entered a town and walked its streets like a human being, he made a remarkable discovery about himself: he had lost the ability to fear.

There seemed to be nothing that could possibly frighten him. If hungry, he would steal; if chased, he would hide; if threatened, he would kill. There was nothing he wanted. Nothing hurt much anymore. Love, pride, desire and compassion were forgotten emotions.

They all came back, eventually; except the fear.

He exchanged his rags for things that looked more or less like clothes, then he remembered how to keep himself clean. He stopped eating garbage and got back into the habit of sitting at a table and using a knife. He began to speak to people and worked as a laborer for a while. One day he found a book, and remembered how to read; and then he knew he had come back from the grave.

He returned a full-blooded revolutionist. It seemed incredible to him that once he had scrupled to throw bombs at the noblemen who maintained those Siberian convict mines, for clearly they deserved much worse than death. He joined a revolutionary cell, and learned to handle explosives, and carried out an assassination without the slightest misgiving. He became a valued member of the group, but he never got close to any of the others, for there was in his eyes something that made them nervous. Then the group was betrayed, as all such groups were sooner or later; and the secret police came to their homes in the middle of the night, and they were all arrested except Feliks, who killed one policeman and maimed another and escaped.

After that he had to leave Russia. He went to Switzerland, where there were many Russian revolutionists of various types. There he became even more civilized. He drank beer instead of vodka, used a fork as well as a knife, wore a collar and a tie, and went to concerts of orchestral music. He got a job in a bookshop, and was deeply discontented.

Russia was in turmoil. Czar Nicolas II was the most incompetent and asinine ruler a degenerate aristocracy could produce. The parliament was impotent, the oil workers were at war with the Cossacks, and a million people were on strike. The country was a powder barrel waiting for a spark, and Feliks wanted to be that spark. But it was fatal to go back. Joe Stalin had gone back, and no sooner had he set foot on Russian soil than he had been sent to Siberia. The secret police knew the exiled revolutionists better than they knew the ones who were still at home.

Feliks was chafed by his collar, his leather shoes and his circumstances. When at last he saw a chance to act, he seized it.

It came about through a traitor in the Ochrana, the Czar's secret police. The police hired people to pose as revolutionists, join cells, report on their activities and encourage them to commit bombings and other outrages. But some of the people they hired really were revolutionists, and others were converted by what they heard at the meetings they were supposed to spy on; so the Ochrana was riddled with traitors. One of the traitors had learned that Prince Oblomov was going to England to make a military pact with the Earl of Walden, obliging Russia to fight on the English side if there should be a war.

Feliks was incensed. The war would be fought by the Russian peasants. He had spent most of his life among those people. They were hard, surly and narrow-minded, because of the life they led; but their foolish generosity and their occasional spontaneous outbursts of sheer fun gave a hint of how they might be in a decent society. Their concerns were the weather, animals, disease, childbirth and outwitting the landlord. For a few years, in their late teens, they were sturdy and straight, and could smile and run fast and flirt; but soon they became bowed and grey and slow and sullen. Now Prince Oblomov and the Earl of Walden would take those young men in the springtime of their lives and march them in front of cannon to be shot to pieces or maimed forever or crippled with dysentery, no doubt for the very best reasons of international diplomacy.

This was why Feliks was going to England to kill Oblomov and Walden.

In the back room of a workingmen's bar in Zurich the anarchist cell had discussed at length the likely consequences of such an assassination. Firstly and obviously it would bring the negotiation of the murderous treaty to an abrupt halt. Secondly, as soon as it became known that the assassin was an expatriate Russian revolutionist, an old quarrel would flare up again between England and Russia: the question of refugees. England, like Switzerland, had a liberal immigration policy, and would admit political subversives who had been forced to flee Russia. This infuriated the Czar, who said, quite rightly, that the refugees did nothing but plot how they could come home and kill him. The English establishment was not very happy to have such people as guests, for they occasionally robbed banks for funds and were much more ready to use guns than were homegrown thieves; but public opinion, and the conscience of the Liberal government, would not have them sent home to be imprisoned, tortured and executed by the Czar's bestial secret police. The dispute smouldered; and if Oblomov were to be killed by a Russian refugee it would flare up, and prevent the talks continuing with replacement negotiators.

Thirdly, and most importantly, the cell would announce that Oblomov and Walden had been killed because they were scheming to drag the Russian people into a war which was no concern of theirs; and the reaction in Russia to that announcement would not only keep Russia out of the war but might set off an outraged revolt leading ultimately to what the anarchists really wanted: the destruction of the Czarist state.

For some time the rural panorama seen through the window of the railway carriage had been interrupted with increasing frequency by the grimy backs of houses and factories. Now fields disappeared altogether, and Feliks realized the train was passing through the London suburbs.

He thought back to Switzerland again. The discussion of which of them should go to England had been short, he recalled. He had wanted to go more than anyone else, so he was the one. Decisions were made like that in anarchist cells: There was no talk of discipline, organization, or submission to the will of the majority, for those ideas were associated with oppression, not with freedom. It had also been a wise decision, for he had vastly more experience than any of the others at this sort of thing.

They had scraped up the money for his fare—third class all the way—and had bought him a cardboard suitcase. He had no need of the case, for he had traveled half across the world without one, but he took if for the sake of appearances.

Final Draft of Last Section of Chapter One

Feliks Kschessinsky sat in a railway carriage waiting for the train to pull out of Dover Station. The carriage was cold. He was quite still. It was dark outside, and he could see his own reflection in the window: a tall man with a neat moustache, wearing a black coat and a bowler hat. There was a small suitcase on the rack above his head. He might have been the traveling representative of a Swiss watch manufacturer, except that anyone who looked closely would have seen that the coat was cheap, the suitcase was cardboard and the face was not the face of a man who sold watches.

He was thinking about England. He could remember when, in his youth, he had upheld England's constitutional monarchy as the ideal form of government. The thought amused him, and the flat white face reflected in the window gave him the ghost of a smile. He had since changed his mind about the ideal form of government.

The train moved off, and a few minutes later Feliks was watching the sun rise over the orchards and hop fields of Kent. He never ceased to be astonished at how *pretty* Europe was. When he first saw it he had suffered a profound shock, for like any Russian peasant he had been incapable of imagining that the world could look this way. He had been on a train then, he recalled. He had crossed hundreds of miles of Russia's thinly populated northwestern provinces, with their stunted trees, their miserable villages buried in snow and their winding mud roads; then, one morning, he had woken up to find himself in Germany. Looking at the neat green fields, the paved roads, the dainty houses in the clean villages and the flower beds on the sunny station platform, he had thought he was in Paradise. Later, in Switzerland, he had sat on the veranda of a small hotel, warmed by the sun yet within sight of snow-covered mountains, drinking coffee and eating a fresh, crusty roll, and he had thought: People here must be so happy.

Now, watching the English farms come to life in the early morning, he recalled dawn in his home village—a gray, boiling sky and a bitter wind; a frozen swampy field with puddles of ice and tufts of coarse grass rimed with frost; himself in a worn canvas smock, his feet already numb in felt shoes and clogs; his father striding along beside him, wearing the threadbare robes of an impoverished country priest, arguing that God was good. His father had loved the Russian people because God loved them. It has always been perfectly obvious to Feliks that God hated the people, for He treated them so cruelly.

That discussion had been the start of a long journey, a journey which had taken Feliks from Christianity through socialism to anarchist terror, from Tambov province through St. Petersburg and Siberia to Geneva. And in Geneva he had made the decision which brought him to England. He recalled the meeting. He had almost missed it . . .

He almost missed the meeting. He had been to Cracow, to negotiate with the Polish Jews who smuggled the magazine *Mutiny* across the border into Russia. He arrived in Geneva after dark and went straight to Ulrich's tiny back-street printing shop. The editorial committee was in session—four men and two girls, gathered around a candle, in the rear of the shop behind the gleaming press, breathing the smells of newsprint and oiled machinery, planning the Russian Revolution.

Ulrich brought Feliks up to date on the discussion. He had seen Josef, a spy for the Okhrana, the Russian secret police. Josef secretly sympathized with the revolutionaries and gave the Okhrana false information for their money. Sometimes the anarchists would give him true but harmless tidbits, and in return Josef warned them of Okhrana activities.

This time Josef's news had been sensational. "The Czar wants a military alliance with England," Ulrich told Feliks. "He is sending Prince Orlov to London to negotiate. The Okhrana know about it because they have to guard the Prince on the journey through Europe."

Feliks took off his hat and sat down, wondering whether this was true. One of the girls, a sad, shabby Russian, brought him tea in a glass. Feliks took a half-eaten lump of sugar from his pocket, placed it between his teeth and sipped the tea through the sugar in the peasant manner.

"The point being," Ulrich went on, "that England could then have a war with Germany and make the Russians fight it."

Feliks nodded.

The shabby girl said: "And it won't be the princes and counts who get killed—it will be the ordinary Russian people."

She was right, Feliks thought. The war would be fought by the peasants. He had spent most of his life among those people. They were hard, surly and narrow-minded, but their foolish generosity and their occasional spontaneous outbursts of sheer fun gave a hint of how they might be in a decent society. Their concerns were the weather, animals, disease, childbirth and outwitting the landlord. For a few years, in their late teens, they were sturdy and straight, and could smile and run fast and flirt; but soon they became bowed and gray and slow and sullen. Now Prince Orlov would take those young men in the springtime of their lives and march them in front of cannon to be shot to pieces or maimed forever, no doubt for the very best reasons of international diplomacy.

It was things like this that made Feliks an anarchist.

"What is to be done?" said Ulrich.

"We must blaze the news across the front page of *Mutiny!*" said the shabby girl.

They began to discuss how the story should be handled. Feliks listened. Editorial matters interested him little. He distributed the magazine and wrote articles about how to make bombs, and he was deeply discontented. He had become terribly civilized in Geneva. He drank beer instead of vodka, wore a collar and a tie and went to concerts of orchestral music. He had a job in a bookshop. Meanwhile Russia was in turmoil. The oil workers were at war with the Cossacks, the parliament was impotent and a million workers were on strike. Czar Nicholas II was the most incompetent and asinine ruler a degenerate aristocracy could produce. The country was a powder barrel waiting for a spark, and Feliks wanted to be that spark. But it was fatal to go back. Joe Stalin had gone back, and no sooner had he set foot on Russian soil than he had been sent to Siberia. The secret police knew the exiled revolutionaries better than they knew those still at home. Feliks was chafed by his stiff collar, his leather shoes and his circumstances.

He looked around at the little group of anarchists: Ulrich, the printer, with white hair and an inky apron. An intellectual who loaned Feliks books by Proudhon and Kropotkin but also a man of action who had once helped Feliks rob a bank; Olga, the shabby girl, who had seemed to be falling in love with Feliks until, one day, she saw him break a policeman's arm and became frightened of him; Vera, the promiscuous poetess; Yevno, the philosophy student who talked a lot about a cleansing wave of blood and fire; Hans, the watchmaker, who saw into people's souls as if he had them under his magnifying glass; and Pyotr, the dispossessed Count, writer of brilliant economic tracts and inspirational revolutionary editorials. They were sincere and hardworking people, and all very clever. Feliks knew their importance, for he had been inside Russia among the desperate people who waited impatiently for smuggled newspapers and pamphlets and passed them from hand to hand until they fell to pieces. Yet it was not enough, for economic tracts were no protection against police bullets, and fiery articles would not burn palaces.

Ulrich was saying: "This news deserves wider circulation than it will get in *Mutiny*. I want every peasant in Russia to know that Orlov would lead him into a useless and bloody war over something that concerns him not at all."

Olga said: "The first problem is whether we will be believed."

Feliks said: "The first problem is whether the story is true."

"We can check," Ulrich said. "The London comrades could find out whether Orlov arrives when he is supposed to arrive, and whether he meets the people he needs to meet."

"It's not enough to spread the news," Yevno said excitedly. "We must put a stop to this!"

"How?" said Ulrich, looking at young Yevno over the top of his wire-rimmed spectacles.

"We should call for the assassination of Orlov—he is a traitor, betraying the people, and he should be executed."

"Would that stop the talks?"

"It probably would," said Count Pyotr. "Especially if the assassin

were an anarchist. Remember, England gives political asylum to anarchists, and this infuriates the Czar. Now, if one of his princes were
killed in England by one of our comrades, the Czar might well be angry
enough to call off the whole negotiation."

Yevno said: "What a story we would have then! We could say that
Orlov had been assassinated by one of us for treason against the Russian
people."

"Every newspaper in the world would carry *that* report," Ulrich
mused.

"Think of the effect it would have at home. You know how Russian
peasants feel about conscription—it's a death sentence. They hold a
funeral when a boy goes into the army. If they learned that the Czar
was planning to make them fight a major European war, the rivers
would run red with blood . . ."

He was right, Feliks thought. Yevno always talked like that, but
this time he was right.

Ulrich said: "I think you're in dreamland, Yevno. Orlov is on a
secret mission—he won't ride through London in an open carriage
waving to the crowds. Besides, I know the London comrades—they've
never assassinated anyone. I don't see how it can be done."

"I do," Feliks said. They all looked at him. The shadows on their
faces shifted in the flickering candlelight. "I know how it can be done."
His voice sounded strange to him, as if his throat were constricted. "I'll
go to London. I'll kill Orlov."

The room was suddenly quiet, as all the talk of death and destruction suddenly became real and concrete in their midst. They stared at
him in surprise, all except Ulrich, who smiled knowingly, almost as if
he had planned, all along, that it would turn out this way.

Analysis of the Two Versions

The main emphasis in the Walden scene revision was to enlarge and
to enhance the characters. But in this scene's second draft the stress is
on compression and on dramatization, which also of course enhances
character. As in the previous revision, we have descriptive improvements in character, setting, and textural details, but here these are
secondary. Feliks gains definition as a character not because he is
changed in any appreciable way, but because he's presented primarily
within the context of a dramatic scene, and not as in the first draft
exclusively through interior monologue and author narration. In version

two the scenes both in the railway carriage and in the print shop are more vividly set, and Follett also adds a description of Feliks, so we can see him. Factual details such as the name of the Russian double agent, the names and descriptions of Feliks's anarchist co-conspirators, background on the revolutionary newspaper on which he works are also nice added improvements.

But in the second draft, one of the two elemental ameliorations results from what Follett excises and omits. Feliks's three-page life history, starting with his training for the priesthood in St. Petersburg and ending with his killing a policeman when his revolutionary cell is compromised and raided, is gone. This much biography presented in the form of author narrative slows down and all but stops the action, the forward motion of the novel. It's information and not drama, and it's far more information than the reader needs at this point to relate to Feliks and to what he's setting out to do. On the other hand, it is good for the author to have compiled and to know all this background for himself. For example, Feliks's discovery about losing the ability to fear becomes in the final draft of chapter two the basis for a wonderful two-page dramatic flashback. But here, when Feliks is first introduced into the story, what is needed most is for the book's issue quickly to be joined, for the assassination plot to be brought forward and set in motion. For this, a journalistic account of a character's life is an impediment. In the final draft, Follett reduces it all to a short paragraph.

His second key improvement, then, is to expand and transform the few paragraphs of flat author narration about the anarchist cell in Switzerland into an almost four-page climactic dramatic scene. Instead of learning about Feliks through chroniclelike reportage, we now see him in action. He participates in a secret meeting. We share his intense reactions to the big news that's being discussed and to little things such as his feeling chafed by a stiff collar. His co-conspirators are deftly sketched with identities as we learn what he thinks of each one of them. They talk of calling for the assassination of Orlov in their underground magazine, but it's all talk. How could it ever be done? And that, of course, becomes Feliks's cue to come forward and say, "I'll go to London. I'll kill Orlov," shocking them all except Ulrich.

As I pointed out in chapter five, character is revealed through action, what the character does right in front of us and not offstage. Rhett Butler, remember, is disparaged and even castigated all through *Gone*

With the Wind for being disloyal to the South. But whatever such acts he commits are offstage. We never see them. So we form our opinion of him based only or largely on the things that we actually see him do.

Feliks's going to England to kill Oblomov and Walden in version one is woven into the ongoing impersonal narrative as an accomplished fact. Feliks is contrasted with no other characters. He recognizes that there is awful injustice in Russia and this simply is his way to make it right. In the final text, he is presented among his peers. Follett portrays them so that they are soft and he is hard, they wishy-washy and he unyielding. Then, in an electric moment of decision, Feliks steps forward, takes command, asserts that he'll actually go to London and commit murder, something that none of the others would dare to do. They are stunned, as are we, and Feliks as a larger-than-life character is established.

As important as establishing Feliks is the transformation of low-key author narration into vivid dramatic action. Feliks almost misses the meeting, one that brings sensational news. It's within this tense context, set not in the past but in the immediate present, that we now learn why he's become an anarchist. His colleagues discuss what should go into their magazine. He's interested only in writing articles about how to make bombs, in sparking the revolution. Follett contrives a heated situation in which secondary characters act and react against each other while at the same time he sets up Feliks in sharp juxtaposition with them all. With this newly added scene, fresh excitement and suspense are generated.

Now let's make an altogether different comparison, one between the book's finale—chapters thirteen, fourteen and fifteen—and the ending of the fourth outline with its sections twelve through fifteen. If you haven't done so already, you will note numerous changes, some small and several that are huge. Follett's publisher was content with the outline, but the author himself, once he got into the actual writing, clearly was not. Why? We'll focus on only a few improvements that reflect important aspects of novelistic craft, most of which are dealt with or at least touched upon in earlier portions of this book.

In the outline, the emphasis is almost entirely on the plot and counterplot of Felix trying to get to Walden Hall to carry out his murderous mission, and on Walden and his cohorts struggling to prevent this from happening. In the end, Feliks plants a bomb in the Octagon where the treaty is scheduled to be signed. Charlotte refuses to cooperate in allowing her father be killed. Feliks reveals that he is her father. Charlotte, unmoved, runs into the Octagon warning everyone to get out, and Feliks, clutching the about-to-explode bomb, throws himself out a window, killing himself but saving Charlotte.

So what's so terrible? It's not terrible, but neither is it wonderful. This ending is rushed, and it is almost pure melodrama. It does include a heartfelt scene of Lydia's confessing to Walden. Apart from that, however, it fails to deal with and resolve the poisonous secrets and the other delicate human issues that, in the course of the novel, have been dramatically implanted between all the major characters and especially between members of the Walden family. It could be a fitting ending to a potboiler, but not to a novel of character.

As you can see from the book, Follett largely chucks this portion of the outline and in its stead creates a series of episodes that, on the one hand, causally connect with and lead into each other, but on the other, alternate scenes of physical action with intense human revelations and confrontations.

At the beginning of the book's chapter fourteen, for example, Charlotte finds Feliks hiding in the wood and warns him to give up and clear off. With a hundred and fifty men searching for him, he has no chance, and she won't be party to his suicide. It's then, virtually as soon as he arrives at Walden Hall, that he reveals that he's her father. Here, where no bomb is about to explode, there's time and space for this information to turn Charlotte's world upside down. This cementing of their relationship, exciting in itself, can then be used to govern both his and her actions for the remaining fifty or so pages of the denouement. Most directly, this revelation is what causes Charlotte to agree to hide him in the house. Its ramifications then open the way to stirring scenes she now can have with both her parents.

What follows are wonderful examples of how tight character relationships can be used to create high drama. In the outline, during Lydia's confession to Walden, she also reveals that Charlotte has informed Feliks that Oblomov was now at Walden Hall, whereupon Walden confines Charlotte to her room. This news in the book is made into a huge shock, because Charlotte's perfidy is conveyed to her father by an outsider, Basil Thomson. Walden feels disgraced. The two men then confront Charlotte, who reveals nothing, and Thomson threatens to bring her to trial for murder. Alone with his daughter, Walden is devastated and, fearful for her future, will do anything to save her. He pleads for her to trust him, if only because he's her father. She loves him, but she now knows that he's not. His cheeks are wet with tears because he has failed to raise her so that she could believe in him. And she, after he blows his nose, leaves and locks her in, bursts into tears. These two people love each other, long to reach out to one another, and fail, with imminent mayhem or murder looming and about to envelop them. With this new encounter, Follett provides the obligatory scene for the drama between these two characters. It also sets up Walden's desperate race to rescue Charlotte from the flames at the novel's end.

The author then creates equally powerful climaxes of one kind or another for Charlotte and Lydia, Lydia and Feliks, Lydia and Walden, and finally between Feliks and Walden as they charge together into the inferno of the burning house to rescue Charlotte. Although the thrust of the novel is clearly built around the attempt to kill Orlov, in the final draft, Feliks's shooting him is passed over quickly. The assassination attempt is clearly secondary to the climax of biological father and the presumed father joining forces to save their child. The entire ending of the book departs from the outline to utilize and bring to a head the well of deep emotions built up between the characters through all the preceding chapters.

At the same time, note the improvement in the physical action— how compared with the outline, the assassination is planned and carried out in an atmosphere of nail-biting suspense. In the outline, once Feliks is on the estate, he sneaks at night into the Octagon to set a time bomb for the hour when the Treaty is to be signed. Except for overpowering two guards and Lydia, he does nothing until Charlotte rushes in to try and save her father. The novel, on the other hand, sets up the shooting step by step over six short scenes, which are interspersed with the character confrontations discussed above. Feliks's machinations cause suspense to build and build. First, Feliks induces Charlotte to draw him a plan of the house. Later, in the dead of night, he manages to find the gun room and to break free a shotgun. Then he conceives a plan. To get Orlov out of his closely guarded room, so he can get a shot at him, he'll set fire to the house. Outside he finds a hose, which he runs through several rooms and connects to a petrol tank in the barn, clubbing an interfering sentry unconscious while he's at it. In the fourth scene he sets the fire, and in the fifth positions himself outside to shoot Aleks as he emerges. Follett thus, step by careful step, beautifully sets up for when Feliks pulls the trigger. Charlotte's peril is also well prepared for with a prior scene in which Lydia tries to open the door to her daughter's burning room but cannot.

What you should conclude from this, in addition to the structural points already made, is that even a meticulously worked out fourth draft outline usually cannot be slavishly followed in the writing of a high-stakes novel or any novel.

Chapter Fourteen

GETTING IT PUBLISHED
AND ONTO THE
BEST-SELLER LISTS

⸜⸝

YOU HAVE GONE THROUGH YOUR MANUSCRIPT A NUMBER OF TIMES, patiently and carefully restructuring, rewriting and layering into it all or most of the precepts espoused in this book. You think it's pretty damn good, marvelous even. So what do you do next? Send it to an agent or publisher? No. You look for confirmation or, more likely, for professional editorial assistance or guidance.

EDITING

Virtually all popular best-selling novelists need and get help from others in enriching their characters and maximizing the drama of their work. Established writers who are paid large advances, often before they commit even one word to paper, are provided by their publishers with editors who pore over their manuscripts and make detailed comments and suggestions on outlines and successive drafts of a manuscript. Authors sometimes also have editorially skilled agents who work with them or novelist colleagues with whom they exchange critiques. But the genre author, the midlist author, or the new author who lacks these personal connections and who is trying to break into this Top Writer rarified circle—who submits a manuscript that is meritorious but in some respect faulty, slow, obscure, in short, anything less than a mesmerizing knockout—is usually not accorded editorial succor from a publisher and most likely gets rejected.

Editors in publishing houses are overworked. They put in a full day in the office fielding phone calls from authors and agents, from publicity, marketing and production departments within their companies; attending meetings about covers, new acquisitions, production scheduling; interviewing, hiring and firing assistants; and negotiating with management for books they want to acquire, for promotion budgets for these books, and for pay increases and promotions for themselves. The result is that most of their editing and usually all of their reading gets relegated to nights and weekends, of which there are never enough, given the avalanchelike onslaught of manuscripts that keep piling in on them. The bulk of their time has to be devoted to contracted-for projects, books in which their company has already made an often sizeable investment, an investment that has to be nurtured and protected by the editors, who slave to help the author get the book into its optimal condition. All this leaves the editor precious little time or strength for a new author, unless what she presents is somehow marvelous.

Finding an Expert Reader

So you've got this much sweated-over manuscript that you think is marvelous. Your spouse and your best friends are even more enthusiastic. What now? Don't trust yourself or the people who love you. Find a professional novelist, someone you don't know personally and who has no stake in your ego or making you feel good. Offer to pay this person to read your work, to provide you with an honest opinion as to its fine qualities and weaknesses and give you written suggestions as to how you might improve and strengthen it.

How do you find such a person? It's probably easier than you think. The owner or manager of your nearby bookstore or of one in the nearest big city will usually know the local authors. They generally come in for signing parties when their books are published or at the very least to autograph their copies in stock. Check out these authors' writing and choose one whose work has some affinity to yours. Then contact her. Be prepared to pay what it takes. If you've invested a year or several years in writing a novel, one you're hoping will bring you a worldwide readership and make you financially comfortable, you owe it to yourself to protect and bolster your investment of time with cash. You ought to be able to get a read-through and general letter for $500 to $1,000, and a detailed critique with a marked-up manuscript for $2,000 to $5,000, depending on the length of your novel and the eminence of the author you're approaching.

If you're low on cash or simply cannot find an established novelist who will, even for a price, critique your manuscript, then I suggest that you join or form a novel workshop. Most universities have them, but they also can be purely private and meet in lodges, churches and writers' homes. In such a group, you would read your chapters aloud to other authors or would-be authors, and the group (which sometimes will have a novelist or an editor as a leader) would comment and make suggestions, letting you know which of your characters are engaging, repellent, or boring, which episodes in your story are riveting and which are dull, and whether the strands of your plot hang together from beginning to end.

In your role as self-critic, you must then sift through this criticism and advice, whether from a known novelist or from a group in a work-shop, and make your own decisions about which suggestions to imple-ment and how to implement them and which suggestions to ignore. Keep in mind, though, that none of us can be objective about our own work. So, if you get complaints, the likelihood is strong that there are problems, even though the suggestions you've been given on how to address these problems may or may not be exactly right.

PUBLISHING

After you've worked over your novel with the help of an individual or a group, you would be wise to get a reading from a second professional who has never seen it before. The first person who worked with you is likely to be all caught up in the improvements you've made and aware of how much better the book is. But that's not the same as being coolly objective. A person who is reading your work cold will be better equipped to advise you if your novel is or isn't ready to submit.

Okay, you have torn apart the manuscript and rewritten it from beginning to end. Your novelist-mentor or your workshop colleagues or, better yet, your second outside professional has now told you that you've done one hell of a job, your novel is as good as anything on the *New York Times* best-seller list, and you are as ready to shoot for the big time as you ever will be. Now what?

Finding an Agent

You need an agent, and not just any agent. *Literary Marketplace* (LMP) is the bible and almanac of the U.S. and Canadian publishing industries. It lists several hundred literary agencies and agents. But of these, only twenty or so represent 90 percent of our best-selling novelists. Submis-sions coming from this small group of agents usually get prompt and serious consideration at publishing houses' highest levels. These agents are personally familiar with the literary tastes and predilections of the leading editors and publishers and are best equipped to make the big deals that help push a book by a relative unknown to best-sellerdom. So, if your book is a gem, and you can get one of these agents to take you on, you have at least a chance at a blockbuster.

So who are these agents, you ask, and how do I get to one? Again, it's not so hard. Pick an author you admire and whose writing you believe has a kinship with yours. To find out who represents that author, go to the bookstore (or library) and ask to see the current catalog of that author's publisher. Most publishers' catalogs contain "rights information," i.e., who (invariably the author's agent) controls motion picture and/or translation rights. This information is sometimes at the bottom of the page on which the author's new book is described or in a special section in the rear of the catalog. If the catalog contains no such disclosure, which is occasionally the case, then look up the name of the publisher's Subsidiary Rights Director in *LMP*, call or write that person, and tell her you're interested in acquiring motion picture rights to your author's novel. You will then be directed to the agency or agent.

Now you know the name of the agent. What do you do about it? Top agents are as busy or busier than the orthopedist for whom you might have to wait three months for an appointment. Their first obligation is to the authors they already represent, the ones whose incomes provide the agents' livelihoods. These authors keep turning in outlines and manuscripts that have to be read, getting offers from publishers and movie companies that have to be negotiated, and experiencing an endless stream of problems with publishers about payments, jackets, deadlines, publication dates, publicity tours, titles, editorial content, personality conflicts, printing errors, all of which the agent must attend to and struggle to sort out before he can consider work from a potential new client. So don't be surprised if your attempt to communicate doesn't get a prompt reply.

The crux now is how you communicate. First, don't bother trying to telephone. Heavyweight agents just don't have the time to listen to a spiel from someone they don't know, unless the caller has "name recognition," either his own or that of someone (usually an author or an editor) known to the agent. It's almost always far better to write. Fiction is a written medium, and if you manage to write an enticing letter, the agent may feel there's a chance you've written a good book. Your letter should be brief, about a page, and should include a few lines about the story; a short paragraph about why it's wonderful, hard-hitting, unique, a novel millions would want to read; and a few sentences about your prior experiences and credits as a writer.

If you've published fiction before, either novels or short stories, the agent will be inclined to consider you more seriously than if you haven't. And if you enclose a letter of recommendation from a published novelist, from a teacher of writing, or best of all, from a client of the agent, that too will help stimulate a response. Experience in nonfiction, journalism or screenwriting has more value than no professional writing background, but writers whose prior work is in these areas often have a tough time making a go of the novel form. If you never have had anything published, it may be premature of you to be thinking about an agent. My advice would be first to try and place some short stories or excerpts from your novel in literary or mass-circulation magazines. Once you succeed in this, you'll have the beginnings of a literary track record that should encourage an agent to want to consider your novel.

Once an agent takes on your manuscript, there's not much you can do until either he lets you know he has struck out with it, or he calls you with an offer for publication. If your work is declined, don't give up. If a good agent liked your novel well enough to expend time, energy and money in making a bunch of submissions, there is a decent chance that, with a careful analysis of the publishers' rejection letters and further help from a freelance editor, you may be able to successfully revise it. On the other hand, if a call comes with an offer, and your agent advises acceptance, take it. One of the things you're paying him for, after all, is his expert advice.

MARKETING

Your first step in the publication process will be additional revision. I have placed novels by relatively unknown writers for sums in the neighborhood of $1,000,000, and even these manuscripts required a fair bit of rewriting. Once this work is completed, about a year goes by between the manuscript's "final acceptance" and its appearance in bookstores. Ideally, you will have been paid a substantial advance, in which case the publisher's publicity and promotion departments are likely to be making major efforts to ballyhoo you and your amazingly wonderful book. But keep in mind that publicizing a novel is not an easy thing to do. The best way to sell a book and to propel it onto the best-seller list is television, say, an appearance on *Oprah* or *Donahue*.

But these talk-show hosts prefer authors with issue-oriented nonfiction works, experts who can readily expound on subjects of broad general interest without requiring an audience to have read their books to appreciate and understand them, as opposed to novelists whose plots and characters seem restrictive and obscure within the format of a five- or seven-minute televised chitchat.

But if your novel is concerned with, or even touches upon, some subject of general interest such as codependency, sexual obsession, or protection of the environment, or if you yourself have had an extraordinary life, you can be pitched for television either by your publisher or by a public relations firm that you can retain, and there's a decent chance that you may get booked for local if not nationwide shows. To attract TV attention, a stimulating and provocative press kit can be a help; it can also be useful in obtaining print coverage and interviews. This usually is prepared by your publisher's publicity department, but I have known authors who have arranged on their own for such a kit to be put together and sent out press releases, which were then picked up by the media. Other authors have sent catchy bits about their books to gossip columnists or gotten themselves written up in *Publishers Weekly*. Bear in mind that a major publisher's catalog for a four-month spring, fall or winter season contains thirty to fifty titles. Your book, even if you are paid a large advance, can be allotted only so much of a publicity department's time and attention, so it behooves you to try and help in every way that you can.

To give the sales of your novel a lift when it is first launched, first, print up a card with the book's jacket on it and a bit of information on you and your story and send it to literally everyone you know or ever have known—high school or college classmates, church or synagogue congregants, PTA acquaintances, fellow lodge or club members—and ask all your close friends and relatives to send out twenty or thirty of these to the people closest to them. A personal note on the card should urge all its recipients to buy the book, preferably at a chain bookstore and during a particular week, probably the third week after you see it in the stores, by which time its national distribution should be complete. By doing this, you may well be able to generate a sale of one or two thousand copies. Except for during the Christmas season, this is usually enough to push a hardcover novel onto at least the bottom of the best-seller list. Once a book gets on the list, readers, bookstore owners and managers, discount houses and price clubs, librarians, etc., all take notice of it, and if they love it, good sales are likely to follow.

One other thing you can do is to ingratiate yourself with as many bookstores as you can get to. People who work in bookstores usually love books and are pleased if not excited to meet authors. You want these people to read your book, love it, and recommend it to their customers. If you can afford it—and, again, think of this as an investment in yourself and your career—one good approach is to introduce yourself, buy a copy of your own book, present it to the owner or chief clerk, and urge her to read it. Publishers, also looking for such recommendations to customers, deluge bookstores with promotional reading copies that, because of their sheer volume, mostly go unread. A personally presented volume, however, one that you autograph and inscribe to the bookseller, will most likely be read and, hopefully, recommended to the store's clientele. You also might offer to autograph all copies the store has in stock. Readers who buy books often take pleasure in acquiring autographed copies, especially as gifts.

Another way to get booksellers interested in you and in your book is to throw a nice party for them. In a city like New York where authors abound and where store managers lead harried lives, this is not an easy thing to pull off. But in any other sizeable city, if you have a close friend or relative who is willing to make his or her home available to you, you will have surmounted your biggest obstacle. Usually you can get the names and addresses of the booksellers from your publisher's local sales representative, a person whom you should try to enlist as an ally in this venture, since reps and booksellers often are personally close. The party itself need not be elaborate. Ideally, after meeting you in this friendly setting, the bookseller should go away wanting to read your book.

Endorsements, blurbs printed on the back jacket or in ads in which well-known writers or celebrities say how terrific your novel is, also help. Usually these are obtained by publishers or agents, but any that you can procure by whatever means can advance your cause.

A FINAL WORD

Keep in mind, though, that all the information in this chapter is, as it were, frosting on the cake. Your main job is to write an unforgettable novel on a subject that has wide appeal. If you can manage to do that, your agent and publisher (with some help from you) should be able to guide your book to the success it deserves.

INDEX

∽

More Great Books
for Writers!

Guerilla Marketing for Writers—Packed with proven insights and techniques, this practical manual shows you 100 no-cost, low-cost ways to sell your books, before and after they're published. Written by the master of Guerilla Marketing, Jay Conrad Levinson! *#10667/$14.99/224 pages/paperback*

Get Organized, Get Published—In this lively, inspirational, browsable book, you'll find a plethora of easy-to-find, easy-to-use tips for organizing and managing the writing life, staying motivated and getting published. *#10689/$18.99/240 pages/hardcover*

Writing the Breakout Novel—Successful novelist and agent Donald Maass shows you how to give your novel the best chance of succeeding in a crowded marketplace. Examples and case studies illustrate the elements that all breakout novels have in common, while savvy advice helps you write stories that are equally as powerful. *#10751/$19.99/256 pages/hardcover*

Jump Start Your Book Sales—Here is the information you need to generate thousands of additional sales - fantastic ideas for booking author events, signings, TB appearances and radio interviews, and promoting on the Web. *#10623/$19.95/320 pages/paperback*

Formatting & Submitting Your Manuscript—Throughout this easy-to-use guide, dozens of charts, lists, models and sidebars show you everything you need to know to submit your work correctly and enhance your chances of being published. *#10618/$18.99/208 pages/paperback*

Word Painting—In this extraordinary guide, Rebecca McClanahan leads you through an exploration of the descriptive writing process, combining direct instruction with engaging word exercises that challenge you to elevate your writing to new levels of richness and clarity. *#10709/$14.99/ 256 pages/paperback*

The Marshall Plan for Novel Writing—A successful literary agent, Evan Marshall breaks down the novel-writing process into small, manageable tasks that even the most inexperienced writer can achieve. Each task is illuminated with insightful, informed advice, diagrams and charts designed to show you how to find a hook, create a conflict, develop a protagonist and more. Also included is information about writing query letters and manuscript submission. *#10740/$15.99/240 pages/ paperback*

The Marshall Plan Workbook—This companion volume to The Marshall Plan for Novel Writing details the process of building a novel's plot with more than 40 pages of fill-in sheets that become a veritable blue-print for any novel. *#10738/$19.99/256 pages/paperback*
